M000249983

Mastering Puppet

Pull the strings of Puppet to configure enterprise-grade
environments for performance optimization

Thomas Uphill

PUBLISHING

BIRMINGHAM - MUMBAI

Mastering Puppet

Copyright © 2014 Packt Publishing

All rights reserved. No part of this book may be reproduced, stored in a retrieval system, or transmitted in any form or by any means, without the prior written permission of the publisher, except in the case of brief quotations embedded in critical articles or reviews.

Every effort has been made in the preparation of this book to ensure the accuracy of the information presented. However, the information contained in this book is sold without warranty, either express or implied. Neither the author, nor Packt Publishing, and its dealers and distributors will be held liable for any damages caused or alleged to be caused directly or indirectly by this book.

Packt Publishing has endeavored to provide trademark information about all of the companies and products mentioned in this book by the appropriate use of capitals. However, Packt Publishing cannot guarantee the accuracy of this information.

First published: July 2014

Production reference: 1090714

Published by Packt Publishing Ltd.
Livery Place
35 Livery Street
Birmingham B3 2PB, UK.

ISBN 978-1-78398-218-9

www.packtpub.com

Cover image by Gagandeep Sharma (er.gagansharma@gmail.com)

Credits

Author
Thomas Uphill

Reviewers
Ugo Bellavance
C. N. A. Corrêa
Jeroen Hooyberghs
Johan De Wit

Commissioning Editor
Edward Gordon

Acquisition Editor
Meeta Rajani

Content Development Editor
Sharvari Tawde

Technical Editors
Veena Pagare
Anand Singh

Copy Editors
Sarang Chari
Mradula Hegde

Project Coordinator
Danuta Jones

Proofreaders
Faye Coulman
Maria Gould

Indexers
Mariammal Chettiyar
Tejal Soni
Priya Subramani

Graphics
Sheetal Aute
Ronak Dhruv

Production Coordinator
Shantanu Zagade

Cover Work
Shantanu Zagade

About the Author

Thomas Uphill is an RHCA who has been using Puppet since version 0.24. He has been a system administrator for nearly 20 years, more than 10 of which have been with Red Hat Linux and its derivatives. He has presented tutorials on Puppet at LOPSA-East and has spoken at PuppetConf 2013. He enjoys teaching others how to use Puppet to automate as much system administration tasks as possible. When he's not at the Seattle Puppet Meetup, you can find him at http://ramblings.narrabilis.com.

I am very thankful to my friend and colleague Joško Plazonić for introducing me to Puppet and getting me started on this journey. I would like to thank my wife Priya Fernandes for putting up with the long nights and weekends it took to finish this book. Thanks to Nate Tade for his encouragement while I worked on this book, the rest of my team for trying my crazy ideas, and Shawn Foley for a few not-so-crazy ideas. Thanks to Theresa, David, and Ben for their support.

About the Reviewers

Ugo Bellavance has done most of his studies in e-commerce. He started using Linux from RedHat 5.2, got Linux training from Savoir-faire Linux at age 20, and got his RHCE on RHEL 6 in 2011. He's been a consultant in the past, but he's now an employee for a provincial government agency for which he manages the IT infrastructure (servers, workstations, network, security, virtualization, SAN/NAS, and PBX). He's a big fan of open source software and its underlying philosophy. He has worked with Debian, Ubuntu, and SUSE, but what he knows best is RHEL-based distributions. He's known for his contributions to the MailScanner project (he has been a technical reviewer for *MailScanner User Guide and Training Manual, Julian Field*), but he has also given time to different open source projects such as Mondo Rescue, OTRS, SpamAssassin, pfSense, and a few others. He's been a technical reviewer for *Centos 6 Linux Server Cookbook, Jonathan Hobson, Packt Publishing* and *Puppet 3 Beginner's Guide, John Arundel, Packt Publishing*.

I thank my lover, Lysanne, who accepted to allow me some free time slots for this review even with two dynamic children to take care of. The presence of these three human beings in my life is simply invaluable.

I must also thank my friend Sébastien, whose generosity is only matched by his knowledge and kindness. I would never have reached this high in my career if it wasn't for him.

C. N. A. Corrêa (@cnacorrea) is an IT operations manager and consultant. He is also a Puppet enthusiast and an old-school Linux hacker. He has a master's degree in Systems Virtualization and holds the CISSP and RHCE certifications. Backed by a 15-year career on systems administration, Carlos leads IT operations teams for companies in Brazil, Africa, and the USA. He is also a part-time professor for graduate and undergraduate courses in Brazil. Carlos co-authored several research papers on network virtualization and OpenFlow, presented on peer-reviewed IEEE and ACM conferences worldwide.

I thank God for all the opportunities of hard work and all the lovely people I always find on my way. I thank the sweetest of them all, my wife Nanda, for all her loving care and support that pushes me forward. I would also like to thank my parents, Nilton and Zélia, for being such a big inspiration for all the things I do.

Jeroen Hooyberghs has eight years of professional experience in many different Linux environments. Currently, he's employed as an Open Source and Linux Consultant at Open-Future in Belgium. Since the past year, a lot of his time has been going into implementing and maintaining Puppet installations for clients.

I would like to thank my two girls, Eveline and Tess, for understanding that a passion for open source requires evenings and weekends spent on it.

Johan De Wit was an early Linux user, and he still remembers the day he built a 0.9x Linux kernel on his brand new 486 computer that took an entire night. His love for the UNIX operating systems existed before Linux was announced. It is not surprising that he started a career as a UNIX system administrator.

He doesn't remember precisely when he started working with open source software, but since 2009, he is working as an Open Source Consultant at Open-Future, where he got the opportunity to work with Puppet. Right now, Puppet has become Johan's biggest interest. He also loves to teach Puppet as one of the few official Puppet trainers in Belgium.

Johan started the Belgian Puppet User Group a year ago, where he tries to bring some Puppeteers together having great and interesting meetups. When he takes time writing some Puppet-related blogs, he mostly does that at `http://puppet-be.github.io/`, the BPUG website. Also, from time to time, he tries to spread some hopefully wise Puppet words by presenting talks at Puppet camps across in Europe.

Besides having fun at work, he spends a lot of his free time with his two lovely kids, his two Belgian draft horses, and if time and the weather permits, he likes to (re)build and drive his old-school chopper.

www.PacktPub.com

Support files, eBooks, discount offers, and more

You might want to visit www.PacktPub.com for support files and downloads related to your book.

Did you know that Packt offers eBook versions of every book published, with PDF and ePub files available? You can upgrade to the eBook version at www.PacktPub.com and as a print book customer, you are entitled to a discount on the eBook copy. Get in touch with us at service@packtpub.com for more details.

At www.PacktPub.com, you can also read a collection of free technical articles, sign up for a range of free newsletters and receive exclusive discounts and offers on Packt books and eBooks.

http://PacktLib.PacktPub.com

Do you need instant solutions to your IT questions? PacktLib is Packt's online digital book library. Here, you can access, read and search across Packt's entire library of books.

Why subscribe?

- Fully searchable across every book published by Packt
- Copy and paste, print and bookmark content
- On demand and accessible via web browser

Free access for Packt account holders

If you have an account with Packt at www.PacktPub.com, you can use this to access PacktLib today and view nine entirely free books. Simply use your login credentials for immediate access.

Table of Contents

Preface

Every project changes when you scale it out. Puppet is no different. Working on a small number of nodes with a small team of developers is a completely different task than working with thousands of nodes with a large group of developers.

Mastering Puppet deals with the issues faced with larger deployments, such as scaling and duplicate resource definitions. It will show you how to fit Puppet into your organization and keep everyone working. The concepts presented can be adopted to suit organizations of any size.

What this book covers

Chapter 1, Dealing with Load/Scale, deals with scaling out your Puppet infrastructure to handle a large number of nodes. Using proxying techniques, a sample deployment is presented.

Chapter 2, Organizing Your Nodes and Data, is where we examine different methods of applying modules to nodes. In addition to ENCs (external node classifiers), we use hiera and `hiera_include` to apply modules to nodes.

Chapter 3, Git and Environments, shows you how to use Git hooks to deploy your code to your Puppet masters and enforce access control for your modules.

Chapter 4, Public Modules, presents several supported modules from the Puppet Forge and has real-world example use cases.

Chapter 5, Custom Facts and Modules, is all about extending facter with custom facts and rolling your own modules to solve problems.

Chapter 6, Custom Types, covers how to implement defined types and create your own custom types where appropriate.

Chapter 7, *Reporting and Orchestration*, says that without reporting you'll never know when everything is broken. We explore two popular options for reporting, Foreman and Puppet Dashboard. We then configure and use the marionette collective (mcollective or mco) to perform orchestration tasks.

Chapter 8, *Exported Resources*, is an advanced topic where we have resource definitions on one node applying to another node. We start by configuring puppetdb and more onto real-world exported resources examples with Forge modules.

Chapter 9, *Roles and Profiles*, is a popular design paradigm used by many large installations. We show how this design can be implemented using all of the knowledge from the previous chapters.

Chapter 10, *Troubleshooting*, is a necessity. Things will always break, and we will always need to fix them. This chapter shows some common techniques for troubleshooting.

What you need for this book

All the examples in this book were written and tested using an Enterprise Linux 6.5 derived installation such as CentOS 6.5, Scientific Linux 6.5, or Springdale Linux 6.5. Additional repositories used were EPEL (Extra Packages for Enterprise Linux), the Software Collections (SCL) Repository, the Foreman repository, and Puppet Labs repository. The version of Puppet used was the latest 3.4 series at the time of writing.

Who this book is for

This book is for system administrators and Puppeteers writing Puppet code in an enterprise setting. Puppet masters will appreciate the scaling and troubleshooting chapters and Puppet implementers will find useful tips in the customization chapters.

Conventions

In this book, you will find a number of styles of text that distinguish between different kinds of information. Here are some examples of these styles, and an explanation of their meaning.

Puppet code words in text, module names, folder names, filenames, dummy URLs, and user input are shown as follows: "The file `/var/lib/puppet/classes.txt` contains a list of the classes applied to the machine."

A block of code is set as follows:

```
class base {
  file {'one':
    path   => '/tmp/one',
    ensure => 'directory',
  }
  file {"two":
    path   => "/tmp/one$one",
    ensure => 'file',
  }
}
```

When we wish to draw your attention to a particular part of a code block, the relevant lines or items are set in bold:

```
service {'nginx':
  require => Package['nginx'],
  ensure  => true,
  enable  => true,
}
```

Any command-line input or output is written as follows:

```
$ mco ping
worker1.example.com                    time=86.03 ms
node2.example.com                      time=96.21 ms
node1.example.com                      time=97.64 ms
---- ping statistics ----
3 replies max: 97.64 min: 86.03 avg: 93.29
```

New terms and **important words** are shown in bold. Words that you see on the screen, in menus or dialog boxes for example, appear in the text like this: "Then navigate to the settings section and update the **trusted_puppetmaster_hosts** setting."

Warnings or important notes appear in a box like this.

Tips and tricks appear like this.

Reader feedback

Feedback from our readers is always welcome. Let us know what you think about this book—what you liked or may have disliked. Reader feedback is important for us to develop titles that you really get the most out of.

To send us general feedback, simply send an e-mail to feedback@packtpub.com, and mention the book title via the subject of your message.

If there is a topic that you have expertise in and you are interested in either writing or contributing to a book, see our author guide on www.packtpub.com/authors.

Customer support

Now that you are the proud owner of a Packt book, we have a number of things to help you to get the most from your purchase.

Downloading the example code

You can download the example code files for all Packt books you have purchased from your account at http://www.packtpub.com. If you purchased this book elsewhere, you can visit http://www.packtpub.com/support and register to have the files e-mailed directly to you.

Errata

Although we have taken every care to ensure the accuracy of our content, mistakes do happen. If you find a mistake in one of our books—maybe a mistake in the text or the code—we would be grateful if you would report this to us. By doing so, you can save other readers from frustration and help us improve subsequent versions of this book. If you find any errata, please report them by visiting http://www.packtpub.com/submit-errata, selecting your book, clicking on the **errata submission form** link, and entering the details of your errata. Once your errata is verified, your submission will be accepted and the errata will be uploaded on our website, or added to any list of existing errata, under the Errata section of that title. Any existing errata can be viewed by selecting your title from http://www.packtpub.com/support.

Piracy

Piracy of copyright material on the Internet is an ongoing problem across all media. At Packt, we take the protection of our copyright and licenses very seriously. If you come across any illegal copies of our works, in any form, on the Internet, please provide us with the location address or website name immediately so that we can pursue a remedy.

Please contact us at `copyright@packtpub.com` with a link to the suspected pirated material.

We appreciate your help in protecting our authors, and our ability to bring you valuable content.

Questions

You can contact us at `questions@packtpub.com` if you are having a problem with any aspect of the book, and we will do our best to address it.

1
Dealing with Load/Scale

A large deployment will have a large number of nodes. If you are growing your installation from scratch, you may have started with a single Puppet master running the built-in WEBrick server and moved up to a passenger installation. At a certain point in your deployment, a single Puppet master just won't cut it—the load will become too great. In my experience, this limit was around 600 nodes. Puppet agent runs begin to fail on the nodes, and catalogs fail to compile. There are two ways to deal with this problem: divide and conquer or conquer by dividing.

That is, we can either split up our Puppet master and divide the workload among several machines or we can make each of our nodes apply our code directly using Puppet agent (this is known as a masterless configuration). We'll examine each of these solutions separately.

Divide and conquer

When you start to think about dividing up your Puppet server, the main thing to realize is that many parts of Puppet are simply HTTP SSL transactions. If you treat those things as you would a web service, you can scale out to any size required using HTTP load balancing techniques.

The first step in splitting up the Puppet master is to configure the Puppet master to run under passenger. To ensure we all have the same infrastructure, we'll install a stock passenger configuration together and then start tweaking the configuration. We'll begin building on an x86_64 Enterprise 6 rpm-based Linux; the examples in this book were built using CentOS 6.5 and Springdale Linux 6.5 distributions. Once we have passenger running, we'll look at splitting up the workload.

Puppet with passenger

In our example installation, we will be using the name puppet.example.com for our Puppet server. Starting with a server installation of Enterprise Linux version 6, we install httpd and mod_ssl using the following code:

```
# yum install httpd mod_ssl
Installed:
  httpd-2.2.15-29.el6_4.x86_64
  mod_ssl-2.2.15-29.el6_4.x86_64
```

Downloading the example code

You can download the example code files for all Packt books you have purchased from your account at http://www.packtpub.com. If you purchased this book elsewhere, you can visit http://www.packtpub.com/support and register to have the files e-mailed directly to you.

In each example, I will install the latest available version for Enterprise Linux 6.5 and display the version for the package requested (some packages may pull in dependencies—those versions are not shown).

To install mod_passenger, we pull in the **Extra Packages for Enterprise Linux (EPEL)** repository available at https://fedoraproject.org/wiki/EPEL. Install the EPEL repository by downloading the rpm file from http://download.fedoraproject.org/pub/epel/6/x86_64/repoview/epel-release.html or use the following code:

```
# yum install http://dl.fedoraproject.org/pub/epel/6/x86_64/epel-release-6-8.noarch.rpm
Installed:
  epel-release-6-8.noarch
```

Once EPEL is installed, we install mod_passenger from that repository using the following code:

```
# yum install mod_passenger
Installed:
  mod_passenger-3.0.21-5.el6.x86_64
```

Next, we will pull in Puppet from the `puppetlabs` repository available at `http://docs.puppetlabs.com/guides/puppetlabs_package_repositories.html#for-red-hat-enterprise-linux-and-derivatives` using the following code:

```
# yum install http://yum.puppetlabs.com/el/6/products/x86_64/puppetlabs-release-6-7.noarch.rpm
Installed:
  puppetlabs-release-6-7.noarch
```

With the `puppetlabs` repository installed, we can then install Puppet using the following command:

```
# yum install puppet
Installed:
  puppet-3.3.2-1.el6.noarch
```

The Puppet rpm will create the `/etc/puppet` and `/var/lib/puppet` directories. In `/etc/puppet`, there will be a template `puppet.conf`; we begin by editing that file to set the name of our Puppet server (`puppet.example.com`) in the certname setting using the following code:

```
[main]
  logdir = /var/log/puppet
  rundir = /var/run/puppet
  vardir = /var/lib/puppet
  ssldir = $vardir/ssl
  certname = puppet.example.com
  [agent]
  server = puppet.example.com
  classfile = $vardir/classes.txt
  localconfig = $vardir/localconfig
```

The other lines in this file are defaults. At this point, we would expect `puppet.example.com` to be resolved with a DNS query correctly, but if you do not control DNS at your organization or cannot have this name resolved properly at this point, edit `/etc/hosts`, and put in an entry for your host pointing to `puppet.example.com`. In all the examples, you would substitute `example.com` for your own domain name.

```
127.0.0.1    localhost localhost.localdomain puppet
  puppet.example.com
```

We now need to create certificates for our master; to ensure the Certificate Authority (CA) certificates are created, run Puppet cert list using the following command:

```
# puppet cert list
Notice: Signed certificate request for ca
```

In your enterprise, you may have to answer requests from multiple DNS names, for example, `puppet.example.com`, `puppet`, and `puppet.devel.example.com`. To make sure our certificate is valid for all those DNS names, we will pass the `dns-alt-names` option to `puppet certificate generate`; we also need to specify that the certificates are to be signed by the local machine using the following command:

```
puppet# puppet certificate generate --ca-location local --dns-alt-names
puppet,puppet.prod.example.com,puppet.dev.example.com puppet.example.com
Notice: puppet.example.com has a waiting certificate request
true
```

Now, to sign the certificate request, first verify the certificate list using the following commands:

```
puppet# puppet cert list
  "puppet.example.com" (SHA256) E5:F7:26:0A:6C:41:26:FA:80:02:E5:A6:A1
:DB:F4:E0:9D:9C:5B:2D:A5:BF:EC:D1:FA:84:51:F4:8C:FD:9B:AF (alt names:
"DNS:puppet", "DNS:puppet.dev.example.com", "DNS:puppet.example.com",
"DNS:puppet.prod.example.com")
```

```
puppet# puppet cert sign puppet.example.com
```

```
Notice: Signed certificate request for puppet.example.com
```

```
Notice: Removing file Puppet::SSL::CertificateRequest puppet.example.com
at '/var/lib/puppet/ssl/ca/requests/puppet.example.com.pem'
```

 We specified the `ssldir` directive in our configuration. To interactively determine where the certificates will be stored using the following command line:

`$ puppet config print ssldir`

One last task is to copy the certificate that you just signed into `certs` by navigating to `/var/lib/puppet/ssl/certs`. You can use Puppet certificate find to do this using the following command:

```
# puppet certificate find puppet.example.com --ca-location local
-----BEGIN CERTIFICATE-----
MIIF1TCCA72gAwIBAgIBAjANBgkqhkiG9w0BAQsFADAoMSYwJAYDVQQDDB1QdXBw
...
-----END CERTIFICATE-----
```

When you install Puppet from the `puppetlabs` repository, the rpm will create an Apache configuration file called `apache2.conf`. Locate this file and copy it into your Apache configuration directory using the following command:

```
# cp /usr/share/puppet/ext/rack/example-passenger-vhost.conf /etc/httpd/
conf.d/puppet.conf
```

We will now show the Apache config file and point out the important settings using the following configuration:

```
PassengerHighPerformance on
PassengerMaxPoolSize 12
PassengerPoolIdleTime 1500
# PassengerMaxRequests 1000
PassengerStatThrottleRate 120
RackAutoDetect Off
RailsAutoDetect Off
```

The preceding lines of code configure passenger for performance. `PassengerHighPerformance` turns off some compatibility that isn't required. The other options are tuning parameters. For more information on these settings, see `http://www.modrails.com/documentation/Users%20guide%20Apache.html`.

Next we will need to modify the file to ensure it points to the newly created certificates. We will need to edit the lines for `SSLCertificateFile` and `SSLCertificateKeyFile`. The other SSL file settings should point to the correct certificate, chain, and revocation list files as shown in the following code:

```
Listen 8140
<VirtualHost *:8140>
  ServerName puppet.example.com
  SSLEngine on
  SSLProtocol -ALL +SSLv3 +TLSv1
  SSLCipherSuite ALL:!ADH:RC4+RSA:+HIGH:+MEDIUM:-LOW:-SSLv2:-EXP

  SSLCertificateFile /var/lib/puppet/ssl/certs/puppet.example.com.pem
  SSLCertificateKeyFile /var/lib/puppet/ssl/private_keys/puppet.
example.com.pem
  SSLCertificateChainFile /var/lib/puppet/ssl/ca/ca_crt.pem
  SSLCACertificateFile /var/lib/puppet/ssl/ca/ca_crt.pem
  # If Apache complains about invalid signatures on the CRL, you can
try disabling
  # CRL checking by commenting the next line, but this is not
recommended.
  SSLCARevocationFile /var/lib/puppet/ssl/ca/ca_crl.pem
  SSLVerifyClient optional
  SSLVerifyDepth 1
  # The `ExportCertData` option is needed for agent certificate
expiration warnings
  SSLOptions +StdEnvVars +ExportCertData
  RequestHeader set X-SSL-Subject %{SSL_CLIENT_S_DN}e
  RequestHeader set X-Client-DN %{SSL_CLIENT_S_DN}e
  RequestHeader set X-Client-Verify %{SSL_CLIENT_VERIFY}e

  DocumentRoot /etc/puppet/rack/public/
```

```
    RackBaseURI /
<Directory /etc/puppet/rack/>
  Options None
  AllowOverride None
  Order allow,deny
  allow from all
</Directory>
</VirtualHost>
```

In this VirtualHost we listen on 8140 and configure the SSL certificates in the SSL lines. The RequestHeader lines are used to pass certificate information to the Puppet process spawned by passenger. The DocumentRoot and RackBaseURI settings are used to tell passenger where to find its configuration file `config.ru`. We create `/etc/puppet/rack` and it's subdirectories and then copy the example `config.ru` into that directory using the following commands:

```
# mkdir -p /etc/puppet/rack/{public,tmp}
```

```
# cp /usr/share/puppet/ext/rack/files/config.ru /etc/puppet/rack
```

```
# chown puppet:puppet /etc/puppet/rack/config.ru
```

We change the owner of `config.ru` to `puppet:puppet` as the passenger process will run as the owner of `config.ru`. Our `config.ru` will contain the following code:

```
$0 = "master"


# if you want debugging:
# ARGV << "--debug"


ARGV << "--rack"
ARGV << "--confdir" << "/etc/puppet"
ARGV << "--vardir"  << "/var/lib/puppet"


require 'puppet/util/command_line'
run Puppet::Util::CommandLine.new.execute
```

In this example, we have used the repository rpms supplied by Puppet and EPEL. In a production installation, you would use `reposync` to copy these repositories locally so that your Puppet machines do not need to access the Internet directly.

The `config.ru` file sets the command-line arguments for Puppet. The ARGV lines are used to set additional parameters to the puppet process. As noted in the Puppet master main page, any valid configuration parameter from `puppet.conf` can be specified as an argument here. Only the options that affect where Puppet will look for files should be specified here. Once puppet knows where to find `puppet.conf`, adding arguments here could be confusing.

With this configuration in place, we are ready to start Apache as our Puppet master. Simply start Apache with a service `httpd` start.

SELinux

Security Enhanced Linux (SELinux) is a system for Linux that provides support for **mandatory access controls (MA**C). If your servers are running with SELinux enabled, great! You will need to make some policy changes to allow Puppet to work within passenger. The easiest way to build up your policy is to use *audit2allow*, which is provided in policycoreutils-python. Rotate the audit logs to get a clean log file, and then start a Puppet run. After the Puppet run, get audit2allow to build a policy module for you and insert it. Then turn SELinux back on. Refer to `https://bugzilla.redhat.com/show_bug.cgi?id=1051461` for more information.

```
# setenforce 0
# service auditd rotate
# service httpd restart
(start a puppet run remotely)
# audit2allow -i /var/log/audit/audit.log -M puppet_
passenger
# semodule -i puppet_passenger.pp
# setenforce 1
```

If necessary, repeat the process until everything runs cleanly. `semodule` will sometimes suggest enabling the `allow_ypbind` Boolean; this is a very bad idea. The `allow_ypbind` Boolean allows so many things that it is almost as bad as turning SELinux off.

Now that Puppet is running, you'll need to open the local firewall (`iptables`) on port 8140 to allow your nodes to connect. Then you'll need an example `site.pp` to get started. For testing we will create a basic `site.pp` that defines a default node with a single class attached to the default node as shown in the following code:

```
node default {
  include example
}

class example {
  notify {"This is an example": }
}
```

You can start a practice node or two and run their agent against the Puppet server either using `--server puppet.example.com` or editing the agents `puppet.conf` file to point at your server. Agents will by default look for an unqualified host called Puppet. Then search based on your DNS configuration (`search` in `/etc/resolv.conf`), and if you do not control DNS, you may have to edit the local `/etc/hosts` file to specify the IP address of your Puppet master. A sample run, for a node called `node1`, should look something like the following commands:

```
[root@node1 ~]# puppet agent -t
Info: Creating a new SSL key for node1
Info: Caching certificate for ca
Info: Creating a new SSL certificate request for node1
Info: Certificate Request fingerprint (SHA256): C4:0D:7A:54:ED:C8:E8:CC:6
8:D0:A6:13:C4:91:28:3D:B1:66:71:48:57:85:D8:99:AF:D0:81:54:B9:64:AB:F2
Exiting; no certificate found and waitforcert is disabled
```

Sign the certificate on the Puppet master and run again; the run should look like the following commands:

```
[root@puppet ~]# puppet cert sign node1
Notice: Signed certificate request for node1
Notice: Removing file Puppet::SSL::CertificateRequest node1 at '/var/lib/
puppet/ssl/ca/requests/node1.pem'


[root@node1 ~]# puppet agent -t
Info: Caching certificate for node1
Info: Caching certificate_revocation_list for ca
Info: Retrieving plugin
Info: Caching catalog for node1
Info: Applying configuration version '1386310193'
Notice: This is an example
Notice: /Stage[main]/Example/Notify[This is an example]/message: defined
'message' as 'This is an example'
Notice: Finished catalog run in 0.03 seconds
```

You now have a working passenger configuration. This configuration can handle a much larger load than the default WEBrick server provided with puppet. Puppet Labs suggests the WEBrick server is appropriate for *small* installations; in my experience that number is much less than 100 nodes, maybe even less than 50. You can tune the passenger configuration and handle a large number of nodes, but to handle a very large installation (1000s of nodes), you'll need to start splitting up the workload.

Splitting up the workload

Puppet is a web service. But there are several different components supporting that web service, as shown in the following diagram:

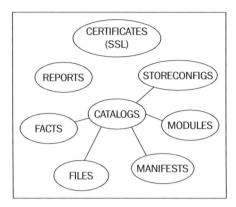

Each of the different components in your Puppet infrastructure: SSL CA, Reporting, Storeconfigs, and Catalog compilation can be split up into their own server or servers.

Certificate signing

Unless you are having issues with certificate signing consuming too many resources, it's simpler to keep the signing machine a single instance, possibly with a hot spare. Having multiple certificate signing machines means that you have to keep certificate revocation lists synchronized.

Reporting

Reporting should be done on a single instance if possible. Reporting options will be shown in *Chapter 7, Reporting and Orchestration*.

Storeconfigs

Storeconfigs should be run on a single server, storeconfigs allows for exported resources and is optional. The recommended configuration for storeconfigs is puppetdb, which can handle several thousand nodes in a single installation.

Catalog compilation

Catalog compilation is the one task that can really bog down your Puppet installation. Splitting compilation among a pool of workers is the biggest win for scaling your deployment. The idea here is to have a primary point of contact for all your nodes—the Puppet master. Then, using proxying techniques, the master will direct requests to specific worker machines within your Puppet infrastructure. From the perspective of the nodes checking into the Puppet master, all the interaction appears to come from the main proxy machine.

To understand how we are going to achieve this load balancing, we first need to look at how the agents request data from our Puppet master. The request URL sent to our Puppet master has the format `https://puppetserver:8140/environment/resource/key`. The "environment" in the request URL is the Puppet environment in use by the node. It defaults to production but can be other values as we will see in later chapters. The resource being requested can be any of the accepted REST API calls, such as: catalog, certificate, resource, report, `file_metadata`, or `file_content`. A complete listing of the `http_api` is available at `http://docs.puppetlabs.com/guides/rest_api.html`.

Requests from nodes to the Puppet masters follow a pattern that we can use to configure our proxy machine. The pattern is as follows:

`/environment/resource/key`

For example, when `node1.example.com` requests its catalog in the production environment, it connects to the server and requests the following (using URL encoding):

`https://puppet.example.com:8140/production/catalog/node1.example.com`.

Knowing that there is a pattern to the requests, we can configure Apache to redirect requests based on regular expression matches to different machines in our Puppet infrastructure.

Our first step in splitting up our load will be to clone our Puppet master server twice to create two new worker machines, which we will call `worker1.example.com` and `worker2.example.com`. In this example, we will use `192.168.100.101` for worker1 and `192.168.100.102` for worker2. Create a private network for all the Puppet communication on `192.168.100.0/24`. Our Puppet master will use the address `192.168.100.100`. It is important to create a private network for the worker machines as our proxy configuration removes the SSL encryption, which means that communication between the workers and the master proxy machine is unencrypted.

Our new Puppet infrastructure is shown in the following diagram:

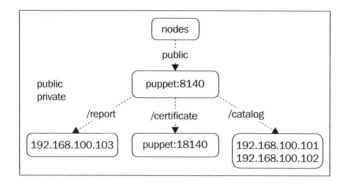

On our Puppet server, we will change the Apache `puppet.conf` as follows. Instead of listening on 8140, we will listen on 18140, and importantly, only listen on our private network as this traffic will be unencrypted. Next, we will not enable SSL on 18140. And finally we will remove any header settings we were making in our original file as shown in the following configuration:

```
PassengerHighPerformance on
PassengerMaxPoolSize 12
PassengerPoolIdleTime 1500
# PassengerMaxRequests 1000
PassengerStatThrottleRate 120
RackAutoDetect Off
RailsAutoDetect Off

Listen 127.0.0.1:18140
Listen 192.168.100.100:18140

<VirtualHost *:18140>
  ServerName puppet.example.com
  DocumentRoot /etc/puppet/rack/public/
  RackBaseURI /
  <Directory /etc/puppet/rack/>
    Options None
    AllowOverride None
    Order allow,deny
    allow from all
  </Directory>
</VirtualHost>
```

The configuration for this VirtualHost is much simpler. Now, on the worker machines, create `/etc/httpd/conf.d/puppet.conf` files that are identical to the previous files but have different `Listen` directives shown as follows:

- On worker1:

```
Listen 192.168.100.101:18140
```

- On worker2:

```
Listen 192.168.100.102:18140
```

Remember to open port 18140 on the worker machines' firewalls (`iptables`) and start `httpd`.

Returning to the Puppet master machine, create a `proxy.conf` file in the Apache `conf.d` directory (`/etc/httpd/conf.d`) to point at the workers. We will create two proxy pools. The first is for certificate signing, called puppetca, as shown in the following configuration:

```
<Proxy balancer://puppetca>
BalancerMember http://127.0.0.1:18140
</Proxy>
```

A second proxy pool is for catalog compilation, called puppetworker, as shown in the following configuration:

```
<Proxy balancer://puppetworker>
BalancerMember http://192.168.100.102:18140
BalancerMember http://192.168.100.101:18140
</Proxy>
```

Next recreate the Puppet VirtualHost listener for 8140 with the SSL and certificate information used previously, as shown in the following configuration:

```
LoadModule ssl_module modules/mod_ssl.so


Listen 8140
<VirtualHost *:8140>
ServerName puppet.example.com
        SSLEngine on
        SSLProtocol -ALL +SSLv3 +TLSv1
        SSLCipherSuite ALL:!ADH:RC4+RSA:+HIGH:+MEDIUM:-LOW:-SSLv2:-
        EXP
```

```
    SSLCertificateFile

    /var/lib/puppet/ssl/certs/puppet.example.com.pem

    SSLCertificateKeyFile

  /var/lib/puppet/ssl/private_keys/puppet.example.com.pem

    SSLCertificateChainFile /var/lib/puppet/ssl/ca/ca_crt.pem

    SSLCACertificateFile    /var/lib/puppet/ssl/ca/ca_crt.pem

    # If Apache complains about invalid signatures on the CRL, you can
try disabling

    # CRL checking by commenting the next line, but this is not
recommended.

    SSLCARevocationFile     /var/lib/puppet/ssl/ca/ca_crl.pem

    SSLVerifyClient optional

    SSLVerifyDepth  1

    # The `ExportCertData` option is needed for agent certificate
expiration warnings

    SSLOptions +StdEnvVars +ExportCertData

    # This header needs to be set if using a loadbalancer or proxy

    RequestHeader unset X-Forwarded-For

    RequestHeader set X-SSL-Subject %{SSL_CLIENT_S_DN}e

    RequestHeader set X-Client-DN %{SSL_CLIENT_S_DN}e

    RequestHeader set X-Client-Verify %{SSL_CLIENT_VERIFY}e
```

Since we know that we want all certificate requests going to the puppetca balancer, we use `ProxyPassMatch` to match URLs that have a certificate as the second phrase following the environment as shown in the next configuration. Our regular expression searches for a single word followed by `/certificate.*`, and any match is sent to our puppetca balancer.

```
ProxyPassMatch ^/([^/]+/certificate.*)$ balancer://puppetca/$1
```

The only thing that remains is to send all noncertificate requests to our load balancing pair, worker1 and worker2, as shown in the following configuration:

```
ProxyPass / balancer://puppetworker/

ProxyPassReverse / balancer://puppetworker

</VirtualHost>
```

At this point, we can restart Apache on the Puppet master.

SELinux

You'll need to allow Puppet to bind to port 18140 at this point since the default puppet SELinux module allows for 8140 only. You will also need to allow Apache to connect to the worker instances; there is a Boolean for that, `httpd_can_network_connect`.

Now, when a node connects, if it requests for a certificate, it will be redirected to the VirtualHost on port 18140 on the Puppet master. If the node requests a catalog, it will be redirected to one of the worker nodes. To convince yourself that this is the case, edit `/etc/puppet/manifests/site.pp` on your worker1 node and insert `notify` as shown in the following configuration:

```
node default {
  include example
  notify {'Compiled on worker1': }
}
```

Do the same on worker2 with the message `Compiled on worker2`, run puppet agent again on your node, and see where the catalog is being compiled using the following commands:

```
[root@node1 ~]# puppet agent -t
Info: Retrieving plugin
Info: Caching catalog for node1
Info: Applying configuration version '1386312527'
Notice: Compiled on worker1
Notice: /Stage[main]//Node[default]/Notify[Compiled on worker1]/message:
defined 'message' as 'Compiled on worker1'
Notice: This is an example
Notice: /Stage[main]/Example/Notify[This is an example]/message: defined
'message' as 'This is an example'
Notice: Finished catalog run in 0.10 seconds
```

You may see "Compiled on worker2", which is expected.

To verify that certificates are being handled properly, clean the certificate for your example node, remove it from the node, and restart the agent.

- On the master:

    ```
    master# puppet cert clean node1
    ```

- On the node:

```
node1# \rm -r /var/lib/puppet/ssl/*
node1# puppet agent -t
```

Alternatively to this configuration, you could use the puppetca setting in `puppet.conf` on your nodes to get clients to use a specific machine for signing requests.

Since this is an enterprise installation, we should have a dashboard of some kind running to collect reports from workers.

If your reports setting on the master is either HTTP or `puppetdb`, then this section won't affect you.

We'll clone our worker again to make a new server called reports (192.168.100.103), which will collect our reports. We then have to add another line to our Apache `proxy.conf` configuration file to use the new server, and we need to place this line directly after the certificate proxy line. Since reports must all be sent to the same machine to be useful, we won't use a balancer line as before, and we will simply set the proxy to the address of the reports machine directly.

```
ProxyPassMatch ^/([^/]+/certificate.*)$ balancer://puppetca/$1
ProxyPassMatch ^/([^/]+/report/.*)$ http://192.168.100.103/$1
ProxyPass / balancer://puppetworker/
```

Keep the `/etc/httpd/conf.d/proxy.conf` balancer section updated to send reports to `192.168.100.103`.

Again, restart Apache and make sure that `report=true` is set on the node in the `[agent]` section of `puppet.conf`. Run Puppet agent on the node, and verify that the report gets sent to 192.168.100.103 (look in `/var/lib/puppet/reports/`).

If you are still seeing problems with client catalog compilation timeouts after creating multiple catalog workers, it may be that your client is timing out the connection before the worker has a chance to compile the catalog. Try experimenting with the `configtimeout` parameter in the `[agent]` section of `puppet.conf`

```
configtimeout=300
```

Setting this higher may resolve your issue. You will need to change the `ProxyTimeout` directive in the `proxy.conf` configuration for Apache as well. This will be revisited in *Chapter 10, Troubleshooting*.

Keeping the code consistent

At this point, we are able to scale out our catalog compilation to as many servers as we need, but we've neglected one important thing: we need to make sure that the Puppet code on all the workers remains in sync. There are a few ways we can do this, and when we cover integration with Git in *Chapter 3, Git and Environments*, we will see how to use Git to distribute the code.

Rsync

A simple way to distribute the code is with rsync; this isn't the best solution, but just for example, you will need to run rsync whenever you change the code. This will require changing the Puppet user's shell from `/sbin/nologin` to `/bin/bash` or `/bin/rbash`, which is a potential security risk.

 If your puppet code is on a filesystem that supports ACLs, then creating an rsync user and giving that user rights to that filesystem is a better option. Using `setfacl`, it is possible to grant write access to the filesystem for a user other than Puppet.

First we create an ssh-key for rsync to use to ssh between the worker nodes and the master. We then copy the key into the `authorized_keys` file of the Puppet user on the workers using the `ssh-copy-id` command as follows:

```
puppet# ssh-keygen -f puppet_rsync
(creates puppet_rsync.pub puppet_rsync)

worker1# mkdir /var/lib/puppet/.ssh
# cp puppet_rsync.pub /var/lib/puppet/.ssh/authorized_keys
# chown -R puppet:puppet /var/lib/puppet/.ssh
# chmod 700 /var/lib/puppet/.ssh
# chmod 600 /var/lib/puppet/.ssh/authorized_keys
# chsh -s /bin/bash puppet

puppet# rsync -e 'ssh -i puppet_rsync' -az /etc/puppet/ puppet@worker1:/etc/puppet
```

 Creating SSH Keys and using rsync

The trailing slash on the first part `/etc/puppet/` and the absence of the slash on the second part, `puppet@worker1:/etc/puppet` is by design. That way, we get the contents of `/etc/puppet` on the master placed into `/etc/puppet` on the worker.

Using rsync is not a good enterprise solution, and the concept of using SSH Keys and transferring the files as the Puppet user is the important part of this method.

NFS

A second option to keep the code consistent is to use NFS. If you already have an NAS appliance, then using the NAS to share out the Puppet code may be the simplest solution. If not, using the Puppet master as an NFS server is another, but this does make your Puppet master a big, single point of failure. NFS is not the best solution to this sort of problem.

Clustered filesystem

Using a clustered filesystem such as `gfs2` or `glusterfs` is a good way to maintain consistency between nodes. This also removes the problem of the single point of failure with NFS.

Git

A third option is to have your version control system keep the files in sync with a post-commit hook or scripts that call Git directly, such as `r10k` or `puppet-sync`. We will cover how to configure Git to do some housekeeping for us in a later chapter. Using Git to distribute the code is a popular solution since it only updates the code when a commit is made, the continuous delivery model. If your organization would rather push code at certain points, then using the scripts mentioned earlier on a routine basis is the solution I would suggest.

One more split

Now that we have our Puppet infrastructure running on two workers and the master, you might notice that the main Apache virtual machine need not be on the same machine as the certificate-signing machine. At this point, there is no need to run passenger on that main gateway machine, and you are open to use whatever load balancing solution you see fit. In this example I will be using nginx as the main proxy point.

Using nginx is not required, but you may wish to use nginx as the proxy machine. This is because nginx has more configuration options for its proxy module, such as redirecting based on client IP address.

The important thing to remember here is that we are just providing a web service. We'll intercept the SSL part of the communication with nginx and then forward it onto our worker and CA machines as necessary. Our configuration will now look like the following diagram:

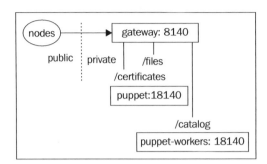

We will start with a blank machine this time; we do not need to install passenger or Puppet on the machine. To make use of the latest SSL-handling routines, we will download nginx from the nginx repository.

```
# yum install http://nginx.org/packages/rhel/6/noarch/RPMS/nginx-release-rhel-6-0.el6.ngx.noarch.rpm
Installed:
  nginx-release-rhel.noarch 0:6-0.el6.ngx
# yum install nginx
Installed:
  nginx-1.4.4-1.el6.ngx.x86_64
```

Now we need to copy the SSL CA files from the Puppet master to this gateway using the following commands:

```
puppet# scp /var/lib/puppet/ssl/ca/ca_crl.pem gateway:/etc/nginx

puppet# scp /var/lib/puppet/ssl/ca/ca_crt.pem gateway:/etc/nginx

puppet# scp /var/lib/puppet/ssl/certs/puppet.example.com.pem gateway:/etc/nginx

puppet# scp /var/lib/puppet/ssl/private_keys/puppet.example.com.pem gateway:/etc/nginx/puppet.example.com.key
```

Now we need to create a gateway configuration for `nginx`, which we will place in `/etc/ngninx/conf.d/puppet-proxy.conf`

We will define the two proxy pools as we did before, but using nginx syntax this time.

```
upstream puppetca {
  server 192.168.100.100:18140;
}

upstream puppetworkers {
  server 192.168.100.101:8140;
  server 192.168.100.102:8140;
}
```

Next, we create a server stanza, specifying that we handle the SSL connection, and we need to set some headers before passing on the communication to our proxied servers.

```
server {
  listen 8140 ssl;
  server_name puppet.example.com;

  default_type application/x-raw;

  ssl on;
  ssl_certificate     puppet.example.com.pem;
  ssl_certificate_key puppet.example.com.key;
  ssl_trusted_certificate  ca_crt.pem;
  ssl_crl       ca_crl.pem;

  ssl_session_cache   shared:SSL:5m;
  ssl_session_timeout  5m;

  ssl_protocols     SSLv2 SSLv3 TLSv1;
  ssl_ciphers
  ALL:!ADH:!EXPORT56:RC4+RSA:+HIGH:+MEDIUM:+LOW:+SSLv2:+EXP;
  ssl_prefer_server_ciphers on;
  ssl_verify_client optional_no_ca;
```

Setting `ssl_verify_client` to `optional_no_ca` is important, since on the first connection, the client will not have a signed certificate, so we need to accept all connections but mark a header with the verification status.

```
proxy_set_header   Host        $host;
proxy_set_header   X-Real-IP  $remote_addr;
proxy_set_header    X-Forwarded-For $proxy_add_x_forwarded_for;
proxy_set_header   X-Client-Verify  $ssl_client_verify;
proxy_set_header   X-Client-DN     $ssl_client_s_dn;
proxy_set_header   X-SSL-Subject    $ssl_client_s_dn;
proxy_set_header    X-SSL-Issuer     $ssl_client_i_dn;
proxy_read_timeout  1000;
```

The header `X-Client-Verify` will hold success or failure at this point, so our Puppet master will know if the certificate is valid. Now we need to look for certificate requests and hand those off to the `puppetca` pool:

```
location ~* ^/.*/certificate {
  proxy_pass     http://puppetca;
  proxy_redirect    off;
  proxy_read_timeout  1000;
}
```

Then we can send all other requests to our worker pool

```
location / {
  proxy_pass     http://puppetworkers;
  proxy_redirect     off;
  proxy_read_timeout  1000;
}
```

Now we need to start nginx on the gateway machine, open up port 8140 on the firewall, and open up 18140 on the Puppet master firewall (gateway will now need to communicate with that port).

Running puppet again on your node will now produce the same results as before, but you are now able to leverage the load balancing of nginx over that of Apache.

You will need to synchronize the SSL CA Certificate Revocation List (CRL) from the Puppet master to the gateway machine. Without synchronization, the keys that are removed from the Puppet master will not be revoked on the gateway machine.

One last split or maybe a few more

We have already split our workload into a certificate-signing machine (the master or puppetca), a pool of catalog machines, and a report-gathering machine. What is interesting as an exercise at this point is that we can also serve files up using our gateway machine.

Based on what we know about the puppet HTTP API, we know that requests for `file_buckets`, and files have specific URIs that we can serve directly from nginx without using passenger or Apache or even puppet. To test the configuration, alter the definition of the example class to include a file as follows:

```
class example {
  notify { 'This is an example': }
  file {'/tmp/example':
    mode => 644,
    owner => 100,
    group => 100,
    source => 'puppet:///modules/example/example',
  }
}
```

Create the example file in `/etc/puppet/modules/example/files/example`.

This file lives on the workers. On the gateway machine, rsync your Puppet module code from the workers into `/var/lib/nginx/puppet`. Now, to prove that the file is coming from the gateway, edit the example file after you run the rsync.

The `/etc/puppet/modules/example/files/example` file lives on the gateway. At this point, we can start serving up files from nginx by putting in a location clause as follows; we will do two stanzas, one for files outside modules and the other for module-provided files at `/etc/nginx/conf.d/gateway.conf`.

```
location ~* ^/.*/file_content/modules {
  rewrite ^/([^/]+)/file_content/modules/([^/]+)/(.*) /$2/files/$3;
  break;
  root /var/lib/nginx/puppet/modules/;
}
location ~* ^/.*/file_content/ {
  rewrite ^/([^/]+)/file_content/([^/]+)/(.*) /$2/files/$3;
  break;
  root /var/lib/nginx/puppet/;
}
```

Restart nginx on the gateway machine, and then run Puppet on the node using the following command:

```
[root@node1 ~]# puppet agent -t
...
Notice: /Stage[main]/Example/File[/tmp/example]/ensure: defined content
as '{md5}c83849f23a139c41edfbcd8473a81ac1'
...
Notice: Finished catalog run in 0.16 seconds
[root@node1 ~]# cat /tmp/example
This file lives on the gateway
```

As we can see, although the file living on the workers has the contents "This file lives on the workers," our node is getting the file directly from nginx on the gateway.

> Our node will keep changing /tmp/example to the same file each time because the catalog is compiled on the worker machine with contents different from those of the gateway. In a production environment, all the files would need to be synchronized.

One important thing to consider is security, as any configured client can retrieve files from our gateway machine. In production, you would want to add ACLs to the file location.

As we have seen, once the basic proxying is configured, further splitting up of the workload becomes a routine task. We can split the workload to scale to handle as many nodes as we require.

Conquer by dividing

Depending on the size of your deployment and the way you connect to all your nodes, a masterless solution may be a good fit. In a masterless configuration, you don't run the Puppet agent; rather, you push the Puppet code to a node, and then run Puppet apply. There are a few benefits to this method and a few drawbacks.

Benefits	Drawbacks
No single point of failure	Can't use built-in reporting tools such as dashboard.
Simpler configuration	Exported resources requires nodes have write access to the database.
Finer-grained control on where code is deployed	Each node has access to all the code
Multiple simultaneous runs do not affect each other (reduces contention)	More difficult to know when a node is failing to apply catalog correctly
Connection to Puppet master not required (offline possible)	No certificate management
No certificate management	

The idea with a masterless configuration is that you distribute the Puppet code to each node individually and then kick off a puppet run to apply that code. One of the benefits of Puppet is that it keeps your system in a known good state, so when choosing masterless it is important to build your solution with this in mind. A cron job configured by your deployment mechanism that can apply Puppet to the node on a routine schedule will suffice.

The key parts of a masterless configuration are: distributing the code, pushing updates to the code, and ensuring the code is applied routinely to the nodes. Pushing a bunch of files to a machine is best done with some sort of package management.

 Many masterless configurations use Git to have clients pull the files, this has the advantage of clients pulling changes.

For Linux systems, the big players are rpm and dpkg, whereas for MacOS, Installer package files can be used. It is also possible to configure the nodes to download the code themselves from a web location. Some large installations use Git to update the code as well.

The solution I will outline is that of using an rpm deployed through yum to install and run Puppet on a node. Once deployed, we can have the nodes pull updated code from a central repository rather than rebuild the rpm for every change.

Creating an rpm

To start our rpm, we will make an rpm spec file, we can make this anywhere since we don't have a master in this example. Start by installing rpm-build, which will allow us to build the rpm.

```
# yum install rpm-build
Installing
  rpm-build-4.8.0-37.el6.x86_64
```

It will be important later to have a user to manage the repository, so create a user called builder at this point. We'll do this on the Puppet master machine we built earlier. Create an rpmbuild directory with the appropriate subdirectories, and then create our example code in this location.

```
# sudo -iu builder
$ mkdir -p rpmbuild/{SPECS,SOURCES}
$ cd SOURCES
$ mkdir -p modules/example/manifests
$ cat <<EOF>modules/example/manifests/init.pp
class example {
notify {"This is an example.": }
file {'/tmp/example':
mode => '0644',
owner => '0',
group => '0',
content => 'This is also an example.'
}
}
EOF
$ tar cjf example.com-puppet-1.0.tar.bz2 modules
```

Next, create a spec file for our rpm in rpmbuild/SPECS as shown in the following commands:

```
Name:           example.com-puppet
Version: 1.0
Release: 1%{?dist}
Summary: Puppet Apply for example.com

Group: System/Utilities
```

```
License: GNU
Source0: example.com-puppet-%{version}.tar.bz2
BuildRoot: %(mktemp -ud %{_tmppath}/%{name}-%{version}-%{release}-XXXXXX)

Requires: puppet
BuildArch:      noarch

%description
This package installs example.com's puppet configuration
and applies that configuration on the machine.


%prep

%setup -q -c
%install
mkdir -p $RPM_BUILD_ROOT/%{_localstatedir}/local/puppet
cp -a . $RPM_BUILD_ROOT/%{_localstatedir}/local/puppet

%clean
rm -rf %{buildroot}

%files
%defattr(-,root,root,-)
%{_localstatedir}/local/puppet

%post
# run puppet apply
/bin/env puppet apply --logdest syslog --modulepath=%{_localstatedir}/
local/puppet/modules %{_localstatedir}/local/puppet/manifests/site.pp

%changelog
* Fri Dec 6 2013 Thomas Uphill <thomas@narrabilis.com> - 1.0-1
- initial build
```

Then use `rpmbuild` to build the rpm based on this spec, as shown in the following command:

```
$ rpmbuild -ba example.com-puppet.spec
...
Wrote: /home/builder/rpmbuild/SRPMS/example.com-puppet-1.0-1.el6.src.rpm
Wrote: /home/builder/rpmbuild/RPMS/noarch/example.com-puppet-1.0-1.el6.
noarch.rpm
```

Now, deploy a node and copy the rpm onto that node. Verify that the node installs Puppet and then does a Puppet apply run.

```
# yum install example.com-puppet-1.0-1.el6.noarch.rpm
Loaded plugins: downloadonly
...
Installed:
  example.com-puppet.noarch 0:1.0-1.el6
Dependency Installed:
  augeas-libs.x86_64 0:1.0.0-5.el6
. . .
  puppet-3.3.2-1.el6.noarch
...
Complete!
```

Verify that the file we specified in our package has been created by using the following command:

```
# cat /tmp/example
This is also an example.
```

Now, if we are going to rely on this system of pushing Puppet to nodes, we have to make sure we can update the rpm on the clients and we have to ensure that the nodes still run Puppet regularly so as to avoid configuration drift (the whole point of Puppet). There are many ways to accomplish these two tasks. We can put the cron definition into the post section of our rpm:

```
%post
# install cron job
/bin/env puppet resource cron 'example.com-puppet' command='/bin/
env puppet apply --logdest syslog --modulepath=%{_localstatedir}/
local/puppet/modules %{_localstatedir}/local/puppet/manifests/site.pp'
minute='*/30' ensure='present'
```

We could have a cron job be part of our `site.pp`, as shown in the following command:

```
cron { 'example.com-puppet':
  ensure      => 'present',
  command => '/bin/env puppet apply --logdest syslog --modulepath=/var/
local/puppet/modules /var/local/puppet/manifests/site.pp',
  minute  => ['*/30'],
  target  => 'root',
  user  => 'root',
}
```

To ensure the nodes have the latest version of the code, we can define our package in the `site.pp`.

```
package {'example.com-puppet':  ensure => 'latest' }
```

In order for that to work as expected, we need to have a yum repository for the package and have the nodes looking at that repository for packages.

Creating the YUM repository

Creating a YUM repository is a very straightforward task. Install the `createrepo` rpm and then run `createrepo` on each directory you wish to make into a repository.

```
# mkdir /var/www/html/puppet
# yum install createrepo
...
Installed:
 createrepo.noarch 0:0.9.9-18.el6
# chown builder /var/www/html/puppet
# sudo -iu builder
$ mkdir /var/www/html/puppet/{noarch,SRPMS}
$ cp /home/builder/rpmbuild/RPMS/noarch/example.com-puppet-1.0-1.el6.
noarch.rpm /var/www/html/puppet/noarch
$ cp rpmbuild/SRPMS/example.com-puppet-1.0-1.el6.src.rpm /var/www/html/
puppet/SRPMS
$ cd /var/www/html/puppet
$ createrepo noarch
$ createrepo SRPMS
```

Our repository is ready, but we need to export it with the web server to make it available to our nodes. This rpm contains all our Puppet code, so we need to ensure that only the clients we wish get access to the files. We'll create a simple listener on port 80 for our Puppet repository

```
Listen 80
<VirtualHost *:80>
  DocumentRoot /var/www/html/puppet
</VirtualHost>
```

Now, the nodes need to have the repository defined on them so they can download the updates when they are made available via the repository. The idea here is that we push the rpm to the nodes and have them install the rpm. Once the rpm is installed, the yum repository pointing to updates is defined and the nodes continue updating themselves.

```
yumrepo { 'example.com-puppet':
  baseurl  => 'http://puppet.example.com/noarch',
  descr    => 'example.com Puppet Code Repository',
  enabled  => '1',
  gpgcheck => '0',
}
```

So to ensure that our nodes operate properly, we have to make sure of the following things:

- Install code
- Define repository
- Define cron job to run Puppet apply routinely
- Define package with *latest* tag to ensure it is updated

A default node in our masterless configuration requires that the cron task and the repository be defined. If you wish to segregate your nodes into different production zones (such as development, production, and sandbox), I would use a repository management system like Pulp. Pulp allows you to define repositories based on other repositories and keeps all your repositories consistent.

> You should also setup a gpg key on the builder account that can sign the packages it creates. You would then distribute the gpg public key to all your nodes and enable gpgcheck on the repository definition.

Summary

Dealing with scale is a very important task in enterprise deployments. As your number of nodes increases beyond the proof-of-concept stage (> 50 nodes), the simple WEBrick server cannot be used. In the first section, we configured a Puppet master with passenger to handle a larger load. We then expanded that configuration with load balancing and proxying techniques realizing that Puppet is simply a web service. Understanding how nodes request files, catalogs, and certificates allows you to modify the configuration and bypass or alleviate bottlenecks.

In the last section, we explored masterless configuration, wherein instead of checking into Puppet to retrieve new code, the nodes check out the code first and then run against it on a schedule.

Now that we have dealt with the load issue, we need to turn our attention to managing the modules to be applied to nodes. We will cover organizing the nodes in the next chapter.

2
Organizing Your Nodes and Data

Now that we can deal with a large number of nodes in our installation, we need a way of organizing which classes we apply to each node.

There are quite a few solutions to the problem of attaching classes to nodes; in this chapter, we will examine the following node organization methods:

- An **External Node Classifier (ENC)**
- LDAP backend
- Hiera

Getting started

For the remainder of this chapter, we will assume your Puppet infrastructure is configured with a single Puppet master used for signing and a worker machine used for catalog compilation, as pictured in the following diagram:

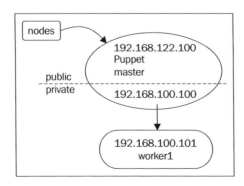

Any Puppet master configuration will be sufficient for this chapter; the previous configuration is only provided for reference.

Organizing the nodes with ENC

An ENC is a script that is run on the Puppet master, or the host compiling the catalog, to determine which classes are applied to the node. The ENC script can be written in any language, and it receives as a command-line argument `certname` (certificate name) from the node. In most cases, this will be the **Fully Qualified Domain Name (FQDN)** of the node; we will assume that the `certname` setting has not been explicitly set and that the FQDN of our nodes is being used.

We will only use the hostname portion as the FQDN can be unreliable in some instances. Across your enterprise, the naming convention of the host should not allow for multiple machines to have the same hostname. The FQDN is determined by a fact; this fact is the union of the hostname fact and the domain fact. The domain fact on Linux is determined by running the command `hostname -f`. If DNS is not configured correctly or reverse records do not exist, the domain fact will not be set and the FQDN will also not be set, as shown in the following commands:

```
# facter domain
example.com
# facter fqdn
node1.example.com
# mv /etc/resolv.conf /etc/resolv.conf.bak
# facter domain
# facter fqdn
#
```

The output of the ENC script is a YAML file, which defines the classes, variables, and environment for the node.

Unlike `site.pp`, the ENC script can only assign classes, make top-scope variables, and set the environment of the node. Environment is only set from ENC on version 3 and above of Puppet.

A simple example

To use ENC, we need to make one small change in our Puppet worker machine. We'll add the `node_terminus` and `external_nodes` lines to the `[master]` section of `puppet.conf`, as shown in the following code (we only need make this change on the worker machines as this is concerned with catalog compilation only):

```
[master]
    node_terminus = exec
    external_nodes = /usr/local/bin/simple_node_classifier
```

 The `puppet.conf` files need not be the same across our installation; workers and CA machines may have different settings.

Our first example, as shown in the following code snippet, will be written in Ruby and live in the file `/usr/local/bin/simple_node_classifier`:

```ruby
#!/bin/env ruby
require 'yaml'


# create an empty hash to contain everything
@enc = Hash.new
@enc["classes"] = Hash.new
@enc["classes"]["base"] = Hash.new
@enc["parameters"] = Hash.new
@enc["environment"] = 'production'
#convert the hash to yaml and print
puts @enc.to_yaml
exit(0)
```

Make this script executable and test it on the command line as shown in the following snippet:

```
# chmod 755 /usr/local/bin/simple_node_classifier
# /usr/local/bin/simple_node_classifier
---
classes:
  base: {}
environment: production
parameters: {}
```

This script returns a properly formatted YAML file.

 YAML files start with three dashes (---); they use colons (:) to separate parameters from values, and hyphens (-) to separate multiple values (arrays). For more information on YAML, visit http://www.yaml.org/.

If you use a language such as Ruby or Python, you do not need to know the syntax of YAML as the built-in libraries take care of the formatting for you. The following is the same example in Python. To use the Python example, you will need to install PyYAML, that is, the Python YAML interpreter as shown in the following commands:

```
# yum install PyYAML
Installed:
  PyYAML.x86_64 0:3.10-3.el6
```

The Python version starts with an empty dictionary. We then use sub-dictionaries to hold the classes, parameters, and environment. We will call our Python example /usr/local/bin/simple_node_classifier_2. The following is our example:

```
#!/bin/env python
import yaml
import sys
# create an empty hash
enc = {}
enc["classes"] = {}
enc["classes"]["base"] = {}
enc["parameters"] = {}
enc["environment"] = 'production'
# output the ENC as yaml
print "---"
print yaml.dump(enc)
sys.exit(0)
```

Make /usr/local/bin/simple_node_classifier_2 executable and run it using the following commands:

```
worker1# chmod 755 /usr/local/bin/simple_node_classifier_2
worker1# /usr/local/bin/simple_node_classifier_2
---
classes:
  base: {}
environment: production
parameters: {}
```

 The order of the lines below the --- may be different on your machine; when Python dumps the hash of values, the order is not specified.

The Python script outputs the same YAML as the Ruby code. We will now define the base class referenced in our ENC script, as shown in the following code snippet:

```
class base {
  file {'/etc/motd':
    mode => '0644',
    owner => '0',
    group => '0',
    content => inline_template("Managed Node: <%= hostname %>\nManaged
by Puppet version <%= puppetversion %>\n"),
  }
}
```

Now that our base class is defined, when we run Puppet on our node, we will see that our message of the day (/etc/motd) has been updated using an inline template, as shown in the following command-line output:

```
node1# puppet agent -t
Info: Retrieving plugin
Info: Caching catalog for node1
Info: Applying configuration version '1386748797'
Notice: /File[/etc/motd]/ensure: defined content as '{md5}
ad29f471b2cbf5754c706cdc0a54684b'
Notice: Compiled on worker1
```

```
Notice: /Stage[main]//Node[default]/Notify[Compiled on worker1]/message:
defined 'message' as 'Compiled on worker1'
Notice: This is an example
Notice: /Stage[main]/Example/Notify[This is an example]/message: defined
'message' as 'This is an example'
Notice: Finished catalog run in 0.11 seconds
node1# cat /etc/motd
Managed Node: node1
Managed by Puppet version 3.3.2
```

Since ENC is only given one piece of data ever, that is, FQDN (`certname`), we need to create a naming convention that provides us with enough information to determine which classes should be applied to the node.

Hostname strategy

In an enterprise, it's important that your hostnames are meaningful. By meaningful I mean that the hostname should give you as much information as possible about the machine; when encountering a machine in a large installation, it is very likely that you did not build the machine. You need to know as much as possible about the machine just from its name. The following key points should be readily determined from the hostname:

- Operating system
- Application/role
- Location
- Environment
- Instance

It is important that the convention is standardized and consistent. In our example, let us suppose that the application is the most important component for our organization, so we put that first, and the physical location comes next (which datacenter), followed by the operating system, environment, and instance number. The instance number will be used when you have more than one machine with the same role, location, environment, and operating system. Since we know that the instance number will always be a number, we can omit the underscore between the operating system and environment, making the hostname a little easier to type and remember.

Your enterprise may have more or less information, but the principle will remain the same. To delineate our components, we will use underscores (_); some companies rely on a fixed length for each component of the hostname so as to mark the individual components of the hostname by position alone.

In our example, we will have the following environments:

- p: This stands for production
- n: This stands for non-production
- d: This stands for development/testing/lab

Our applications will be of the following types:

- web
- db

Our operating system will be Linux, which we will shorten to just l, and our location will be our main datacenter (main). So, a production web server on Linux in the main datacenter would have the hostname web_main_lp01.

 If you think you are going to have more than 99 instances of any single service, you might want to have another leading zero to the instance number (001).

Now this looks pretty good. We know that this is a web server in our main datacenter. It's running on Linux, and it's the first machine like this in production. Now that we have a nice convention like this, we need to modify our ENC to use the convention to glean all this information from the hostname.

Modified ENC using hostname strategy

We'll build our Python ENC script (/usr/local/bin/simple_node_classifier_2) and update it to use the new hostname strategy as shown in the following commands:

```
#!/bin/env python
# Python ENC
# receives fqdn as argument

import yaml
import sys
```

```
"""output_yaml renders the hash as yaml and exits cleanly"""
def output_yaml(enc):
    # output the ENC as yaml
    print "---"
    print yaml.dump(enc)
    quit()
```

Python is very particular about spacing; if you are new to Python, take care to copy the indenting exactly as given in the previous snippet.

We define a function to print the YAML and exit the script as shown in the following commands; if the hostname doesn't match our naming standards, we'll exit the script early:

```
# create an empty hash
enc = {}
enc["classes"] = {}
enc["classes"]["base"] = {}
enc["parameters"] = {}


try:
    hostname=sys.argv[1]
except:
    # need a hostname
    sys.exit(10)
```

Exit the script early if the hostname is not defined. This is a minimum requirement, we should never reach this point.

We split the hostname using underscores (_) in an array called `parts`; we then assign indexes of `parts` to `role`, `location`, `os`, `environment`, and `instance`, as shown in the following commands:

```
# split hostname on _
try:
    parts = hostname.split('_')
    role = parts[0]
    location = parts[1]
    os = parts[2][0]
    environment = parts[2][1]
    instance = parts[2][2:]
```

We are expecting hostnames to conform to the standard; if you cannot guarantee this, then you would have to use something like the regular expression module to deal with exceptions to the naming standard.

```
except:
  # hostname didn't conform to our standard
  # include a class which notifies us of the problem
  enc["classes"]["hostname_problem"] = hostname
  output_yaml(enc)
  raise SystemExit
```

We wrapped the previous assignments in a `try` statement; in this `except` statement, we exit printing the YAML and assign a class named `hostname_problem`. This class would be used to alert us in the console or reporting system that this host has a problem.

The environment is a single character in the hostname; hence, we use a dictionary to assign a full name to the environment, as shown in the following snippet:

```
# map environment from hostname into environment
environments = {}
environments['p'] = 'production'
environments['n'] = 'nonprod'
environments['d'] = 'devel'
environments['s'] = 'sbx'
try:
  enc["environment"] = environments[environment]
except:
  enc["environment"] = 'undef'
```

The following commands are used to map a role from hostname into role:

```
# map role from hostname into role
enc["classes"][role] = {}
```

Next, we assign top scope variables to the node based on the values we obtained from the `parts` array previously:

```
# set top scope variables
enc["parameters"]["enc_hostname"] = hostname
enc["parameters"]["role"] = role
enc["parameters"]["location"] = location
```

```
enc["parameters"]["os"] = os
enc["parameters"]["instance"] = instance


output_yaml(enc)
```

Heading back to `web_main_lp01`, we run Puppet, sign the certificate on our puppetca machine, and then run Puppet again to verify that the `web` class is applied, as shown in the following commands:

```
web_main_lp01# puppet agent -t
Info: Retrieving plugin
Info: Caching catalog for web-main-lp01
Info: Applying configuration version '1386834979'
Notice: /File[/etc/motd]/ensure: defined content as '{md5}
a828f52c2447032b1864405626f4e3a4'
Notice: /Stage[main]/Web/Package[httpd]/ensure: created
Notice: /Stage[main]/Web/Service[httpd]/ensure: ensure changed 'stopped'
to 'running'
Info: /Stage[main]/Web/Service[httpd]: Unscheduling refresh on
Service[httpd]
Notice: Finished catalog run in 10.14 seconds
```

Our machine has been installed as a web server without any intervention on our part; the system knew which classes to apply to the machine based solely on the hostname. Now, if we try to run Puppet against our `node1` machine created earlier, our ENC includes the class `hostname_problem` with the parameter of the hostname passed to it. We can create this class to capture the problem and notify us. Create the `hostname_problem` module in `/etc/puppet/modules/hostname_problem/ manifests/init.pp`, as shown in the following snippet:

```
class hostname_problem ($enc_hostname) {
  notify {"WARNING: $enc_hostname ($::ipaddress) doesn't conform to
naming standards": }
}
```

Now when we run Puppet on our `node1` machine, we will get a useful warning that `node1` isn't a good hostname for our enterprise, as you can see in the following commands:

```
node1# puppet agent -t
Info: Retrieving plugin
Info: Caching catalog for node1
Info: Applying configuration version '1386916930'
```

```
Notice: WARNING: node1 (192.168.122.132) doesn't conform to naming
standards
Notice: /Stage[main]/Hostname_problem/Notify[WARNING: node1
  (192.168.122.132) doesn't conform to naming standards]/message:
  defined 'message' as 'WARNING: node1 (192.168.122.132) doesn't
  conform to naming standards'
Notice: Finished catalog run in 0.05 seconds
```

Your ENC can be customized much further than this simple example; you have the power of Python, Ruby, or any other language you wish to use. You could connect to a database and run some queries to determine classes to install. For example, if you have a CMDB at your enterprise, you could connect to the CMDB and retrieve information based on the FQDN of the node and apply classes based on that information. You could connect to a URI and retrieve a catalog (dashboard and foreman do something similar). There are many ways to expand this concept. In the next section, we'll look at using LDAP to store class information.

LDAP backend

If you already have an LDAP implementation in which you can extend the schema, then you can use the LDAP node terminus that ships with Puppet. Using this schema adds a new `objectclass` called `puppetclass`. Using this `objectclass`, you can set the environment, set top scope variables, and include classes. The LDAP schema that ships with Puppet includes `puppetClass`, `parentNode`, `environment`, and the `puppetVar` attributes that are assigned to the `objectclass` named `puppetClient`. LDAP experts should note that all four of these attributes are marked as optional and the `objectclass` named `puppetClient` is non-structural. To use the LDAP terminus, you must have a working LDAP implementation, apply the Puppet schema to that installation and add the `ruby-ldap` package to your workers (to allow Puppet to query for node information).

OpenLDAP configuration

We'll begin by setting up a fresh OpenLDAP implementation and adding a `puppet` schema. Create a new machine and install `openldap-servers`; my installation installed the version `openldap-servers-2.4.23-32.el6_4.1.x86_64`. This version requires configuration with OLC (**OpenLDAP Configuration** or runtime configuration); further information on OLC can be obtained at `http://www.openldap.org/doc/admin24/slapdconf2.html`. OLC configures LDAP using LDAP.

After installing `openldap-servers`, your configuration will be in `/etc/openldap/slapd.d/cn=config`. There is a file named `olcDatabase={2}.bdb.ldif` in this directory. Edit the file and change the following lines:

`olcSuffix: dc=example,dc=com`

`olcRootDN: cn=Manager,dc=example,dc=com`

`olcRootPW: packtpub`

> The `olcRootPW` line is not present in the default file, you will have to add it here. If you're going into production with LDAP, you should set `olcDbConfig` parameters as outlined at http://www.openldap.org/doc/admin24/slapdconf2.html.

These lines set the top-level location for your LDAP and the password for `RootDN`. This password is in plain text; a production installation would use SSHA encryption. You will be making schema changes, so you must also edit `olcDatabase={0}config.ldif` and set `rootDN` and `rootPW`. For our example, we will use the default `rootDN` value and set the password to `packtpub`, as shown in the following commands:

`olcRootDN: cn=config`

`olcRootPW: packtpub`

> You would want to keep this `RootDN` value and the previous `RootDN` values separate so that this `RootDN` value is the only one that can modify schema and top-level configuration parameters.

Next, use `ldapsearch` (provided by the `openldap-clients` package, which has to be installed separately) to verify that LDAP is working properly. Start `slapd` with `service slapd start`, and then verify with the following `ldapsearch` command:

```
# ldapsearch -LLL -x -b'dc=example,dc=com'
No such object (32)
```

This result indicates that LDAP is running but the directory is empty. To import the `puppet` schema into this version of OpenLDAP, copy the `puppet.schema` from `/usr/share/puppet/ext/ldap/puppet.schema` to `/etc/openldap/schema`. Then create a configuration file named `/tmp/puppet-ldap.conf` with an `include` line pointing to that schema, as shown in the following snippet:

```
include /etc/openldap/schema/puppet.schema
```

Then run `slaptest` against that configuration file, specifying a temporary directory as storage for the configuration files created by `slaptest`, as shown in the following commands:

```
# mkdir /tmp/puppet-ldap
# slaptest -f puppet-ldap.conf -F /tmp/puppet-ldap/
config file testing succeeded
```

This will create an OLC structure in `/tmp/puppet-ldap`; the file we need is in `/tmp/puppet-ldap/cn=config/cn=schema/cn={0}puppet.ldif`. To import this file into our LDAP instance, we need to remove the ordering information (the braces and numbers (`{0}`, `{1}`, ...) in this file). We also need to set the location for our schema, `cn=schema,cn=config`. All the lines after `structuralObjectClass` should be removed. The final version of the file will be in `/tmp/puppet-ldap/cn=config/cn=schema/cn={0}puppet.ldif` and will be as follows:

```
dn: cn=puppet,cn=schema,cn=config
objectClass: olcSchemaConfig
cn: puppet
olcAttributeTypes: ( 1.3.6.1.4.1.34380.1.1.3.10 NAME 'puppetClass' DESC
'Pu
ppet Node Class' EQUALITY caseIgnoreIA5Match SYNTAX
1.3.6.1.4.1.1466.115.121.
1.26 )
olcAttributeTypes: ( 1.3.6.1.4.1.34380.1.1.3.9 NAME 'parentNode' DESC
'Pupp
et Parent Node' EQUALITY caseIgnoreIA5Match SYNTAX
1.3.6.1.4.1.1466.115.121.1
.26 SINGLE-VALUE )
olcAttributeTypes: ( 1.3.6.1.4.1.34380.1.1.3.11 NAME 'environment' DESC
'Pu
ppet Node Environment' EQUALITY caseIgnoreIA5Match SYNTAX
1.3.6.1.4.1.1466.11
5.121.1.26 )
olcAttributeTypes: ( 1.3.6.1.4.1.34380.1.1.3.12 NAME 'puppetVar' DESC 'A
va
riable setting for puppet' EQUALITY caseIgnoreIA5Match SYNTAX
1.3.6.1.4.1.146
6.115.121.1.26 )
olcObjectClasses: ( 1.3.6.1.4.1.34380.1.1.1.2 NAME 'puppetClient' DESC
'Pup
pet Client objectclass' SUP top AUXILIARY MAY ( puppetclass $ parentnode
$ en
vironment $ puppetvar ) )
```

Now add this new schema to our instance using `ldapadd` as follows using the RootDN value `cn=config`:

```
# ldapadd -x -f cn\=\{0\}puppet.ldif -D'cn=config' -W
Enter LDAP Password:
adding new entry "cn=puppet,cn=schema,cn=config"
```

Now we can start adding nodes to our LDAP installation. We'll need to add some containers and a top-level organization to the database before we can do that. Create a file named `start.ldif` with the following contents:

```
dn: dc=example,dc=com
objectclass: dcObject
objectclass: organization
o: Example
dc: example
dn: ou=hosts,dc=example,dc=com
objectclass: organizationalUnit
ou: hosts
dn: ou=production,ou=hosts,dc=example,dc=com
objectclass: organizationalUnit
ou: production
```

> If you are unfamiliar with how LDAP is organized, review the information at http://en.wikipedia.org/wiki/Lightweight_ Directory_Access_Protocol#Directory_structure.

Now add the contents of `start.ldif` to the directory using `ldapadd` as follows:

```
# ldapadd -x -f start.ldif -D'cn=manager,dc=example,dc=com' -W
Enter LDAP Password:
adding new entry "dc=example,dc=com"
adding new entry "ou=hosts,dc=example,dc=com"
adding new entry "ou=production,ou=hosts,dc=example,dc=com"
```

At this point, we have a container for our nodes at ou=production,ou=hosts,dc=example,dc=com; we can add an entry to our LDAP with the following LDIF, which we will name web_main_lp01.ldif:

```
dn: cn=web_main_lp01,ou=production,ou=hosts,dc=example,dc=com
objectclass: puppetClient
objectclass: device
environment: production
puppetClass: web
puppetClass: base
puppetvar: role='Production Web Server'
```

We then add this LDIF to the directory using ldapadd again, as shown in the following commands:

```
# ldapadd -x -f web_main_lp01.ldif -D'cn=manager,dc=example,dc=com' -W
Enter LDAP Password:
adding new entry "cn=web_main_lp01,ou=production,ou=hosts,dc=example,dc=com"
```

With our entry in LDAP, we are ready to configure our worker nodes to look in LDAP for node definitions. Change /etc/puppet/puppet.conf to have the following lines in the [master] section:

```
node_terminus = ldap
ldapserver = ldap.example.com
ldapbase = ou=hosts,dc=example,dc=com
```

We are almost ready; we need ruby-ldap installed on the worker machine before Puppet can use LDAP to look up the node information. We can install it using the following steps:

```
#yum install ruby-ldap
Installed:
ruby-ldap-0.9.7-10.el6.x86_64
```

Now restart `httpd` to have the changes picked up. To convince yourself that the node definition is now coming from LDAP, modify the base class in `/etc/puppet/ modules/base/manifests/init.pp` to include the role variable, as shown in the following snippet:

```
class base {
  file {'/etc/motd':
    mode => '0644',
    owner => '0',
    group => '0',
    content => inline_template("Role: <%= role %>\nManaged Node: <%=
hostname %>\nManaged by Puppet version <%= puppetversion %>\n"),
  }
}
```

 You will also need to open port 389, the standard LDAP port, on `ldap. example.com`, to allow the Puppet masters to query the LDAP machine.

Then run Puppet on `web_main_lp01` and verify the contents of `/etc/motd` using the following commands:

```
# cat /etc/motd
Role: 'Production Web Server'
Managed Node: web_main_lp01
Managed by Puppet version 3.4.0
```

Keeping your class and variable information in LDAP makes sense if you already have all your nodes in LDAP for other purposes, such as DNS or DHCP. One potential drawback of this is that all of the class information for the node has to be stored within a single LDAP entry. It is useful to be able to apply classes to machines based on criteria. In the next section, we look at hiera, a system which allows for this type of criteria-based application.

Before starting the next section, comment out the LDAP ENC lines in `/etc/puppet. conf` as follows:

```
#   node_terminus = ldap
#   ldapserver = puppet.example.com
#   ldapbase = ou=hosts,dc=example,dc=com
```

Hiera

Hiera allows you to create a hierarchy of node information. Using hiera, you can separate your variables and data from your modules. You start by defining what that hierarchy will be by ordering lookups in the main configuration file, `hiera.yaml`. The hierarchy is based on facts. Any fact can be used, even your own custom facts may be used. The values of the facts are then used as values for the YAML files stored in a directory, usually called `hieradata`. More information on hiera may be found on the Puppet Labs website at `http://docs.puppetlabs.com/hiera/1`.

> Facts are case sensitive in hiera and templates; this could be important when writing your `hiera.yaml` script.

Configuring hiera

Hiera only needs to be installed on your worker nodes. Using the Puppet Labs repo, the package to install is hiera; our installation pulled down `hiera-1.3.0-1.el6.noarch`. The command-line hiera tool looks for the hiera configuration file, `hiera.yaml`, in `/etc/hiera.yaml`. Puppet will by default look for `hiera.yaml` in `/etc/puppet/hiera.yaml`. To use the command-line utility consistently with Puppet, symlink one to the other. I suggest making `/etc/puppet/hiera.yaml` the main file and `/etc/hiera.yaml` the link.

> If you wish to use the `/etc/hiera.yaml` file, you can also specify `hiera_config=/etc/hiera.yaml` in `/etc/puppet.conf`.

The `hieradata` directory should also be under the `/etc/puppet` directory. We will create a directory to hold `hieradata` at `/etc/puppet/hieradata` and make the symlink between the `hiera.yaml` configuration files, as shown in the following commands:

```
worker1# mkdir /etc/puppet/hieradata
worker1# rm /etc/hiera.yaml
worker1# ln -s /etc/puppet/hiera.yaml /etc/hiera.yaml
```

Now we can create a simple `hiera.yaml` in `/etc/puppet/hiera.yaml` to show how the hierarchy is applied to a node, as shown in the following code snippet:

```
---
:hierarchy:
- "hosts/%{::hostname}"
- "roles/%{::role}"
```

```
- "%{::kernel}/%{::osfamily}/%{::lsbmajdistrelease} "
- "is_virtual/%{::is_virtual} "
- common
:backends:
- yaml
:yaml:
:datadir: '/etc/puppet/hieradata'
```

The `lsbmajdistrelease` fact requires that the **Linux System Base (LSB)** package be installed (`redhat-lsb`).

This hierarchy is quite basic. Hiera will look for a variable starting with the hostname of the node in the host's directory and then move to the top scope variable role in the directory roles. If a value is not found in roles, it will look in the directory `/etc/puppet/hieradata/kernel/osfamily/` for a file named `lsbmajdistrelease.yaml`. On my test node, this would be `/etc/puppet/hieradata/Linux/RedHat/6.yaml`. If the value is not found there, then hiera will continue to look in `hieradata/is_virtual/true.yaml` (as my node is a virtual machine, the value of `is_virtual` will be `true`). If the value is still not found, the default file `common.yaml` will be tried. If the value is not found in common, then the command-line utility will return `nil`.

> When using hiera in manifests, always set a default value, as failure to find anything in hiera will lead to a failed catalog (although having the node fail when this happens is also an often employed tactic).

As an example, we will set a variable `syslogpkg` to indicate which syslog package is used on our nodes. For EL6 machines, the package is `rsyslog`; for EL5, the package is `syslog`. Create two YAML files, one for EL6 at `/etc/puppet/hieradata/Linux/RedHat/6.yaml` using the following code:

```
---
syslogpkg: rsyslog
```

Create another YAML file for EL5 at `/etc/puppet/hieradata/Linux/RedHat/5.yaml` using the following code:

```
---
syslogpkg: syslog
```

With these files in place, we can test our hiera by setting top scope variables (facts) from the command line. We run hiera three times, changing the value of `lsbmajdistrelease` each time, as shown in the following commands:

```
worker1# hiera syslogpkg ::kernel=Linux ::osfamily=RedHat
::lsbmajdistrelease=6

rsyslog

worker1# hiera syslogpkg ::kernel=Linux ::osfamily=RedHat
::lsbmajdistrelease=5

syslog

worker1# hiera syslogpkg ::kernel=Linux ::osfamily=RedHat
::lsbmajdistrelease=4

nil
```

In the previous commands, we change the value of `lsbmajdistrelease` from 6 to 5 to 4 to simulate the nodes running on EL6, EL5, and EL4. We do not have a `4.yaml` file, so there is no setting of `syslogpkg` and `hiera` that returns `nil`.

Now to use hiera in our manifests, we can use the hiera function inline or set a variable using hiera. When using hiera, the syntax is `hiera('variable','default')`. The `variable` value is the key you are interested in looking at; the `default` value is the value to use when nothing is found in the hierarchy. Create a `syslog` module in `/etc/puppet/modules/syslog/manifest/init.pp` that starts syslog and makes sure the correct syslog is installed, as shown in the following code:

```
    class syslog {
      $syslogpkg = hiera('syslogpkg','syslog')
      package {"$syslogpkg":
        ensure => 'installed',
      }
      service {"$syslogpkg":
        ensure => true,
        enable => true,
      }
    }
```

Then create an empty `/etc/puppet/manifests/site.pp` file that includes syslog, as shown in the following code:

```
node default {
  include syslog
}
```

In this code, we set our default node to include the `syslog` module, and then we define the `syslog` module. The `syslog` module looks for the hiera variable `syslogpkg` to know which syslog package to install. Running this on our test node, we see that `rsyslog` is started as we are running EL6, as shown in the following commands:

```
node1# puppet agent -t
Info: Retrieving plugin
Info: Caching catalog for node1
Info: Applying configuration version '1388785169'
Notice: /Stage[main]/Syslog/Service[rsyslog]/ensure: ensure changed
'stopped' to 'running'
Info: /Stage[main]/Syslog/Service[rsyslog]: Unscheduling refresh on
Service[rsyslog]
Notice: Finished catalog run in 0.71 seconds
```

 If you didn't already disable the LDAP ENC we configured in the previous section, instructions are provided at the end of the *LDAP backend* section from this chapter.

In the enterprise, you want a way to automatically apply classes to nodes based on facts. This is part of a larger issue of separating the code of your modules from the data used to apply them. We will examine this issue in greater depth in *Chapter 9, Roles and Profiles*. Hiera has a function that makes this very easy—`hiera_include`. Using `hiera_include` you can have hiera apply classes to a node based upon the hierarchy.

Using hiera_include

To use `hiera_include`, we set a hiera variable to hold the name of the classes we would like applied to the nodes. By convention, this is called `classes`, but it could be anything. We'll also set a variable role that we'll use in our new base class. We modify `site.pp` to include all classes defined in the hiera variable classes. We also set a default value should no values be found; this way we guarantee that catalogs will compile and that all nodes receive at least the base class. Edit `/etc/puppet/manifest/site.pp` as follows:

```
node default {
  hiera_include('classes', 'base')
}
```

For the base class, we'll just set the `motd` file as we've done previously. We'll also set a welcome string in hiera; in `common.yaml`, we'll set this to something generic and override the value in a hostname-specific YAML file. Edit the base class in `/etc/puppet/modules/base/manifests/init.pp` as follows:

```
class base {
  $welcome = hiera('welcome','Welcome')
  file {'/etc/motd':
    mode => '0644',
    owner => '0',
    group => '0',
    content => inline_template("<%= welcome %>\nManaged Node: <%=
hostname
%>\nManaged by Puppet version <%= puppetversion %>\n"),
  }
}
```

This is our base class; it uses an inline template to set up the "message of the day" file (`/etc/motd`). We then need to set the welcome information in `hieradata`; edit `/etc/puppet/hieradata/common.yaml` to include the default welcome message, as shown in the following code snippet:

```
---
welcome: 'Welcome to Example.com'
classes: - 'base'
syslog: 'nothing'
```

Now we can run Puppet on our `node1` machine; after the successful run, our `/etc/motd` has the following contents:

```
Welcome to Example.com
Managed Node: node1
Managed by Puppet version 3.4.1
```

Now to test if our hierarchy is working as expected, we'll create a YAML file specifically for `node1`, `/etc/puppet/hieradata/hosts/node1.yaml` as follows:

```
---
welcome: 'Welcome to our default node'
```

Again, we run Puppet on `node1` and examine the contents of `/etc/motd`, as shown in the following code:

```
Welcome to our default node
Managed Node: node1
Managed by Puppet version 3.4.1
```

Now that we have verified that our hierarchy performs as we expect, we can use hiera to apply a class to all nodes based on a fact. In this example we'll use the `is_virtual` fact to do some performance tuning on our virtual machines. We'll create a virtual class in `/etc/puppet/modules/virtual/manifests/init.pp`, which installs the `tuned` package. It then sets the tuned profile to `virtual-guest` and starts the `tuned` service, as shown in the following code:

```
class virtual {
  # performance tuning for virtual machine
  package {'tuned':
    ensure => 'present',
  }
  service {'tuned':
    enable => true,
    ensure => true,
    require => Package['tuned']
  }
  exec {'set tuned profile':
    command => '/usr/sbin/tuned-adm profile virtual-guest',
    unless => '/bin/grep -q virtual-guest /etc/tune-profiles/
activeprofile',
  }
}
```

In a real-world example, we'd verify that we only apply this to nodes running on EL6.

This module ensures that the tuned package is installed and the tuned service is started. It then verifies that the current tuned profile is set to `virtual-guest` (using a `grep` statement in the `unless` parameter to the `exec`), if the current profile is not `virtual-guest`, the profile is changed to `virtual-guest` using `tuned-adm`.

Tuned is a tuning daemon included on enterprise Linux systems, which configures several kernel parameters related to scheduling and I/O operations.

To ensure that this class is applied to all virtual machines, we simply need to add it to the `classes` hiera variable in `/etc/puppet/hieradata/is_virtual/true.yaml`, as shown in the following snippet:

```
---
classes: - 'virtual'
```

Now our test node `node1` is indeed virtual, so if we run Puppet now, the virtual class will be applied to the node, and we will see that the tuned profile is set to `virtual-guest`. Running `tuned-admin active` on the host returns the currently active profile; when we run it initially the command is not available as the tuned rpm has not been installed yet, as you can see in the following commands:

```
node1# tuned-adm active
-bash: tuned-adm: command not found
node1# puppet agent -t
Info: Retrieving plugin
Info: Caching catalog for node1
Info: Applying configuration version '1388817444'
Notice: /Stage[main]/Virtual/Package[tuned]/ensure: created
Notice: /Stage[main]/Virtual/Exec[set tuned profile]/returns: executed
successfully
Notice: Finished catalog run in 9.65 seconds
node1# tuned-adm active
Current active profile: virtual-guest
Service tuned: enabled, running
Service ktune: enabled, running
```

This example shows the power of using hiera with `hiera_include` and a well-organized hierarchy. Using this method, we can have classes applied to nodes based on facts and reduce the need for custom classes on nodes. We do, however, have the option of adding classes per node since we have a `hosts/%{::hostname}` entry in our hierarchy. If you had, for instance, a module that only needed to be installed on 32-bit systems, you could make an entry in `hiera.yaml` for `%{::architecture}` and only create an `i686.yaml` file that contained the class in question. Building up your classes in this fashion reduces the complexity of your individual node configurations.

Another great feature of hiera is its ability to automatically fill in values for parameterized class attributes. For this example, we will create a class called `resolver` and set the search parameter for our `/etc/resolv.conf` file using **augeas**.

 Augeas is a tool for modifying configuration files as though they were objects. For more information on augeas, visit the project website at `http://augeas.net`. In this example, we will use augeas to modify only a section of the `/etc/resolv.conf` file.

First, we will create a `resolver` class as follows in `/etc/puppet/modules/resolver/manifests/init.pp`:

```
class resolver($search = "example.com") {
  augeas { 'set resolv.conf search':
    context => '/files/etc/resolv.conf',
    changes => [
      "set search/domain '${search}'"
    ],
  }
}
```

Then we add `resolver` to our classes in `/etc/puppet/hieradata/hosts/node1.yaml` so as to have `resolver` applied to our node, as shown in the following code:

```
---
welcome: 'Welcome to our default node'
classes: - resolver
```

Now we run Puppet on `node1` as shown in the following commands; augeas will change the `resolv.conf` file to have the search domain set to the default `example.com`.

```
node1# puppet agent -t
Info: Retrieving plugin
Info: Caching catalog for node1
Info: Applying configuration version '1388818864'
Notice: Augeas[set resolv.conf search] (provider=augeas):
--- /etc/resolv.conf   2014-01-04 01:59:43.769423982 -0500
+++ /etc/resolv.conf.augnew   2014-01-04 02:00:09.552425174 -0500
@@ -1,2 +1,3 @@
; generated by /sbin/dhclient-script
nameserver 192.168.122.1
+search example.com


Notice: /Stage[main]/Resolver/Augeas[set resolv.conf search]/returns:
executed successfully
Notice: Finished catalog run in 1.09 seconds
```

Now, to get hiera to override the default parameter for the parameterized class `resolver`, we simply set the hiera variable `resolver::search` in our `/etc/puppet/hieradata/hosts/node1.yaml` file, as shown in the following code:

```
---
welcome: 'Welcome to our default node'
classes: - resolver
resolver::search: 'devel.example.com'
```

Running `puppet agent` another time on `node1` will change the search from `example.com` to `devel.example.com` using the value from the hiera hierarchy file, as you can see in the following commands:

```
[root@node1 ~]# puppet agent -t
Info: Retrieving plugin
Info: Caching catalog for node1.example.com
Info: Applying configuration version '1388818864'
Notice: Augeas[set resolv.conf search] (provider=augeas):
--- /etc/resolv.conf   2014-01-04 02:09:00.192424927 -0500
+++ /etc/resolv.conf.augnew   2014-01-04 02:13:24.815425173 -0500
@@ -1,4 +1,4 @@
; generated by /sbin/dhclient-script
nameserver 192.168.122.1
domain example.com
-search example.com
+search devel.example.com


Notice: /Stage[main]/Resolver/Augeas[set resolv.conf search]/returns:
executed successfully
Notice: Finished catalog run in 1.07 seconds
```

By building up your catalog in this fashion, it's possible to override parameters to any class. At this point, our `node1` machine has the `virtual`, `resolver` and `base` classes, but our site manifest (`/etc/puppet/manifests/site.pp`) only has a `hiera_include` line, as shown in the following code:

```
node default {
  hiera_include('classes',base)
}
```

In the enterprise, this means that you can add new hosts without modifying your site manifest and that you can customize the classes and any parameters to those classes.

Two other functions exist for using hiera; they are `hiera_array` and `hiera_hash`. These functions do not stop at the first match found in hiera and instead return either an array or hash of all the matches. This can also be used in powerful ways to build up definitions of variables. One good use of this is in setting the nameservers a node will query. Using `hiera_array` instead of `hiera` function, you can not only set nameservers based on the hostname of the node or some other facts, but also have the default name servers from your `common.yaml` file applied to the node.

Summary

The classes that are applied to nodes should be as automatic as possible. By using a hostname convention and an ENC script, it is possible to have classes applied to nodes without any node-level configuration.

Using LDAP as a backend for class information may be a viable alternative at your enterprise. The LDAP schema included with Puppet can be successfully applied to an OpenLDAP instance or integrated into your existing LDAP infrastructure.

Hiera is a powerful tool for separating data from your module definitions. By utilizing a hierarchy of facts, it is possible to dynamically apply classes to nodes based on their facts.

The important concept in the enterprise is to minimize the customization required in the modules and push that customization up into the node declaration. To separate the code required to deploy your nodes from the specific data, through either LDAP, a custom ENC, or clever use of hiera. If starting from scratch, hiera is the most powerful and flexible solution to this problem.

In the next chapter, we will see how we can utilize Puppet environments to make hiera even more flexible. We will cover using Git to keep our modules under version control.

3
Git and Environments

When working in a large organization, changes can break things. Every developer will need a sandbox to test their code. A single developer may have to work on two or three issues independently throughout the day but may not apply the working code to any nodes. It would be great if you could work on a module and verify it in a development environment or even on a single node before pushing it to the rest of your fleet. Environments allow you to carve up your fleet into as many development environments as needed. Environments allow nodes to work from different versions of your code. Keeping track of the different versions with Git allows for some streamlined workflows. Other versioning systems can be used, but the bulk of integration in Puppet is done with Git.

Environments

When every node requests an object from the Puppet master, they inform the Puppet master of their environment. Depending on how the master is configured, the environment can change the set of modules, the contents of hiera, or the site manifest (`site.pp`). The environment is set on the agent in their `puppet.conf` file or on the command line with `puppet agent --environment`.

In addition, environment may also be set from both the ENC and the LDAP node terminus. In Puppet version 3, setting the environment from the ENC overrides the setting in `puppet.conf`. If no environment is set, then `production`, which is the default environment, is applied.

On the master, if a configuration block's name matches the environment's name, then the settings in that block will take effect for the nodes that use that environment.

 Environment names cannot be the same as that of the main config blocks of the `puppet.conf` file (`main`, `master`, `agent`, and so on).

The configuration block can contain the location of the site manifest (`manifest`), the path to find modules (`modulepath`), the path to find manifests (`manifestdir`), and the path to find templates (`templatedir`). Alternatively, the `$environment` variable can be used in `puppet.conf` to have dynamic paths based on the environment rather than hard coding specific environments.

> The configuration of environments with sections is known as **config file environments** and is soon to be deprecated. Environments based on the setting `environmentpath` will replace configuration file environments. These are equivalent to the dynamic environments we define later in the chapter. If you are using a version of Puppet greater than or equal to 3.6, you will receive deprecation warning when setting `manifestdir` and `modulepath` in `/etc/puppet/puppet.conf`. The new method to configure environments, directory environments, uses the variable `environmentpath` to specify a directory containing environments. Each directory in `environmentpath` is assumed to have `modules` and `manifests` directories. In addition, `modulepath` and `manifest` may be overridden using an `environment.conf` file within any given environment directory. More information on this change is available on Puppet Labs at `http://docs.puppetlabs.com/puppet/latest/reference/environments.html`.

In the remainder of this chapter we will not use the ENC script we configured in *Chapter 2, Organizing Your Nodes and Data*, modify `/etc/puppet/puppet.conf` on worker1, and comment out the two ENC-related settings which we configured in *Chapter 2, Organizing Your Nodes and Data*. Next, add two new sections for the production and development environments, as shown in the following snippet:

```
[production]
    modulepath = $confdir/production/modules
    manifestdir = $confdir/production/manifests
[development]
    modulepath = $confdir/development/modules
    manifestdir = $confdir/development/manifests
```

Next, create the two new environment directories (production and development) and copy our modules and site manifest into the new directories using the following commands:

```
worker1# cd /etc/puppet
worker1# mkdir production development
worker1# cp -a manifests modules production
worker1# cp -a manifests modules development
```

Restart `httpd` for the changes to `puppet.conf` to take effect. Then, go to `/etc/puppet/production/modules/base/manifests/init.pp`, and change the `motd` to show that the node is in the `production` environment, as shown in the following code:

```
class base {
  $welcome = hiera('welcome','Unwelcome')
  file {'/etc/motd':
    mode => '0644',
    owner => '0',
    group => '0',
    content => inline_template("PRODUCTION\n<%= welcome
      %>\nManaged Node: <%= hostname %>\nManaged by Puppet
      version <%= puppetversion %>\n"),
  }
} (The environment is also available as a variable, we could
    have used <%= environment.upcase %> in the above example)
```

Now, run `puppet agent` on `node1` and verify whether the production module is being used, as shown in the following commands:

```
node1# puppet agent -t
...
Notice: /Stage[main]/Base/File[/etc/motd]/content:
--- /etc/motd   2014-01-06 01:54:43.933328053 -0500
+++ /tmp/puppet-file20140106-15383-1476fsl-0    2014-01-06
01:54:48.204327062 -0500
@@ -1,3 +1,4 @@
+PRODUCTION
 Welcome to our default node
 Managed Node: node1
 Managed by Puppet version 3.4.1
...
Notice: Finished catalog run in 1.18 seconds
```

Now, go to the `development` module and change the `motd` for development (`/etc/puppet/development/modules/base/manifests/init.pp`), as shown in the following snippet:

```
class base {
  $welcome = hiera('welcome','Unwelcome')
  file {'/etc/motd':
    mode => '0644',
```

```
        owner => '0',
        group => '0',
        content => inline_template("DEVELOPMENT\n<%= welcome
          %>\nManaged Node: <%= hostname %>\nManaged by Puppet version
          <%= puppetversion %>\n"),
    }
  }
```

Then, run `puppet agent` on `node1` with the `environment` set to `development`, as shown in the following command:

```
node1# puppet agent -t --environment development
...
Notice: /Stage[main]/Base/File[/etc/motd]/content:
--- /etc/motd  2014-01-06 02:15:29.547327060 -0500
+++ /tmp/puppet-file20140106-19402-14qquyt-0    2014-01-06
  02:17:38.502327062 -0500
@@ -1,4 +1,4 @@
-PRODUCTION
+DEVELOPMENT
  ...
Notice: Finished catalog run in 1.25 seconds
```

This will perform a one-time compilation in the `development` environment; in the next Puppet run, where the environment is not explicitly set, this will default to `production` again. To permanently move the node to the `development` environment, edit `/etc/puppet/puppet.conf` and set the environment, as shown in the following code:

```
    [agent]
        environment = development
```

Environments and hiera

Hiera's main configuration file can also use `environment` as a variable. This leads to two options: a single hierarchy with the environment as a hierarchy item, and multiple hierarchies where the path to the `hieradata` directory comes from the environment setting. To have separate `hieradata` trees, you can use the environment in the `datadir` setting for the backend, or to have parts of the hierarchy tied to your environment, put `%{::environment}` in the hierarchy.

Multiple hierarchies

To have a separate data tree, we will first copy the existing `hieradata` directory into the `production` and `development` directories, as shown in the following commands:

```
worker1# cp -a hieradata production
worker1# cp -a hieradata development
```

Now edit `/etc/puppet/hiera.yaml` and change `:datadir` as follows:

```
:yaml:
  :datadir: '/etc/puppet/%{::environment}/hieradata'
```

Now, edit the welcome message in the `node1.yaml` file of the `production` (`/etc/puppet/production/hieradata/hosts/node1.yaml`) `hieradata` tree, as shown in the following line:

```
---
welcome: 'Careful, this is a production node'
```

Also, edit the `development` (`/etc/puppet/development/hieradata/hosts/node1.yaml`) `hieradata` tree to reflect the different environments, as shown in the following line:

```
---
welcome: 'This is a development node, play away'
```

Now, run Puppet on `node1` to see the `/etc/motd` file change according to the environment. First, we run the agent without setting an environment, so the default setting of production is applied, as shown in the following command:

```
node1# puppet agent -t
...
Notice: /Stage[main]/Base/File[/etc/motd]/content:
--- /etc/motd   2014-01-07 00:40:03.349098133 -0500
+++ /tmp/puppet-file20140107-22532-1murkny-0    2014-01-07
00:46:41.822098133 -0500
@@ -1,4 +1,4 @@
 PRODUCTION
-Welcome to our production node
+Careful, this is a production node
...
Notice: Finished catalog run in 1.28 seconds
```

If you previously set the environment value to development by adding environment=development in puppet.conf, remove that setting.

Then, we run agent with environment set to development to see the change, as shown in the following command:

```
node1# puppet agent -t --environment development
...
Notice: /Stage[main]/Base/File[/etc/motd]/content:
--- /etc/motd  2014-01-07 00:46:41.849098133 -0500
+++ /tmp/puppet-file20140107-22797-oe04zc-0    2014-01-07
00:48:03.134098133 -0500
@@ -1,4 +1,4 @@
-PRODUCTION
-Careful, this is a production node
+DEVELOPMENT
+This is a development node, play away
 Managed Node: node1
 Managed by Puppet version 3.4.1
...
Notice: Finished catalog run in 1.17 seconds
```

Configuring hiera in this fashion will allow you to keep completely distinct hieradata trees for each environment. You can, however, configure hiera to look for environment-specific information in a single tree.

Single hierarchy for all environments

To have one hierarchy for all environments, edit hiera.yaml as follows:

```
---
:hierarchy:
  - "environments/%{::environment}"
  - "hosts/%{::hostname}"
  - "roles/%{::role}"
  - "%{::kernel}/%{::osfamily}/%{::lsbmajdistrelease}"
  - "is_virtual/%{::is_virtual}"
  - common
:backends:
  - yaml
:yaml:
  :datadir: "/etc/puppet/hieradata"
```

Next, create an environment directory in `/etc/puppet/hieradata` and create
the following two YAML files: one for `production` (`/etc/puppet/hieradata/`
`environments/production.yaml`) and another for `development` (`/etc/puppet/`
`hieradata/environments/development.yaml`). The following will be the
welcome message for the `production` file:

```
---
welcome: 'Single tree production welcome'
```

The following will be the welcome message for the `development` file:

```
---
welcome: 'Development in Single Tree'
```

Restart `httpd` on `worker1` and run Puppet on `node1` again to see the new `motd` for
`production`, as shown in the following commands:

```
node1# puppet agent -t
...
Notice: /Stage[main]/Base/File[/etc/motd]/content:
--- /etc/motd   2014-01-07 00:48:03.160098133 -0500
+++ /tmp/puppet-file20140107-23083-4z1ztk-0     2014-01-07
00:57:48.273098134 -0500
@@ -1,4 +1,4 @@
-DEVELOPMENT
-This is a development node, play away
+PRODUCTION
+Single tree production welcome
 Managed Node: node1
 Managed by Puppet version 3.4.1
...
Notice: Finished catalog run in 1.20 seconds
puppet run against the single tree hieradata
```

Having the `production` and `development` environments may be sufficient for a
small operation (a *manageable* amount of nodes, typically less than a thousand),
but in an enterprise, you will need many more such environments to help admins
avoid stumbling upon one another. In the next section, we'll configure Puppet to
use dynamic environments.

Dynamic environments

Our configuration for hiera did not specify production or development environments in hiera.yaml. We used the value environment to fill in a path on the filesystem. We can do the same thing in puppet.conf and allow for environments to be defined dynamically. While doing this, it's important to always account for the production environment since that is the default setting for any node where environment is not explicitly set. Note that the modulepath can include multiple directories; it is possible to put environment-specific modules first and always have the production modules included, as shown in the following code:

```
modulepath = /etc/puppet/environments/$environment/modules:/etc/
puppet/environments/production/modules
```

A useful configuration for modulepath is to include a set of standard modules (modules that your company and coworkers will not be changing) in another directory and append that to the path, for example, the stdlib module from Puppet Labs, as shown in the following code

```
[master]
modulepath = /etc/puppet/environments/$environment/modules:/etc/
puppet/environments/production/modules:/etc/puppet/public/modules
```

> In version 3.6 and above, Puppet will look in $environmentpath/
> modules then /etc/puppet/modules unless a modulepath
> is specified in an environment.conf file within any given
> environment directory.

With this configuration, when we change our environment, the modulepath will first look in the new environment directory, then the production directory, followed by our public module directory. With this scenario, any developer can change the modules applied to a node but cannot modify the site.pp file. To allow developers to modify the site.pp file, change manifestdir as well, as shown in the following code:

```
manifestdir = $confdir/environments/$environment/manifests
```

Now, create a new environment, sandbox, by creating a copy of the production directory using the following commands:

```
# mkdir /etc/puppet/environments
# mv  /etc/puppet/production /etc/puppet/environments/
# cp -a /etc/puppet/environments/production /etc/puppet/environments/
sandbox
```

We can now edit the files in `sandbox` and change the behavior of Puppet, starting with the default node definition in `/etc/puppet/environments/sandbox/manifests/site.pp`, as shown in the following code:

```
node default {
  hiera_include('classes',base)
  notify {"Playing in the sandbox":}
}
```

Then, when we run `puppet agent` on `node1` with the `environment` value set to `sandbox`, we see the new notice, as shown in the following commands:

```
node1# puppet agent -t --environment sandbox
...
Notice: Playing in the sandbox
Notice: /Stage[main]/Main/Node[default]/Notify[Playing in the sandbox]/
message: defined 'message' as 'Playing in the sandbox'
Notice: Finished catalog run in 1.04 seconds
```

This type of playing around with environments is great for a single developer, but when you work in a large team, you'll need some version control and automation to convert this to a workable solution. In the next section, we'll use Git to automatically create environments and share environments between developers.

For further reading on environments, refer to the Puppet Labs website at `http://docs.puppetlabs.com/guides/environment.html`.

Git

Git is a version control system, written by Linus Torvalds, which is used to work on the Linux Kernel source code. Its support for rapid branching and merging make it the perfect choice for a Puppet implementation. Each commit has references to its parent commits; to reconstruct a branch, you only need to follow the trail back. We will be exploiting the rapid branch support to have environments defined from Git branches.

 It is possible to use Git without a server and to make copies of repositories using only local Git commands.

In your organization, you likely have some version control software. The software in question isn't too important, but the methodology used is important. Long running branches or a stable trunk are the terms used in the industry to describe the development cycle. In our implementation, we will assume that `development` and `production` are long running branches. By long running we mean that these branches will persist throughout the lifetime of the repository. Most other branches are dead ends—they solve an immediate issue, then get merged into the long running branches and cease to exist, or they fail to solve the issue and are destroyed.

Why Git?

Git is the defacto standard version control software with Puppet because of its implementation of rapid branching. There are numerous other reasons for using Git in general. Each user of Git is given a complete copy of the revision history whenever they clone a Git repository. Each developer is capable of backing up the entire repository should the need arise. Git allows each developer to work independently from the master repository, allowing developers to work off site and even without network connectivity.

This section isn't intended to be an exhaustive guide to using Git. We'll cover enough commands to get your job done, but I recommend you do some reading on the subject to get well acquainted with the tool.

> The main page for Git documentation is `http://git-scm.com/documentation`. Also worth reading is the information on getting started by GitHub at `http://try.github.io`.

To get started with Git, we need to create a bare repository. By bare we mean that only the meta information and checksums will be stored; the files will be in the repository but only in the checksum form. Only the main location for the repository needs to be stored in this fashion.

In the enterprise, you likely want the Git server to be a separate machine, independent of your Puppet master. Perhaps, your Git server isn't even specific to your Puppet implementation. The great thing about Git is that it doesn't really matter at this point; we can put the repository wherever we wish.

To make things easier to understand, we'll work on our single worker machine for now, and in the final section, we will create a new Git server to hold our Git repository.

A simple Git workflow

On our worker machine, install Git using yum, as shown in the following commands:

```
worker1# yum install -y git
...
Installed:  git.x86_64 0:1.7.1-3.el6_4.1
```

Now, decide on a directory to hold all your Git repositories. We'll use /var/lib/git in this example. A directory under /srv may be more appropriate at your organization. The /var/lib/git path more closely resembles the paths used by other EL packages. Since running everything as root is unnecessary, we will create a Git user and make that user the owner of the Git repositories.

Create the directory to contain our repository first (/var/lib/git) and then create an empty Git repository (git init --bare) in that location, as shown in the following commands:

```
worker1# useradd git -c 'Git Repository Owner' -d /var/lib/git
worker1# sudo -iu git
git@worker1$ pwd
/var/lib/git
git@worker1$ git init --bare puppet.git
Initialized empty Git repository in /var/lib/git/puppet.git/
git@worker1$ cd /tmp
git@worker1$ git clone /var/lib/git/puppet.git
Initialized empty Git repository in /tmp/puppet/.git/
warning: You appear to have cloned an empty repository.
git@worker1$ cd puppet
git@worker1$ git status
# On branch master
#
# Initial commit
#
nothing to commit (create/copy files and use "git add" to track)
```

Now that our repository is created, we should start adding files to the repository; however, we should first configure Git. Git will store our username and e-mail address with each commit. These settings are controlled with `git config`. We will add the `--global` option to ensure the `config` file in `~/.git` is modified, as shown in the following commands:

```
git@worker1$ git config --global user.name 'Git Repository Owner'
git@worker1$ git config --global user.email 'git@example.com'
```

Now, we'll copy in our `production` modules and commit them; we'll copy the files from the `/etc/puppet/environments/production` directory of our worker machines and then add them to the repository using `git add`, as shown in the following commands:

```
git@worker1$ cp -a /etc/puppet/environments/production/*.
git@worker1$ ls
hieradata  manifests  modules
git@worker1$ git status
# On branch master
#
# Initial commit
#
# Untracked files:
#   (use "git add <file>..." to include in what will be committed)
#
#   hieradata/
#   manifests/
#   modules/
nothing added to commit but untracked files present (use "git add" to
track)
```

We've copied our `hieradata`, `manifests`, and `modules` directories, but Git doesn't know anything about them. We now need to add them to the Git repository and commit to the default branch master. This is done with two Git commands, first using `git add` and then using `git commit`, as shown in the following commands:

```
git@worker1$ git add hieradata manifests modules
git@worker1$ git commit -m "initial commit"
[master (root-commit) 153426e] initial commit
 15 files changed, 87 insertions(+), 0 deletions(-)
...
 create mode 100644 hieradata/Linux/RedHat/6.yaml
```

To see the files that will be committed when you issue `git commit`, use
`git status` after the `git add` command.

At this point, we've committed our changes to our local copy of the repository.
To ensure that we understand what is happening, we'll clone the initial location
again into another directory (`/tmp/puppet2`), as shown in the following commands:

```
git@worker1$ cd /tmp
git@worker1$ mkdir puppet2
git@worker1$ cd puppet2
git@worker1$ git clone /var/lib/git/puppet.git.
Initialized empty Git repository in /tmp/puppet2/.git/
warning: You appear to have cloned an empty repository.
git@worker1$ ls
```

Our second copy doesn't have the files we just committed, and they only exist in
the first local copy of the repository. One of the powerful features of Git is that it
is a self-contained environment. Going back to our first clone (`/tmp/puppet`),
examine the contents of the `.git/config` file. The `url` setting for the `remote`
`"origin"` points to the remote master that our repository is based on
(`/var/lib/git/puppet.git`), as shown in the following code:

```
[core]
  repositoryformatversion = 0
  filemode = true
  bare = false
  logallrefupdates = true
[remote "origin"]
  fetch = +refs/heads/*:refs/remotes/origin/*
  url = /var/lib/git/puppet.git
[branch "master"]
  remote = origin
  merge = refs/heads/master
```

In Git, `origin` is where the original remote repository lives; in this example, it is a
local location (`/var/lib/git/puppet.git`), but it could also be an HTTPS URI or
SSH URI.

To push the local changes to the remote repository, we use git push; the default push operation is to push to the first remote repository called origin to the currently selected branch. The default branch in Git is always called master as we can see in the [branch "master"] section. To emphasize what we are doing, we'll type in the full arguments to push (although git push will achieve the same result in this case), as you can see in the following commands:

```
git@worker1$ cd /tmp/puppet
git@worker1$ git push origin master
Counting objects: 40, done.
Compressing objects: 100% (15/15), done.
Writing objects: 100% (40/40), 3.05 KiB, done.
Total 40 (delta 0), reused 0 (delta 0)
Unpacking objects: 100% (40/40), done.
To /var/lib/git/puppet.git
 * [new branch]      master -> master
pushing our changes to the remote origin
```

Now that our remote repository has the updates, we can pull them down to our second copy using git pull. Again, we will type in the full argument list (this time, git pull will do the same thing), as shown in the following commands:

```
git@worker1$ cd /tmp/puppet2
git@worker1$ git status
# On branch master
#
# Initial commit
#
nothing to commit (create/copy files and use "git add" to track)
git@worker1$ ls
git@worker1$ git pull origin master
remote: Counting objects: 40, done.
remote: Compressing objects: 100% (15/15), done.
remote: Total 40 (delta 0), reused 0 (delta 0)
Unpacking objects: 100% (40/40), done.
From /var/lib/git/puppet
 * branch          master     -> FETCH_HEAD
git@worker1$ ls
hieradata  manifests  modules
```

Two useful commands to know at this point are `git log` and `git show`. The `git log` command will show you the log entries from Git commits. Using the log entries, you can run `git show` to piece together what your fellow developers have been doing. The following snippet shows the use of these two commands in our example:

```
git@worker1$ git log
commit 1b2bf23df837d4853f911b44823a776956849581
Author: Git Repository Owner <git@example.com>
Date:    Thu Jan 9 01:08:59 2014 -0500
    initial commit

git@worker1$ git show 1b2bf23df837d4853f911b44823a776956849581
...
diff --git a/hieradata/Linux/CentOS/6.yaml b/hieradata/Linux/CentOS/6.
yaml
new file mode 100644
index 0000000..8a79b14
--- /dev/null
+++ b/hieradata/Linux/CentOS/6.yaml
@@ -0,0 +1,2 @@
+---
+welcome: 'CentOS 6'
...
```

The `git show` command takes the commit hash as an optional argument and returns all the changes that were made with that hash.

Now that we have our code in the repository, we need to create a `production` branch for our `production` code. Branches are created using `git branch`; the important concept to note is that they are local until they are pushed to the origin. When `git branch` is run without arguments, it returns the list of available branches with the currently selected branch highlighted with an asterisk, as shown in the following commands:

```
git@worker1$ cd /tmp/puppet
git@worker1$ git branch
* master
git@worker1$ git branch production
git@worker1$ git branch
* master
  production
```

This sometimes confuses people. You have to check the newly created branch after creating it; you can do this in one step using the `git checkout -b <branch_name>` command, but I believe using this shorthand initially leads to confusion. We'll now checkout our `production` branch and make a change which we can commit to the local repository and then push to the remote, as shown in the following commands:

```
git@worker1$ git checkout production
Switched to branch 'production'
git@worker1$ git branch
  master
* production
git@worker1$ cd hieradata/hosts
git@worker1$ sed -i -e 's/Careful/Be very Careful/' node1.yaml
git@worker1$ git add node1.yaml
git@worker1$ git commit -m 'modifying welcome message on node1'
[production 5ba7c42] modifying welcome message on node1
 1 files changed, 1 insertions(+), 1 deletions(-)
git@worker1$ git push origin production
Counting objects: 9, done.
Compressing objects: 100% (4/4), done.
Writing objects: 100% (5/5), 620 bytes, done.
Total 5 (delta 0), reused 0 (delta 0)
Unpacking objects: 100% (5/5), done.
To /var/lib/git/puppet.git
 * [new branch]      production -> production
```

Now, in our second copy of the repository, let's confirm that the `production` branch has been added to the origin using `git fetch` to retrieve the latest metadata from the `remote` origin, as shown in the following commands:

```
git@worker1$ cd /tmp/puppet2
git@worker1$ git branch
* master
git@worker1$ git fetch
remote: Counting objects: 9, done.
remote: Compressing objects: 100% (4/4), done.
remote: Total 5 (delta 0), reused 0 (delta 0)
Unpacking objects: 100% (5/5), done.
From /var/lib/git/puppet
 * [new branch]      production -> origin/production
```

It is important to run `git fetch` routinely to see changes that your teammates may have made and branches that they may have created. Now, we can verify whether the `production` branch has the change we made. We'll display the current contents of `node1.yaml` and then run `git checkout production` to see the `production` version, as shown in the following snippet:

```
git@worker1$ cd hieradata/hosts/
git@worker1$ cat node1.yaml
---
welcome: 'Careful, this is a production node'
classes: - resolver
resolver::search: 'prod.example.com'
git@worker1$ git checkout production
Branch production set up to track remote branch production from origin.
Switched to a new branch 'production'
git@worker1$ cat node1.yaml
---
welcome: 'Be very Careful, this is a production node'
classes: - resolver
resolver::search: 'prod.example.com'
```

As we can see, the welcome message in the `production` branch is different from that of the `master` branch. At this point, we'd like to have the `production` branch in `/etc/puppet/environments/production` and the `master` branch in `/etc/puppet/environments/master`, as shown in the following commands. We'll perform these commands as the `root` user for now:

```
worker1# cd /etc/puppet
worker1# mv environments environments.orig
worker1# mkdir environments
worker1# cd environments
worker1# git clone -b production /var/lib/git/puppet.git production
Initialized empty Git repository in /etc/puppet/environments/production/.git/
remote: Counting objects: 45, done.
remote: Compressing objects: 100% (19/19), done.
remote: Total 45 (delta 0), reused 0 (delta 0)
Receiving objects: 100% (45/45), 3.63 KiB, done.
worker1# cd production
```

```
worker1# ls
hieradata  manifests  modules
worker1# git status
# On branch production
nothing to commit (working directory clean)
```

Now that our production branch is synchronized with the remote, we can do the same for the master branch and verify whether the branches differ, using the following commands:

```
worker1# cd ..
worker1# git clone -b master /var/lib/git/puppet.git master
Initialized empty Git repository in /etc/puppet/environments/master/.git/
remote: Counting objects: 45, done.
remote: Compressing objects: 100% (19/19), done.
remote: Total 45 (delta 0), reused 0 (delta 0)
Receiving objects: 100% (45/45), done.
worker1# cd master
worker1# ls
hieradata  manifests  modules
worker1# git status
# On branch master
nothing to commit (working directory clean)
worker1$ diff hieradata/hosts/node1.yaml ../production/hieradata/hosts/
node1.yaml
2c2
< welcome: 'Careful, this is a production node'
---
> welcome: 'Be very Careful, this is a production node'
verifying that the master and production branches differ.
```

> If you changed hiera.yaml for the single tree example, change it to the following:
>
> ```
> :datadir: "/etc/puppet/environments/%{::environment}/
> hieradata"
> ```

Running Puppet on `node1` in the `production` environment will now produce the change we expect in `/etc/motd` as follows:

```
PRODUCTION
Be very Careful, this is a production node
Managed Node: node1
Managed by Puppet version 3.4.2
```

Run the agent again with the `master` environment to change the motd, as shown in the following command:

```
node1# puppet agent -t --environment master

...

Notice: /Stage[main]/Base/File[/etc/motd]/content:

--- /etc/motd   2014-01-09 02:15:53.961359763 -0500

+++ /tmp/puppet-file20140109-10057-1wbjy4p-0   2014-01-09
02:17:38.611359763 -0500

@@ -1,4 +1,4 @@

 PRODUCTION

-Be very Careful, this is a production node

+Careful, this is a production node
```

So, each branch is mapped to a Puppet environment. As new branches are added, we manually have to set up the directory and push the contents to the new directory. If we were working in a small environment, this arrangement of Git pulls would be fine, but in an enterprise, we would want this to be automatic. Git can run scripts at various points in the commitment of code to the repository—these scripts are called **hooks**.

Git Hooks

Git provides several hook locations that are documented in the `githooks` man page. The hooks of interest are `post-receive` and `pre-receive`. A `post-receive` hook is run after a successful commit to the repository and a `pre-receive` hook is run before any commit is attempted. Git Hooks can be written in any language; the only requirement is that they should be executable. The `post-receive` and `pre-receive` hooks are both passed three parameters via `stdin`: the first is the commit that you are starting from (`oldrev`), the second is the new commit you are creating (`newrev`), and the third is a reference to the type of change that was made to the repository, in that reference is the branch that was updated. Using these hooks, we can automate our workflow. We'll start using the `post-receive` hook to set up our environments for us.

Using post-receive to set up environments

What we would like to happen at this point is a series of steps, discussed as follows:

1.   A developer works on a file in a branch.

2.   The developer commits that change and pushes it to the origin.

3.   If the branch doesn't exist, create it in /etc/puppet/ environments/<branch>.

4.   Pull the updates for the branch into /etc/puppet/environments/<branch>.

In our initial configuration, we will write a post-receive hook that will implement the previously mentioned steps 3 and 4. Later on, we'll ensure that only the correct developers commit to the correct branch with a pre-receive hook. To ensure that our Puppet user has access to the files in /etc/puppet/environments, we will use sudo to run the commits as the Puppet user.

Our hook doesn't need to do anything with the reference other than extract the name of the branch and then update /etc/puppet/environments as necessary. In the interest of simplicity, this hook will be written in bash. Create the script in /var/ lib/git/puppet.git/hooks/post-receive, as follows:

```
#!/bin/bash
PUPPETDIR=/etc/puppet/environments
REPOHOME=/var/lib/git/puppet.git
GIT=/usr/bin/git
umask 0002
unset GIT_DIR
```

We will start by setting some variables for the location of the Git repository and the location of the Puppet environments directory. It will become clear later why we set umask at this point, we want the files created by our script to be group writable. The unset GIT_DIR line is important; the hook will be run by Git after a successful commit where GIT_DIR was set to ".". We unset the variable so that Git doesn't get confused. Next, we will read the variables oldrev, newrev, and refname from stdin (not command-line arguments), as shown in the following code:

```
read oldrev newrev refname
branch=${refname#*\/*\/}
if [ -z $branch ]; then
 echo "ERROR: Updating $PUPPETDIR"
 echo "      Branch undefined"
 exit 10
fi
```

After extracting the branch from the third argument, we will verify whether we were able to extract a branch. If we are unable to parse out the branch name, we will quit the script and warn the user.

Now, we have three scenarios that we will account for in the script, as shown in the following snippet. The first is that the directory exists in /etc/puppet/ environments and that it is a Git repository.

```
# if directory exists, check it is a git repository
if [ -d "$PUPPETDIR/$branch/.git" ]; then
  cd $PUPPETDIR/$branch
  echo "Updating $branch in $PUPPETDIR"
  sudo -u puppet $GIT pull origin $branch
  exit=$?
```

In this case, we will cd to the directory and issue a git pull origin <branchname> command to update the directory. We will run the Git pull command using sudo with -u puppet to ensure that the files are created as the Puppet user.

The second scenario is that the directory exists but it was not created via a Git checkout. We will quit early if we run into this option, as shown in the following snippet:

```
elif [ -d "$PUPPETDIR/$branch" ]; then
  # directory exists but is not in git
  echo "ERROR: Updating $PUPPETDIR"
  echo "      $PUPPETDIR/$branch is not a git repository"
  exit=20
```

The third option is that the directory doesn't exist yet. In this case, we will clone the branch using the git clone command in a new directory as the Puppet user (using sudo again), as shown in the following snippet:

```
else
  # directory does not exist, create
  cd $PUPPETDIR
  echo "Creating new branch $branch in $PUPPETDIR"
  sudo -u puppet $GIT clone -b $branch $REPOHOME $branch
  exit=$?
fi
```

In each case, we retained the return value from Git so that we can exit the script with the appropriate exit code at this point as follows:

```
exit $exit
```

Now, let's see this in action. Change the permissions on the post-receive script to make it executable (chmod 755 post-receive). Now, to ensure that our Git user can run the Git commands as the Puppet user, we need to create a sudoers file. We need the Git user to run /usr/bin/git; so, we put in a rule to allow this in a new file called /etc/sudoers.d/sudoers-puppet as follows:

```
git ALL = (puppet) NOPASSWD: /usr/bin/git *
```

In this example, we'll create a new local branch, make a change in the branch, and then push the change to the origin. Our hook will be called and a new directory will be created in /etc/puppet/environments.

```
worker1# sudo -iu git
git@worker1$ ls /etc/puppet/environments
master   production
git@worker1$ cd /tmp/puppet
git@worker1$ git branch thomas
git@worker1$ git checkout thomas
Switched to branch 'thomas'
git@worker1$ ls
hieradata   manifests   modules
git@worker1$ cd hieradata/hosts/
git@worker1$ sed -i node1.yaml -e "s/welcome:.*/welcome: 'Thomas
Branch'/"
git@worker1$ git add node1.yaml
git@worker1$ git commit -m "Adding thomas branch"
[thomas a266d91] Adding thomas branch
 1 files changed, 1 insertions(+), 1 deletions(-)
git@worker1$ git push origin thomas
Counting objects: 9, done.
Compressing objects: 100% (4/4), done.
Writing objects: 100% (5/5), 625 bytes, done.
Total 5 (delta 0), reused 0 (delta 0)
Unpacking objects: 100% (5/5), done.
remote: Creating new branch thomas in /etc/puppet/environments
remote: Initialized empty Git repository in /etc/puppet/environments/
thomas/.git/
To /var/lib/git/puppet.git
 * [new branch]      thomas -> thomas
git@worker1$ ls /etc/puppet/environments
master   production   thomas
```

Our Git Hook has created a new environment without our intervention; we'll now run puppet agent on the node to see the new environment in action, as shown in the following command:

```
[root@node1 puppet]# puppet agent -t --environment thomas
...
Notice: /Stage[main]/Base/File[/etc/motd]/content:
--- /etc/motd   2014-01-10 01:31:06.286261652 -0500
+++ /tmp/puppet-file20140112-18203-18sjzjb-0   2014-01-12
01:05:34.369163541 -0500
@@ -1,4 +1,4 @@
 PRODUCTION
-Be very Careful, this is a production node
+Thomas Branch
...
Notice: Finished catalog run in 3.10 seconds
```

Using sudo in our post-receive hook guarantees that the users who belong to the pupdevs group do not have write access to /etc/puppet/environments; they are only allowed to run Git as the Puppet user. They may only modify the code by updating the Git repository.

> The users that belong to the pupdevs group can still clone a new repository or add a new remote to gain unauthorized access to your Puppet tree.

Puppet-sync

The problem of synchronizing Git repositories for Puppet is common enough that a script exists on GitHub that can be used for this purpose. The puppet-sync script is available at https://github.com/pdxcat/puppet-sync.

To use puppet-sync, you install the script on your worker machine and edit the post-receive hook to run puppet-sync with appropriate arguments. The updated post-receive hook will have the the following lines:

```
REPO="/var/lib/git/puppet.git"
DEPLOY="/etc/puppet/environments"
[ "$newrev" -eq 0 ] 2> /dev/null && DELETE='--delete' || DELETE=''
sudo -u puppet /usr/bin/puppet-sync \
  --branch "$BRANCH" \
  --repository "$REPO" \
  --deploy "$DEPLOY" \
  $DELETE
```

This process can be extended as a solution to pushing across multiple workers by placing the call to puppet-sync within a for loop which SSHes to each worker and then runs puppet-sync on each of them.

This can be extended further by replacing the call to puppet-sync with a call to **Ansible** to update a group of Puppet workers defined in your Ansible host's file. More information on Ansible is available at http://docs.ansible.com/.

Playing nice with other developers

Up to this point, we've been working with the Git account to make our changes. In the real world, we would want the developers to work as their own user account. We need to worry about permissions at this point. When each developer commits their code, the commit will run as their user, so files will get created with them as the owner, which might prevent other developers from pushing additional updates. Our post-receive hook will run as their user, so they need to be able to use sudo just like the Git user. To mitigate some of these issues, we'll use Git's shareddirectory setting to ensure that the files are group readable in /var/lib/git/puppet.git and use sudo to ensure that the files in /etc/puppet/environments are created and owned by the Puppet user.

We can use Git's built-in sharedrepository setting to ensure that all members of the group have access to the repository, but each user's umask setting may prevent files from being created with group write permissions. Putting a umask setting in our script and running Git using sudo is a more reliable way of ensuring access. To create a Git repository as a shared repository, use shared=group while creating the bare repository, as shown in the following commands:

```
git@worker1$ cd /var/lib/git
git@worker1$ git init --bare --shared=group newrepo.git
Initialized empty shared Git repository in /var/lib/git/
newrepo.git/
```

First, we'll modify our `puppet.git` bare repository to enable shared access, then we'll have to retroactively change the permissions to ensure group access is granted. We'll edit `/var/lib/git/puppet.git/config` as follows:

```
[core]
        repositoryformatversion = 0
        filemode = true
        bare = true
        sharedrepository = 1
```

To illustrate our workflow, we'll create a new group and add a user to that group, as shown in the following commands:

```
worker1# groupadd pupdevs
worker1# useradd -g pupdevs -c "Sample Developer" samdev
worker1# id samdev
uid=502(samdev) gid=502(pupdevs) groups=502(pupdevs)
```

Now, we need to retroactively go back and change the ownership of files in `/var/lib/git/puppet.git` to ensure that the `pupdevs` group have write access to the repository. We'll also set the `setgid` bit on that directory so that new files are group owned by `pupdevs`, as shown in the following commands:

```
worker1# cd /var/lib/git

worker1# find puppet.git -type d -exec chmod g+rwxs {} \;

worker1# find puppet.git -type f -exec chmod g+rw {} \;

worker1# chgrp -R pupdevs puppet.git
```

Now the repository is accessible to anyone in the `pupdevs` group. We now need to add a rule to our `sudoers` file to allow anyone in the `pupdevs` group to run Git as the Puppet user, as shown in the following code:

```
%pupdevs ALL = (puppet) NOPASSWD: /usr/bin/git *
```

With this `sudo` rule in place, `sudo` to `samdev`, clone the repository and modify the production branch, as shown in the following commands:

```
worker1# sudo -iu samdev

samdev@worker1$ git clone /var/lib/git/puppet.git

Initialized empty Git repository in /home/samdev/puppet/.git/

samdev@worker1$ cd puppet

samdev@worker1$ git config --global user.name "Sample Developer"
```

```
samdev@worker1$ git config --global user.email "samdev@example.com"
samdev@worker1$ git checkout production
samdev@worker1$ cd hieradata/hosts
samdev@worker1$ sed -i -e "s/welcome: .*/welcome: 'Sample Developer Made
this change'/" node1.yaml
samdev@worker1$ echo "Example.com Puppet repository" >README
samdev@worker1$ git add node1.yaml README
samdev@worker1$ git commit -m "Sample Developer changing welcome"
sam
samdev@worker1$ git push origin production
Counting objects: 9, done.
...
remote:  2 files changed, 1 insertions(+), 3 deletions(-)
To /var/lib/git/puppet.git
   63c027a..64416fd  production -> production
```

We've updated our `production` branch. Our changes were automatically propagated to the Puppet `environments` directory. Now, we can run Puppet on `node1` (in the `production` environment) to see the change, as shown in the following command:

```
node1# puppet agent -t
...
Notice: /Stage[main]/Base/File[/etc/motd]/content:
--- /etc/motd  2014-01-12 01:05:34.393163541 -0500
+++ /tmp/puppet-file20140113-20261-23hj51-0    2014-01-13
02:06:06.216032724 -0500
@@ -1,4 +1,4 @@
 PRODUCTION
-Thomas Branch
+Sample Developer Made this change
...
Notice: Finished catalog run in 3.72 seconds
```

Now, any user we add to the `pupdevs` group will be able to update our Puppet code and have it pushed to any branch. If we look in `/etc/puppet/environments`, we can see that the owner of the files is also the Puppet user due to the use of `sudo`, as shown in the following commands:

```
worker1# ls -l /etc/puppet/environments
total 8
drwxr-sr-x. 6 puppet pupdevs 4096 Jan 17 02:29 master
drwxr-sr-x. 6 puppet pupdevs 4096 Jan 17 02:13 production
```

Not playing nice with others

Our configuration at this point allows all users in the `pupdevs` group the ability to push changes to all branches. A complaint usually made about Git is that it lacks a good system of access control. Using filesystem ACLs, it is possible to allow only certain users to push changes to specific branches. Another way to control commits is to use a `pre-receive` hook and verify if access will be granted before accepting the commit.

The `pre-receive` hook receives the same information as the `post-receive` hook. The hook runs as the user performing the commit so that we can use that information to block a user from committing to a branch or even doing certain types of commits; merges, for instance, can be denied. To illustrate how this works, we'll create a new user called `newbie` and add them to the `pupdevs` group, as shown in the following commands:

```
worker1# useradd -g pupdevs -c "Rookie Developer" newbie
worker1# sudo -iu newbie
```

We'll have `newbie` check our `production` code; make a commit and then push the change to production, as shown in the following commands:

```
newbie@worker1$ git clone /var/lib/git/puppet.git
Initialized empty Git repository in /home/newbie/puppet/.git/
newbie@worker1$ cd puppet
newbie@worker1$ git config --global user.name "Newbie"
newbie@worker1$ git config --global user.email "newbie@example.com"
newbie@worker1$ git checkout production
Branch production set up to track remote branch production from origin.
Switched to a new branch 'production'
newbie@worker1$ echo "Rookie mistake" >README
newbie@worker1$ git add README
newbie@worker1$ git commit -m "Rookie happens"
[production 8dcf9b0] Rookie happens
 1 files changed, 1 insertions(+), 12 deletions(-)
```

Our rookie managed to wipe out the README file in production; if this were an important file, then the deletion may have caused problems. It would be better if the rookie couldn't make changes to production.

We'll create a `pre-receive` hook that only allows certain users to commit to the `production` branch. Again, we'll use `bash` for simplicity. We will start by defining who will be allowed to commit and which branch we are interested in protecting, as shown in the following snippet:

```
#!/bin/bash

ALLOWED_USERS="samdev git root"
PROTECTED_BRANCH="production"
```

We will then use `whoami` to determine who has run the script (the developer who performed the commit) as follows:

```
user=$(whoami)
```

Now, just like we did in `post-receive`, we'll parse out the branch name, and exit the script if we cannot determine the branch name, as shown in the following code:

```
read oldrev newrev refname
branch=${refname#*\/*\/}
if [ -z $branch ]; then
 echo "ERROR: Branch undefined"
 exit 10
fi
```

We compare the `$branch` variable against our protected branch and exit cleanly if this isn't a branch we are protecting, as shown in the following code. Exiting with an exit code of `0` informs Git that the commit should proceed.

```
if [ "$branch" != "$PROTECTED_BRANCH" ]; then
  # branch not protected, exit cleanly
  exit 0
fi
```

Exiting with an exit code of `0`informs Git that the commit should proceed.

If we make it to this point in the script, we are on the `protected` branch, and the `$user` variable has our username. So, we will just loop through the `$ALLOWED_USERS` variable looking for a user who is allowed to commit to the `protected` branch. If we find a match, we will exit cleanly, as shown in the following code:

```
for allowed in $ALLOWED_USERS
do
  if [ "$user" == "$allowed" ]; then
    # user allowed, exit cleanly
    echo "$PROTECTED_BRANCH change for $user"
    exit 0
  fi
done
```

If the user was not in the $ALLOWED_USERS variable, then their commit is denied and we exit with a non-zero exit code to inform Git that the commit should not be allowed, as shown in the following code:

```
# not an allowed user
echo "Error: Changes to $PROTECTED_BRANCH must be made by $ALLOWED_
USERS"
exit 10
```

Save this file with the name `pre-receive` in `/var/lib/git/puppet.git/hooks/` and then change the ownership to `git`. Make it executable using the following commands:

```
# chmod 755 pre-receive
# chown git:git pre-receive
```

Now, we'll go back and make a simple change to the repository as `root` as shown in the following commands. It is important to always get in the habit of running `git fetch` and `git pull origin <branch>` when you start working on a branch. You need to do this to ensure that you have the latest version of the branch from your origin.

```
worker1# cd puppet2
worker1# git fetch
...
Receiving objects: 100% (110/110), 12.41 KiB, done.
Resolving deltas: 100% (5/5), done.
...
worker1# git branch
  master
* production
worker1# git pull origin production
...
Updating 53ba47b..7a07bed
Fast-forward
...
worker1# echo root >> README
worker1# git add README
worker1# git commit -m README
[production 0766b31] README
 1 files changed, 1 insertions(+), 0 deletions(-)
```

Now, with the simple change made (we appended our username to the README file), we can push the change to the origin using the following command:

```
worker1# git push origin production
...
remote:   README |   1 +
remote:   1 files changed, 1 insertions(+), 0 deletions(-)
...
    7a07bed..0766b31  production -> production
```

As expected, there are no errors and the README file is updated in the production branch by our post-receive hook. Now, we will attempt a similar change as the newbie user, as shown in the following commands:

```
worker1# sudo -iu newbie
newbie@worker1$ cd puppet
newbie@worker1$ git branch
  master
* production
newbie@worker1$ git fetch
...
    1bbf263..0766b31  production -> origin/production
newbie@worker1$ git pull origin production
...
 1 files changed, 7 insertions(+), 0 deletions(-)
newbie@worker1$ echo Again? >README
newbie@worker1$ git add README
newbie@worker1$ git commit -m "oops\!"
[production 77483c2] oops\!
 1 files changed, 1 insertions(+), 8 deletions(-)
```

Our newbie user has wiped out the README file; they meant to append to the file using two less than (>>) signs but instead used a single less than (>) sign and clobbered the file. Now, newbie attempts to push the change to production, as shown in the following commands:

```
newbie@worker1$ git push origin production
Counting objects: 5, done.
Compressing objects: 100% (2/2), done.
Writing objects: 100% (3/3), 340 bytes, done.
Total 3 (delta 0), reused 0 (delta 0)
```

```
Unpacking objects: 100% (3/3), done.
remote: Error: Changes to production must be made by samdev git root
To /var/lib/git/puppet.git
 ! [remote rejected] production -> production (pre-receive hook declined)
error: failed to push some refs to '/var/lib/git/puppet.git'
```

We see the commit beginning — the changes from the local `production` branch in `newbie` are sent to the origin. However, before working with the changes, Git runs the `pre-receive` hook and denies the commit. So, from the origin's perspective, the commit never took place. The commit only exists in the `newbie` user's directory. If the `newbie` user wishes this change to be propagated, they'll need to contact either `samdev`, `git`, or `root`.

Git for everyone

At this point, we've shown how to have Git work from one of the worker machines. In a real enterprise solution, the workers would have some sort of shared storage configured or another method of having the Puppet code updated automatically. In that scenario, the Git repository wouldn't live on a worker but instead be pushed to a worker. Git has a workflow for this which uses SSH keys to grant access to the repository. With minor changes to the shown solution, it is possible to have users SSH to a machine as the Git user to make commits. Git also ships with a restricted shell, `git-shell`, which can be used to only allow a user to update Git repositories. In our configuration, we will change the `git` user's shell to `git-shell` using `chsh`, as shown in the following commands:

```
worker1# chsh -s $(which git-shell) git
Changing shell for git.
Warning: "/usr/bin/git-shell" is not listed in /etc/shells.
Shell changed.
```

Now, we will have our developer generate an SSH key using the following commands:

```
remotedev@host $ ssh-keygen
Generating public/private rsa key pair.
...
Your identification has been saved in /home/remotedev/.ssh/id_rsa.
Your public key has been saved in /home/remotedev/.ssh/id_rsa.pub.
```

Then, copy the key into the `authorized_keys` file for the Git user as shown in the following commands:

```
remotedev@host $ ssh-copy-id -i ~/.ssh/id_rsa git@worker1

/usr/bin/ssh-copy-id: INFO: attempting to log in with the new key(s), to
filter out any that are already installed

/usr/bin/ssh-copy-id: INFO: 1 key(s) remain to be installed -- if you are
prompted now it is to install the new keys


Number of key(s) added: 1
```

Now try logging into the machine, with `ssh 'git@worker1'` and check to make sure that only the key(s) you wanted were added.

If you are copying the keys manually, remember that permissions are important here. They must be restrictive for SSH to allow access. SSH requires that `~git` (Git's home directory) should not be group writable, that `~git/.ssh` be `700`, and also that `~git/.ssh/authorized_keys` be no more than `600`. Check in `/var/log/secure` for messages from SSH if your remote user cannot SSH successfully as the Git user.

When a user attempts to connect to our machine as the `git` user, they will not be able to login, as you can see in the following commands:

```
remotedev@host $ ssh -i .ssh/id_rsa git@worker1

Last login: Sat Jan 18 02:07:29 2014 from 192.168.100.1

fatal: What do you think I am? A shell?

Connection to worker1 closed.
```

However, if they attempted to use Git commands, as shown in the following snippet, they will succeed:

```
remotedev@host $ git clone git@worker1:puppet.git

Cloning into 'puppet'...

remote: Counting objects: 188, done.

remote: Compressing objects: 100% (134/134), done.

remote: Total 188 (delta 12), reused 0 (delta 0)

Receiving objects: 100% (188/188), 19.59 KiB | 0 bytes/s, done.

Resolving deltas: 100% (12/12), done.
```

Now, when a remote user executes a commit, it will run as the `git` user. We need to modify our `sudoers` file to allow `sudo` to run remotely. Add the following line at the top of `/etc/sudoers.d/sudoers-puppet` (possibly using `visudo`):

```
Defaults !requiretty
```

At this point, our `sudo` rule for the `post-receive` hook will work as expected, but we will lose the restrictiveness of our `pre-receive` hook since everything will be running as the `git` user. SSH has a solution to this problem: we can set an `environment` variable in the `authorized_keys` file that is the name of our remote user. Edit `~git/.ssh/authorized_keys` as follows:

```
environment="USER=remotedev" ssh-rsa AAAA...b remotedev@host
```

Finally, edit the `pre-receive` hook, changing the `user=$(whoami)` line to `user=$USER`.

Now, when we use our SSH key to commit remotely, the `environment` variable set in the SSH key is used to determine who ran the commit.

Running an enterprise-level Git server is a complex task in itself; the scenario presented here can be used as a road map to develop your solution.

Summary

In this chapter, we have seen how to configure Puppet to work in different environments. We have seen how having `hieradata` in different environments can allow developers to work independently.

Leveraging the utility of Git and Git Hooks, we can have custom build environments for each developer built automatically when the code is checked into our Git repository. This will allow us to greatly increase our developers' productivity and allow a team full of system administrators to work simultaneously on the same code base.

> When your system administrators work on the same code, they will inevitably run into situations where they have edited the same code as each other. This leads to conflicts. Merging conflicts is a big part of working in a large group. There are numerous resources available only to help resolve merging issues. The Git branching game at `http://pcottle.github.io/learnGitBranching/` is a good place to start.

In the next chapter, we'll see how public modules from the Puppet Forge can be used to accomplish complex configurations on our nodes.

4

Public Modules

The default types shipped with Puppet can be used to do almost everything you need to do to configure your nodes. When you need to perform more tasks than the defaults can provide, you can either write your own custom modules or turn to the Forge (`http://forge.puppetlabs.com/`) and use a public module. The Puppet Forge is a public repository of shared modules. Several of these modules enhance the functionality of Puppet, provide a new type, or solve a specific problem. In this chapter, we will first cover how to keep your public modules organized for your enterprise, then we will go over specific use cases for some popular modules.

Getting modules

Modules are just files and a directory structure. They can be packaged as a ZIP archive or shared via a Git repository. Indeed, most modules are hosted on GitHub in addition to the Puppet Forge. You will find most public modules on the Forge, and the preferred method to keep your modules up to date is to retrieve them from the Forge.

Using GitHub for public modules

If you have a module you wish to use that is only hosted on GitHub, (`github.com` is an online Git service for sharing code using Git) a good way to keep your modules organized is to create a local Git repository and make the GitHub module a submodule of your modules.

We'll start by creating a new Git repository for our public modules:

```
git@worker1$ git init --bare --shared=group public.git
Initialized empty shared Git repository in /var/lib/git/public.git/
```

If your Git user still has git-shell set as its login shell from the previous chapter, change it back to bash, as shown in the following commands:

```
# chsh -s /bin/bash git
Changing shell for git.
Shell changed.
```

The first module we will download from GitHub is puppetdb, which is a module to install and configure puppetdb. This module is available at https://github.com/ puppetlabs/puppetlabs-puppetdb.

With our public repository created, we will clone the repository in another location and create a Git submodule for the puppetlabs-puppetdb repository in a directory called puppetdb, as shown in the following commands. Git submodules are a way of including other Git repositories within your repository. The advantage of a submodule is that when the external repository is updated, your local repository can pull in those changes.

```
git@worker1$ cd /tmp
git@worker1$ git clone /var/lib/git/public.git
Initialized empty Git repository in /tmp/public/.git/
warning: You appear to have cloned an empty repository.
git@worker1$ cd public
git@worker1$ git submodule add https://github.com/puppetlabs/puppetlabs-puppetdb.git puppetdb
Initialized empty Git repository in /tmp/public/puppetdb/.git/
remote: Reusing existing pack: 927, done.
remote: Total 927 (delta 0), reused 0 (delta 0)
Receiving objects: 100% (927/927), 226.25 KiB, done.
Resolving deltas: 100% (385/385), done.
```

As shown in the following commands, we can see that puppetdb has been added to our repository using status:

```
git@worker1$ git status
# On branch master
#
# Initial commit
#
```

```
# Changes to be committed:
#   (use "git rm --cached <file>..." to unstage)
#
#   new file:    .gitmodules
#   new file:    puppetdb
#
```

Now, we need to add `puppetdb` to our repository and commit it as well as the `.gitmodules` file, as shown in the following commands:

```
git@worker1$ git add .gitmodules puppetdb
git@worker1$ git commit -m "adding puppetdb as submodule"
[master (root-commit) 17ad531] adding puppetdb as submodule
 2 files changed, 4 insertions(+), 0 deletions(-)
 create mode 100644 .gitmodules
 create mode 160000 puppetdb
git@worker1$ git push origin master
Counting objects: 3, done.
Compressing objects: 100% (3/3), done.
Writing objects: 100% (3/3), 341 bytes, done.
Total 3 (delta 0), reused 0 (delta 0)
Unpacking objects: 100% (3/3), done.
To /var/lib/git/public.git
 * [new branch]       master -> master
```

The `.gitmodules` file contains references to the upstream Git repositories we use for our submodules; in this case, the `.gitmodules` file will contain the following:

```
[submodule "puppetdb"]
  path = puppetdb
  url = https://github.com/puppetlabs/puppetlabs-puppetdb.git
```

Now, when `puppetlabs-puppetdb` is updated on GitHub, we can pull down the latest commit with `git submodule update`.

 If you create an account on GitHub, you can "watch" this repository and be notified when an update is made.

While working with this workflow, it is important to know that the top-level repository (`public`) only knows where the submodules live, and it doesn't know anything about the contents of the submodules. So, when you checkout the public repository again, the submodules will only be there as stubs, as you can see in the following commands:

```
git@worker1$ cd /tmp/
git@worker1$ git clone /var/lib/git/public.git/ public2
Initialized empty Git repository in /tmp/public2/.git/
git@worker1$ cd public2
git@worker1$ ls -l puppetdb
total 0
```

We need to run `git submodule update --init` to retrieve the latest commit for the submodule, using the following commands:

```
git@worker1$ git submodule update --init
Submodule 'puppetdb' (https://github.com/puppetlabs/puppetlabs-puppetdb.
git) registered for path 'puppetdb'
Initialized empty Git repository in /tmp/public2/puppetdb/.git/
remote: Reusing existing pack: 927, done.
remote: Total 927 (delta 0), reused 0 (delta 0)
Receiving objects: 100% (927/927), 226.25 KiB | 336 KiB/s, done.
Resolving deltas: 100% (385/385), done.
Submodule path 'puppetdb': checked out
'6d5f329e2a329654efbb0e3b036523b3a67c0a2c'
```

This shows a shortcoming of this workflow—each developer will have his/her own version of the submodule based on when he/she checked out the submodule. If you agree to always work on the latest commit, then this solution is workable; however, this can get confusing. Submodules are best used for internal repositories—to allow one group to pull in the work of another one within their enterprise and to allow the teams to work independently on their respective components. If you are primarily using modules available from the Forge, then downloading them directly from the Forge is preferable for this method because only the release versions are posted to the Forge. The modules pulled directly from GitHub can be development releases. Also, you will need to know which modules are required for these modules to work and their dependencies. The `puppetdb` module is a good example to highlight this problem; it requires many Forge modules to function properly, as we will see in the the following section.

Modules from the Forge

Modules on the Puppet Forge can be installed using Puppet's built-in `module` command. The modules on the Forge have files named `Modulefile`, which define their dependencies; so, if you download modules from the Forge using `puppet module install`, then their dependencies will be resolved in a way similar to how `yum` resolves dependencies for `rpm` packages.

To install the `puppetlabs-puppetdb` module, as we did previously, we will simply issue a `puppet module install` command in the appropriate directory. We'll create a new directory in `tmp`; for our example this will be `/tmp/public3`, as shown in the following commands:

```
git@worker1$ mkdir public3
```

```
git@worker1$ cd public3
```

Then, we'll inform Puppet that our `modulepath` is `/tmp/public3` and install the `puppetdb` module, using the following commands:

```
git@worker1 public3$ puppet module install --modulepath=/tmp/public3
puppetlabs-puppetdb
Notice: Preparing to install into /tmp/public3 ...
Notice: Downloading from https://forge.puppetlabs.com ...
Notice: Installing -- do not interrupt ...
/tmp/public3
└─┬ puppetlabs-puppetdb (v3.0.0)
  ├── puppetlabs-firewall (v0.4.2)
  ├── puppetlabs-inifile (v1.0.0)
  ├─┬ puppetlabs-postgresql (v3.2.0)
  │ ├── puppetlabs-apt (v1.4.0)
  │ └── puppetlabs-concat (v1.0.0)
  └── puppetlabs-stdlib (v4.1.0)
```

Using `module install`, we retrieved `puppetlabs-firewall`, `puppetlabs-inifile`, `puppetlabs-postgresql`, `puppetlabs-apt`, `puppetlabs-concat`, and `puppetlabs-stdlib` all at once. So, not only have we satisfied dependencies automatically, but we also have retrieved release versions of the modules as opposed to the development code. We can, at this point, add these modules to a local repository and guarantee that our fellow developers will be using the same versions as we have checked out. Otherwise, we can inform our developers about the version we are using and have them checkout the modules using the same versions.

You can specify the version with `puppet module install` as follows:

```
git@worker1$ \rm -r stdlib

git@worker1$ puppet module install --modulepath=/tmp/public3 puppetlabs-
stdlib --version 3.2.0

Notice: Preparing to install into /tmp/public3 ...

Notice: Downloading from https://forge.puppetlabs.com ...

Notice: Installing -- do not interrupt ...

/tmp/public3
└── puppetlabs-stdlib (v3.2.0)
```

> The \rm in the previous example is a shorthand in Unix to disable shell expansion of variables. rm is usually aliased to rm -i, which would have prompted us when we wanted to delete the directory.

Keeping track of the installed versions can become troublesome; a more stable approach is to use `librarian-puppet` to pull in the modules you require for your site.

Using librarian

Librarian is a bundler for Ruby. It handles dependency checking for you. The project to use librarian with Puppet is called `librarian-puppet` and is available at `http://rubygems.org/gems/librarian-puppet`. To install `librarian-puppet`, we'll use RubyGems since no rpm packages exist in public repositories at this time. To avoid user-installed gems from polluting our Ruby structure, we'll install `librarian-puppet` into the Git user's `.gem` directory, and copy the modules into a directory the Puppet master can use, using the following commands:

```
git@worker1$ gem install --user-install librarian-puppet

WARNING:  You don't have /var/lib/git/.gem/ruby/1.8/bin in your PATH,
    gem executables will not run.

Successfully installed thor-0.18.1

Successfully installed librarian-puppet-0.9.10

2 gems installed

Installing ri documentation for thor-0.18.1...

Installing ri documentation for librarian-puppet-0.9.10...

Installing RDoc documentation for thor-0.18.1...

Installing RDoc documentation for librarian-puppet-0.9.10...
```

Gem was kind enough to remind us that we don't have the new path we just created in our $PATH; we'll now add it using the following command:

```
git@worker1$ echo export PATH=\$PATH:/var/lib/git/.gem/ruby/1.8/bin >>~/.bashrc
git@worker1$ . .bashrc
```

We can now run librarian-puppet as follows:

```
[git@worker1 ~]$ librarian-puppet version
librarian-puppet v0.9.10
```

The librarian-puppet project uses a Puppetfile to define the modules that will be installed. The syntax is the name of the module followed by a comma and the version to install. You can override the location of the Puppet Forge using a forge line as well. Our initial Puppetfile would be the following:

```
    forge "http://forge.puppetlabs.com"
    mod 'puppetlabs/puppetdb', '3.0.0'
    mod 'puppetlabs/stdlib', '3.2.0'
```

We'll create a new public directory in /tmp/public4 and include the Puppetfile in that directory, as shown in the following commands:

```
git@worker1$ cd /tmp
git@worker1$ mkdir public4 && cd public4
git@worker1$ cat <<EOF>Puppetfile
> forge "http://forge.puppetlabs.com"
> mod 'puppetlabs/puppetdb', '3.0.0'
> mod 'puppetlabs/stdlib', '3.2.0'
> EOF
```

Next, we'll tell librarian-puppet to install everything we've listed in the Puppetfile as follows:

```
git@worker1$ librarian-puppet update
git@worker1$ ls
modules  Puppetfile  Puppetfile.lock
```

The Puppetfile.lock file is a file used by librarian-puppet to keep track of installed versions and dependencies; in our example, it contains the following:

```
    FORGE
      remote: http://forge.puppetlabs.com
      specs:
```

```
        puppetlabs/apt (1.4.0)
          puppetlabs/stdlib (>= 2.2.1)
        puppetlabs/concat (1.1.0-rc1)
          puppetlabs/stdlib (>= 3.0.0)
        puppetlabs/firewall (0.4.2)
        puppetlabs/inifile (1.0.0)
        puppetlabs/postgresql (3.2.0)
          puppetlabs/apt (>= 1.1.0, < 2.0.0)
          puppetlabs/concat (>= 1.0.0, < 2.0.0)
          puppetlabs/firewall (>= 0.0.4)
          puppetlabs/stdlib (>= 3.2.0, < 5.0.0)
        puppetlabs/puppetdb (3.0.0)
          puppetlabs/firewall (>= 0.0.4)
          puppetlabs/inifile (~> 1)
          puppetlabs/postgresql (>= 3.1.0, < 4.0.0)
          puppetlabs/stdlib (>= 2.2.0)
        puppetlabs/stdlib (3.2.0)
    DEPENDENCIES
      puppetlabs/puppetdb (= 3.0.0)
      puppetlabs/stdlib (= 3.2.0)
```

Our modules are installed in `/tmp/public4/modules`. Now, we can go back and add all these modules to our initial `Puppetfile` to lockdown the versions of the modules for all our developers. The process for a developer to clone our working tree would be to install `librarian-puppet` and then pull down our `Puppetfile`. We will add the `Puppetfile` to our Git repository to complete the workflow. Thus, each developer will be guaranteed of having the same `public` module structure.

We can then move these modules to `/etc/puppet/public` and change permissions for the Puppet user, using the following commands:

```
worker1# cd /tmp/public4/
worker1# cp -a . /etc/puppet/public
worker1# chown -R puppet:puppet /etc/puppet/public
worker1# ls -l /etc/puppet/public/modules
total 28
drwxrwxr-x. 8 puppet puppet 4096 Jan 21 02:16 apt
...
drwxrwxr-x. 6 puppet puppet 4096 Jan 21 02:16 stdlib
```

This method works fairly well, but we still need to update the modules independently of our Git updates; we need to do these two actions together. This is where **r10k** comes into play.

Using r10k

r10k is an automation tool for Puppet environments. It is hosted on GitHub at
`https://github.com/adrienthebo/r10k`. The project is used to speed up
deployments when there are many environments and many Git repositories in use.
From what we've covered so far, we can think of it as `librarian-puppet` and Git
Hooks in a single package. r10k takes the Git repositories specified in `/etc/r10k.yaml`
and checks out each branch of the repositories into a subdirectory of the `environment`
directory (the `environment` directory is also specified in `/etc/r10k.yaml`). If there is
a `Puppetfile` in the root of the branch, then r10k parses the file in the same way that
`librarian-puppet` does, and it uses `puppet module install` to install the specified
modules in a directory named `modules` under the `environment` directory.

To use r10k, we'll replace our `post-receive` Git Hook from the previous chapter
with a call to r10k, and we'll move our `librarian-puppet` configuration to a place
where r10k is expecting it. Since r10k will only be used by the Puppet user, we'll
install r10k in the Puppet user's home directory and add the user `rubygem` path
to the Puppet users' path.

Set up the Puppet user with a normal shell and login files, as shown in the
following commands:

```
worker1# chsh -s /bin/bash puppet worker1# sudo -iu puppet
puppet@worker1$ cp /etc/skel/.bashrc ~
puppet@worker1$ cp /etc/skel/.bash_profile ~
```

Now, install the r10k gem as shown in the following commands:

```
puppet@worker1$ gem install r10k --user-install
WARNING:  You don't have /var/lib/puppet/.gem/ruby/1.8/bin in your PATH,
    gem executables will not run.
...
Successfully installed r10k-1.1.2
6 gems installed
...
puppet@worker1$ echo "export PATH=\$PATH:~/.gem/ruby/1.8/bin" >>~/.bashrc
puppet@worker1$ exit
logout
worker1# sudo -iu puppet
puppet@worker1$ r10k version
1.1.2
```

Next, we'll create a `/etc/r10k.yaml` file to point to our local Git repository.
We will also specify that our Puppet environments will reside in `/etc/puppet/`
`environments`, as shown in the following snippet:

```
:cachedir: '/var/cache/r10k'
:sources:
 :plops:
   remote: '/var/lib/git/puppet.git'
   basedir: '/etc/puppet/environments'
```

Now, we need to create the `cache` directory and make it owned by the Puppet user.
We will use the following commands to do so:

```
worker1# mkdir /var/cache/r10k
```

```
worker1# chown puppet:puppet /var/cache/r10k
```

Now, we need to checkout our code and add a `Puppetfile` to the root of the
checkout. In each environment, create a `Puppetfile` that contains which modules
you want installed in that environment; we'll copy the previous `Puppetfile` as
shown in the following code:

```
forge "http://forge.puppetlabs.com"
mod 'puppetlabs/puppetdb', '3.0.0'
mod 'puppetlabs/stdlib', '3.2.0'
```

Add the `Puppetfile` to the Git repository using the following commands:

```
samdev@worker1$ git checkout master
samdev@worker1$ git add Puppetfile
samdev@worker1$ git commit -m "adding Puppetfile"
[master 880486a] adding Puppetfile
 1 files changed, 3 insertions(+), 0 deletions(-)
 create mode 100644 Puppetfile
```

Now, r10k expects that the modules specified in the `Puppetfile` will get installed
in `$environment/modules`, but we already have modules in that location. Move the
existing modules into another directory as shown in the following commands; `dist`
or `local` are commonly used:

```
samdev@worker1$ git mv modules dist
samdev@worker1$ git commit -m "moving modules to dist"
[master f0909fc] moving modules to dist
 7 files changed, 0 insertions(+), 0 deletions(-)
...
 rename {modules => dist}/web/manifests/init.pp (100%)
```

Now that our modules are out of the way, we don't want a modules directory to be tracked by Git, so add modules to .gitignore using the following commands:

```
samdev@worker1$ echo "modules/" >>.gitignore
samdev@worker1$ git add .gitignore
samdev@worker1$ git commit -m "adding .gitignore"
[master da71672] adding .gitignore
 1 files changed, 1 insertions(+), 0 deletions(-)
 create mode 100644 .gitignore
```

Ok, we are finally ready to test. Well almost. We want to test r10k, so we need to disable our post-receive hook; just disable the execute bit on the script as shown in the following commands:

```
git@worker1$ cd /var/lib/git/puppet.git/hooks/
git@worker1$ chmod -x post-receive
```

Now we can finally push our changes to the Git repository, as shown in the following commands:

```
git@worker1$ exit
root@worker1# sudo -iu samdev
samdev@worker1$ git push origin master
Counting objects: 6, done.
Compressing objects: 100% (4/4), done.
Writing objects: 100% (5/5), 609 bytes, done.
Total 5 (delta 1), reused 0 (delta 0)
Unpacking objects: 100% (5/5), done.
To /var/lib/git/puppet.git
   1a0d896..da71672  master -> master
```

Note that there are no remote lines in the output since we no longer have a post-receive hook running. We can now clean out the environments directory and test r10k, using the following commands:

```
samdev@worker1$ exit
root@worker1# sudo -iu puppet
puppet@worker1$ cd /etc/puppet
puppet@worker1$ \rm -r environments
puppet@worker1$ mkdir environments
puppet@worker1$ r10k deploy environment -p
```

```
puppet@worker1$ ls environments
master   production   thomas
puppet@worker1$ ls environments/production/
hieradata  manifests  modules  README
puppet@worker1$ ls environments/production/modules
puppet@worker1$ ls environments/master/
dist  hieradata  manifests  modules  Puppetfile  README
puppet@worker1$ ls environments/master/modules/
puppetdb  stdlib
```

As we can see, r10k did a Git checkout of our code in the master, thomas, and production branches. We added a Puppetfile to the master branch; so, when we look in /etc/puppet/environments/master/modules, we will see the puppetdb and stdlib modules defined in the Puppetfile.

To switch our workflow to use r10k, we'll change our post-receive hook to use r10k. Our post-receive hook will be greatly simplified; we'll just call r10k with the name of the branch and exit. Alternatively, we can have r10k run on every environment if we choose to; this way, it will only update a specific branch each time. To make the hook work again, we'll first need to enable the execute bit on the file, as shown in the following commands:

```
root@worker1# sudo -iu git
git@worker1$ cd /var/lib/git/puppet.git/hooks
git@worker1$ chmod +x post-receive
```

Next, we'll replace the contents of post-receive with the following script:

```
#!/bin/bash
r10k=/var/lib/puppet/.gem/ruby/1.8/bin/r10k
read oldrev newrev refname
  branch=${refname#*\/*\/}
  # let r10k take care of everything, all we need is the branch name
  sudo -u puppet $r10k deploy environment $branch -p
  exit=$?
exit $exit
```

Now, we need to edit our sudoers file to allow Git to run r10k as Puppet, as shown in the following code:

```
git ALL = (puppet) NOPASSWD: /var/lib/puppet/.gem/ruby/1.8/bin/r10k
%pupdevs ALL = (puppet) NOPASSWD: /var/lib/puppet/.gem/ruby/1.8/bin/
r10k
```

Now, to test whether everything is working, remove a module from the `master` environment using the following command:

```
[puppet@worker1 puppet]$ \rm -fr environments/master/modules/stdlib/
[puppet@worker1 puppet]$ exit
logout
```

Now, make a change in `master` and push that change to the origin to trigger an r10k run, as shown in the following commands:

```
worker1# sudo -iu samdev
samdev@worker1$ cd puppet
samdev@worker1$ echo "Using r10k in post-recieve" >>README
samdev@worker1$ git add README
samdev@worker1$ git commit -m "triggering r10k rebuild"
[master afad1cd] triggering r10k rebuild
 1 files changed, 1 insertions(+), 0 deletions(-)
samdev@worker1$ git push origin master
Counting objects: 5, done.
Compressing objects: 100% (3/3), done.
Unpacking objects: 100% (3/3), done.
Writing objects: 100% (3/3), 298 bytes, done.
Total 3 (delta 2), reused 0 (delta 0)
To /var/lib/git/puppet.git
   afad1cd..0d1695a  master -> master
```

Finally, verify whether the `stdlib` module was recreated or not using the following command:

```
samdev@worker1$ ls /etc/puppet/environments/master/modules/
puppetdb  stdlib
```

Keeping everything in r10k allows us to have mini labs for developers to work on a copy of our entire infrastructure with a few commands. They will only need a copy of our Git repository and our `r10k.yaml` file to recreate the configuration on a private Puppet master.

Using modules

Many of the modules found on the public Forge are of high quality and have good documentation. The modules we will cover in this section are well-documented. What we will do is use concrete examples to show how to use these modules to solve real-world problems. Though I have covered only those modules I personally found useful, there are many excellent modules that can be found on the Forge. I encourage you to have a look at them first before starting to write their own modules.

The modules that we will cover are as follows:

- concat
- inifile
- firewall
- lvm
- stdlib

These modules extend Puppet with custom types and, therefore, require that pluginsync be enabled on our nodes. Pluginsync copies Ruby libraries from the modules to /var/lib/puppet/lib/puppet and /var/lib/puppet/lib/facter. To enable pluginsync, set pluginsync=true in /etc/puppet/puppet.conf, or add pluginsync to the puppet agent command line.

Pluginsync is enabled by default in Puppet versions 3.0 and higher.

concat

When we distribute files with Puppet, we either send the whole file as is, or we send over a template that has references to variables. The concat module offers us a chance to build up a file from fragments and have it reassembled on the node. Using concat, we can have files, which live locally on the node, incorporated into the final file as sections. More importantly, while working in a complex system, we can have more than one module adding sections to the file. In a simple example, we can have four modules all operating on /etc/issue. The modules are as follows:

- issue – This is the base module that puts a header on /etc/issue
- issue_confidential – This module adds a confidential warning to /etc/issue

- issue_secret – This module adds a secret level warning to /etc/issue
- issue_topsecret – This module adds a top secret level warning to /etc/issue

Using either the file or the template method to distribute the file won't work here because all of the four modules are modifying the same file. What makes this harder still is that we will have machines in our organization that require one, two, three, or all four of the modules to be applied. The concat module allows us to solve this problem in an organized fashion (not a haphazard series of execs with awk and sed). To use concat, you first define the container, which is the file that will be populated with the fragments. concat calls the sections of the file **fragments**. The fragments are assembled based on their order. The order value is assigned to the fragments and should have the same number of digits, that is, if you have 100 fragments, then your first fragment should have 001, and not 1, as the order value. Our first module issue will have the following init.pp manifest file:

```
class issue {
  concat { 'issue':
    path    => '/etc/issue',
  }
  concat::fragment {'issue_top':
    target  => 'issue',
    content => "Example.com\n",
    order   => '01',
  }
}
```

This defines /etc/issue as a concat container and also creates a fragment to be placed at the top of the file (order 01). When applied to a node, the /etc/issue container will simply contain Example.com.

Our next module is issue_confidential. This includes the issue module to ensure that the container for /etc/issue is defined and we have our header. We then define a new fragment to contain the confidential warning, as shown in the following code:

```
class issue_confidential {
  include issue
  concat::fragment {'issue_confidential':
    target  => 'issue',
    content => "Unauthorised access to this machine is strictly
        prohibited. Use of this system is limited to authorised
        parties only.\n",
    order   => '05',
  }
}
```

This fragment has order 05, so it will always appear after the header. The next two modules are issue_secret and issue_topsecret. They both perform the same function as issue_confidential but with different messages and orders, as you can see in the following code:

```
class issue_secret {
  include issue
  concat::fragment {'issue_secret':
    target  => 'issue',
    content => "All information contained on this system is protected,
no information may be removed from the system unless authorised.\n",
    order   => '10',
  }
}
class issue_topsecret {
  include issue
  concat::fragment {'issue_topsecret':
    target  => 'issue',
    content => "You should forget you even know about this system.\n",
    order   => '15',
  }
}
```

Using our hiera configuration from the previous chapter, we will modify the node1.yaml file to contain the issue_confidential class; this will cause the /etc/issue file to contain the header and the confidential warning.

After running this configuration on node1, we see the following while attempting to log in to the system:

Example.com

Unauthorised access to this machine is strictly prohibited. Use of this system is limited to authorised parties only.

node1.example.com login:

Now, we will go back to our node1.yaml file and add issue_secret, as shown in the following snippet:

```
---
welcome: 'Sample Developer Made this change'
classes: - issue_confidential
         - issue_secret
```

After a successful Puppet run, the login looks like the following:

```
Example.com

Unauthorised access to this machine is strictly prohibited. Use of this
system is limited to authorised parties only.

All information contained on this system is protected, no information may
be removed from the system unless authorized.

node1.example.com login:
```

Adding the `issue_topsecret` module is left as an exercise, but we can see the utility of being able to have several modules modify a file. We can also have a fragment defined from a file on the node. We'll create another module called `issue_local` and add a local fragment. To specify a local file resource, we will use the `source` attribute of `concat::fragment`, as shown in the following code:

```
class issue_local {
  include issue
  concat::fragment {'issue_local':
    target => 'issue',
    source => '/etc/issue.local',
    order  => '99',
  }
}
```

Now, we add `issue_local` to `node1.yaml`, but before we can run the `puppet agent` on `node1`, we have to create `/etc/issue.local`, or the catalog will fail. This is a shortcoming of the `concat` module—if you specify a local path, then it has to exist. You can overcome this by having a file resource defined that creates an empty file if the local path doesn't exist, as shown in the following snippet:

```
file {'issue_local':
  path => '/etc/issue.local',
  ensure => 'file',
}
```

Then, modify the `concat::fragment` to require the file resource, as shown in the following snippet:

```
concat::fragment {'issue_local':
  target => 'issue',
  source => '/etc/issue.local',
  order  => '99',
  require => File['issue_local'],
}
```

Now, we can run `puppet agent` on `node1`; nothing will happen but the catalog will compile. Next, add some content to `/etc/issue.local` as shown in the following statement:

```
node1# echo "This is an example node, avoid storing protected material
here" >/etc/issue.local
```

Now after running Puppet, our login prompt will look like this:

```
Example.com
Unauthorised access to this machine is strictly prohibited. Use of this
system is limited to authorised parties only.
All information contained on this system is protected, no information may
be removed from the system unless authorized.
This is an example node, avoid storing protected material here
node1.example.com login:
```

There are many places where you would like to have multiple modules modify a file. When the structure of the file isn't easily determined, `concat` is the only viable solution. If the file is highly structured, then other mechanisms, such as `augeas`, can be used. When the file has a syntax of the `inifile` type, there is a module specifically made for inifiles.

inifile

The `inifile` module modifies the ini-style configuration files, such as those used by Samba, **System Security Services Daemon (SSSD)**, YUM, tuned, and many others, including Puppet. The module uses the `ini_setting` type to modify settings based on their section, name, and value. Consider the `gpgcheck` setting in the following `/etc/yum.conf` file:

```
[main]
cachedir=/var/cache/yum/$basearch/$releasever
keepcache=0
debuglevel=2
logfile=/var/log/yum.log
exactarch=1
obsoletes=1
gpgcheck=1
plugins=1
installonly_limit=3
```

As an example, we will modify that setting using `puppet resource`, as shown in the following commands:

```
node1# puppet resource ini_setting dummy_name path=/etc/yum.conf
section=main setting=gpgcheck value=0
Notice: /Ini_setting[dummy_name]/value: value changed '1' to '0'
ini_setting { 'dummy_name':
  ensure => 'present',
  value  => '0',
}
```

When we look at the file, we will see that the value was indeed changed:

```
[main]
cachedir=/var/cache/yum/$basearch/$releasever
keepcache=0
debuglevel=2
logfile=/var/log/yum.log
exactarch=1
obsoletes=1
gpgcheck=0
plugins=1
installonly_limit=3
```

The power of this module is the ability to change only part of a file and not clobber the work of another module. To show how this can work, we'll modify the SSSD configuration file. SSSD manages access to remote directories and authentication systems. It supports talking to multiple sources; we can exploit this to create modules that only define their own section of the configuration file. In this example, we'll assume there are production and development authentication LDAP directories called prod and devel. We'll create modules called sssd_prod and sssd_devel to modify the configuration file. Starting with sssd_prod, we'll add a [domain/prod] section to the file, as shown in the following snippet:

```
class sssd_prod {
  ini_setting {'krb5_realm_prod':
    path    => '/etc/sssd/sssd.conf',
    section => 'domain/PROD',
    setting => 'krb5_realm',
    value   => 'PROD',
  }
  ini_setting {'ldap_search_base_prod':
    path    => '/etc/sssd/sssd.conf',
```

```
        section => 'domain/PROD',
        setting => 'ldap_search_base',
        value   => 'ou=prod,dc=example,dc=com',
    }
    ini_setting {'ldap_uri_prod':
        path    => '/etc/sssd/sssd.conf',
        section => 'domain/PROD',
        setting => 'ldap_uri',
        value   => 'ldaps://ldap.prod.example.com',
    }
    ini_setting {'krb5_kpasswd_prod':
        path    => '/etc/sssd/sssd.conf',
        section => 'domain/PROD',
        setting => 'krb5_kpasswd',
        value   => 'secret!',
    }
    ini_setting {'krb5_server_prod':
        path    => '/etc/sssd/sssd.conf',
        section => 'domain/PROD',
        setting => 'krb5_server',
        value   => 'kdc.prod.example.com',
    }
}
```

These `ini_setting` resources will create five lines within the `[domain/PROD]` section of the configuration file. We need to add PROD to the list of domains; for this, we'll use `ini_subsetting` as shown in the following snippet. The `ini_subsetting` type allows us to add sub settings to a single setting.

```
    ini_subsetting {'domains_prod':
        path      => '/etc/sssd/sssd.conf',
        section   => 'sssd',
        setting   => 'domains',
        subsetting => 'PROD',
    }
```

Now, we'll add sssd_prod to our node1.yaml file and apply puppet agent on node1 to see the changes, as shown in the following commands:

```
node1# puppet agent -t --pluginsync --environment master
...
Notice: /Stage[main]/Sssd_prod/Ini_subsetting[domains_prod]/ensure:
created
...
Notice: Finished catalog run in 0.68 seconds
```

Now when we look at `/etc/sssd/sssd.conf`, we will see the `[sssd]` and `[domain/PROD]` sections are created (they are incomplete for this example, you will need many more settings to make SSSD work properly), as shown in the following snippet:

```
[sssd]
domains = PROD

[domain/PROD]
krb5_server = kdc.prod.example.com
krb5_kpasswd = secret!
ldap_search_base = ou=prod,dc=example,dc=com
ldap_uri = ldaps://ldap.prod.example.com
krb5_realm = PROD
```

Now, we can create our `sssd_devel` module and add the same setting as we had done for `prod`, changing their values for `devel`, as shown in the following code:

```
class sssd_devel {
  ini_setting {'krb5_realm_devel':
    path    => '/etc/sssd/sssd.conf',
    section => 'domain/DEVEL',
    setting => 'krb5_realm',
    value   => 'DEVEL',
  }
  ini_setting {'ldap_search_base_devel':
    path    => '/etc/sssd/sssd.conf',
    section => 'domain/DEVEL',
    setting => 'ldap_search_base',
    value   => 'ou=devel,dc=example,dc=com',
  }
  ini_setting {'ldap_uri_devel':
    path    => '/etc/sssd/sssd.conf',
    section => 'domain/DEVEL',
    setting => 'ldap_uri',
    value   => 'ldaps://ldap.devel.example.com',
  }
  ini_setting {'krb5_kpasswd_devel':
    path    => '/etc/sssd/sssd.conf',
    section => 'domain/DEVEL',
    setting => 'krb5_kpasswd',
    value   => 'DevelopersDevelopersDevelopers',
  }
  ini_setting {'krb5_server_devel':
```

```
    path    => '/etc/sssd/sssd.conf',
    section => 'domain/DEVEL',
    setting => 'krb5_server',
    value   => 'dev1.devel.example.com',
}
```

Again, we will add DEVEL to the list of domains using ini_subsetting, as shown in the following code:

```
ini_subsetting {'domains_devel':
    path    => '/etc/sssd/sssd.conf',
    section => 'sssd',
    setting => 'domains',
    subsetting => 'DEVEL',
}
```

Now, after adding sssd_devel to node1.yaml, we run puppet agent on node1 and examine the /etc/sssd/sssd.conf file after, as shown in the following snippet:

```
[sssd]
domains = PROD DEVEL

[domain/PROD]
krb5_server = kdc.prod.example.com
krb5_kpasswd = secret!
ldap_search_base = ou=prod,dc=example,dc=com
ldap_uri = ldaps://ldap.prod.example.com
krb5_realm = PROD

[domain/DEVEL]
krb5_realm = DEVEL
ldap_uri = ldaps://ldap.devel.example.com
ldap_search_base = ou=devel,dc=example,dc=com
krb5_server = dev1.devel.example.com
krb5_kpasswd = DevelopersDevelopersDevelopers
```

As we can see, both realms have been added to the domains section, and each realm has had its own configuration section created. To complete this example, we will need an SSSD module that each of these modules calls with include sssd. In that module, we will define the SSSD service and have our changes send a notify signal to the service. I would place the notify signal in the domain's ini_subsetting resource.

Having multiple modules work on the same files simultaneously can make your Puppet implementation a lot simpler. It's counterintuitive, but having the modules coexist means you don't need as many exceptions in your code. The Samba configuration file can be managed by a Samba module, but shares can be added by other modules using inifile and not interfere with the main Samba module.

firewall

If your organization uses host-based firewalls, filters that run on each node filtering network traffic, then the `firewall` module will soon become a friend. On enterprise Linux systems, the `firewall` module can be used to configure **iptables** automatically. Effective use of this module requires having all your iptables rules in Puppet.

 The `firewall` module has some limitations—if your systems require large rulesets, your agent runs may take some time to complete.

The default configuration can be a little confusing—there are ordering issues that have to be dealt with while working with the firewall rules. The idea here is to ensure that there are no rules at the start. This is achieved with `purge`, as shown in the following code:

```
resources { "firewall":
   purge => true
}
```

Next, we need to make sure that any firewall rules we define are inserted after our initial configuration rules and before our final deny rule. To ensure this, we use a resource default definition. Resource defaults are made by capitalizing the resource type. In our example, `firewall` becomes `Firewall`, and we define the `before` and `require` attributes such that they point to the location where we will keep our setup rules (`pre`) and our final `deny` statement (`post`), as shown in the following snippet:

```
Firewall {
   before => Class['example_fw::post'],
   require => Class['example_fw::pre'],
}
```

Because we are referencing `example_fw::pre` and `example_fw::post`, we'll need to include them at this point. The module also defines a `firewall` class that we should include. Rolling all that together, we have our `example_fw` class with the following:

```
class example_fw {
  include example_fw::post
  include example_fw::pre
  include firewall

  resources { "firewall":
    purge => true
  }
  Firewall {
    before => Class['example_fw::post'],
    require => Class['example_fw::pre'],
  }
}
```

Now we need to define our default rules to go to `example_fw::pre`. We will allow all ICMP traffic, all established and related TCP traffic, and all SSH traffic. Since we are defining `example_fw::pre`, we need to override our earlier `require` attribute at the beginning of this class, as shown in the following code:

```
class example_fw::pre {
  Firewall {
    require => undef,
  }
```

Then, we can add our rules using the firewall type provided by the module. When we define the firewall resources, it is important to start the name of the resource with a number, as shown in the following snippet. The numbers are used for ordering by the `firewall` module.

```
firewall { '000 accept all icmp':
  proto => 'icmp',
  action => 'accept',
}
firewall { '001 accept all to lo':
  proto => 'all',
  iniface => 'lo',
  action => 'accept',
}
firewall { '002 accept related established':
  proto => 'all',
```

```
        state => ['RELATED', 'ESTABLISHED'],
        action => 'accept',
    }
    firewall { '022 accept ssh':
        proto => 'tcp',
        port => '22',
        action => 'accept',
    }
}
```

Now, if we finished at this point, our rules would be a series of `allow` statements. Without a final `deny` statement, everything is allowed. We need to define a `drop` statement in our `post` class. Again, since this is `example_fw::post`, we need to override the earlier setting to `before`, as shown in the following code:

```
class example_fw::post {
    firewall { '999 drop all':
        proto => 'all',
        action => 'drop',
        before => undef,
    }
}
```

Now, we can apply this class in our `node1.yaml` file and run Puppet to see the firewall rules getting rewritten by our module. The first thing we will see is the current firewall rules being purged, as shown in the following commands:

```
node1# puppet agent -t --pluginsync --environment master
...
Notice: /Stage[main]/Example_fw/Firewall[9006
32828795e9fcabe60ef2ca2c1d6ccf05]/ensure: removed

Notice: /Stage[main]/Example_fw/Firewall[9004
dc0f1adfee77aa04ef7fdf348860a701]/ensure: removed

Notice: /Stage[main]/Example_fw/Firewall[9005
738c8429dea5edc3ad290a06dc845dc9]/ensure: removed

Notice: /Stage[main]/Example_fw/Firewall[9001
fe701ab7ca74bd49f13b9f0ab39f3254]/ensure: removed

Notice: /Stage[main]/Example_fw/Firewall[9007
9c205c1da32aab86e155ff77334c5fc8]/ensure: removed

Notice: /Stage[main]/Example_fw/Firewall[9002
a627067f779aaa7406fa9062efa4550e]/ensure: removed
```

Next, our `pre` section will apply our initial `allow` rules:

```
Notice: /Stage[main]/Example_fw::Pre/Firewall[002 accept related
established]/ensure: created
```

```
Notice: /Stage[main]/Example_fw::Pre/Firewall[000 accept all icmp]/
ensure: created
```

```
Notice: /Stage[main]/Example_fw::Pre/Firewall[022 accept ssh]/ensure:
created
```

```
Notice: /Stage[main]/Example_fw::Pre/Firewall[001 accept all to lo]/
ensure: created
```

Finally, our `post` section adds a `drop` statement to the end of the rules, as shown in the following commands:

```
Notice: /Stage[main]/Example_fw::Post/Firewall[999 drop all]/ensure:
created
```

```
Notice: Finished catalog run in 5.90 seconds
```

Earlier versions of this module did not save the rules; you would need to execute `iptables-save` after the `post` section. The module now takes care of this so that when we examine `/etc/sysconfig/iptables`, we see our current rules saved, as shown in the following snippet:

```
*filter
:INPUT ACCEPT [0:0]
:FORWARD ACCEPT [0:0]
:OUTPUT ACCEPT [1:180]
-A INPUT -p icmp -m comment --comment "000 accept all icmp" -j ACCEPT
-A INPUT -i lo -m comment --comment "001 accept all to lo" -j ACCEPT
-A INPUT -m comment --comment "002 accept related established" -m
state --state RELATED,ESTABLISHED -j ACCEPT
-A INPUT -p tcp -m multiport --ports 22 -m comment --comment "022
accept ssh" -j ACCEPT
-A INPUT -m comment --comment "999 drop all" -j DROP
COMMIT
```

Now that we have our firewall controlled by Puppet, when we apply our web module to our node, we can have it open port 80 on the node as well, as shown in the following code. Our earlier web module can just use `include example_fw` and define a firewall resource.

```
class web {
  package {'httpd':
    ensure => 'installed'
  }
```

```
    service {'httpd':
      ensure => true,
      enable => true,
      require => Package['httpd'],
    }
    include example_fw
    firewall {'080 web server':
      proto  => 'tcp',
      port   => '80',
      action => 'accept',
    }
}
```

Now when we apply this class to node1, we will see that port 80 is applied after our SSH rule and before our deny rule as expected:

```
*filter
:INPUT ACCEPT [0:0]
:FORWARD ACCEPT [0:0]
:OUTPUT ACCEPT [566:72386]
-A INPUT -p icmp -m comment --comment "000 accept all icmp" -j ACCEPT
-A INPUT -i lo -m comment --comment "001 accept all to lo" -j ACCEPT
-A INPUT -m comment --comment "002 accept related established" -m
state --state RELATED,ESTABLISHED -j ACCEPT
-A INPUT -p tcp -m multiport --ports 22 -m comment --comment "022
accept ssh" -j ACCEPT
-A INPUT -p tcp -m multiport --ports 80 -m comment --comment "080 web
server" -j ACCEPT
-A INPUT -m comment --comment "999 drop all" -j DROP
COMMIT
```

Using this module, it's possible to have very tight host-based firewalls on your systems that are flexible and easy to manage.

lvm

This module allows you to create volume groups, logical volumes, and filesystems with Puppet using the **logical volume manager (lvm)** tools in Linux.

 Having Puppet automatically configure your logical volumes can be a great benefit, but it can also cause problems. The module is very good at not shrinking filesystems, but you may experience catalog failures when physical volumes do not have sufficient free space.

If you are not comfortable with lvm, then I suggest you do not start with this module. This module can be of great help if you have products that require their own filesystems or auditing requirements that require application logs to be on separate filesystems. The only caveat here is that you need to know where your physical volumes reside, that is, which device contains the physical volumes for your nodes. If you are lucky and have the same disk layout for all nodes, then creating a new filesystem for your audit logs, /var/log/audit, is very simple. Assuming we have an empty disk at /dev/sdb, we can create a new volume group for audit items and a logical volume to contain our filesystem. The module takes care of all the steps that have to be performed. It creates the physical volume and creates the volume group using the physical volume. Then, it creates the logical volume and creates a filesystem on that logical volume.

To show the lvm module in action, we'll create node2 that has a boot device and a second drive. On my system, the first device is /dev/vda and the second drive is /dev/sda. We can see the disk layout using lsblk as shown in the following screenshot:

```
node2# lsblk
NAME                           MAJ:MIN RM   SIZE RO TYPE MOUNTPOINT
vda                            252:0    0     8G  0 disk
├─vda1                         252:1    0   500M  0 part /boot
└─vda2                         252:2    0   7.5G  0 part
  ├─VolGroup-lv_root (dm-0)    253:0    0   6.7G  0 lvm  /
  └─VolGroup-lv_swap (dm-1)    253:1    0   816M  0 lvm  [SWAP]
sda                              8:0    0     8G  0 disk
node2#
```

We can see that /dev/sda is available on the system but nothing is installed on it. We'll create a new module called lvm_web, which will create a logical volume of 4 GB, and format it with an ext4 filesystem, as shown in the following code:

```
class lvm_web {
  lvm::volume {"lv_var_www":
    ensure => present,
    vg      => "vg_web",
    pv      => "/dev/sda",
    fstype => "ext4",
    size    => "4G",
  }
}
```

Now we'll create a `node2.yaml` file in `hieradata/hosts/node2.yaml`, as shown in the following snippet:

```
---
welcome: 'lvm node'
classes: - lvm_web
```

Now when we run `puppet agent` on node2, we will see that the `vg_web` volume group is created, followed by the `lv_var_www` logical volume, and the filesystem after that:

```
node2# puppet agent -t --pluginsync --environment master

...

Info: Caching catalog for node2

Info: Applying configuration version '1391408119'

...

Notice: /Stage[main]/Lvm_web/Lvm::Volume[lv_var_www]/Volume_group[vg_
web]/ensure: created

Notice: /Stage[main]/Lvm_web/Lvm::Volume[lv_var_www]/Logical_volume[lv_
var_www]/ensure: created

Notice: /Stage[main]/Lvm_web/Lvm::Volume[lv_var_www]/Filesystem[/dev/vg_
web/lv_var_www]/ensure: created
```

Now when we run `lsblk` again, we will see that the filesystem was created:

```
node2# lsblk
NAME                           MAJ:MIN RM  SIZE RO TYPE MOUNTPOINT
vda                            252:0    0    8G  0 disk
├─vda1                         252:1    0  500M  0 part /boot
└─vda2                         252:2    0  7.5G  0 part
  ├─VolGroup-lv_root (dm-0)    253:0    0  6.7G  0 lvm  /
  └─VolGroup-lv_swap (dm-1)    253:1    0  816M  0 lvm  [SWAP]
sda                            8:0      0    8G  0 disk
└─vg_web-lv_var_www (dm-2)     253:2    0    4G  0 lvm
node2#
```

Note that the filesystem is not mounted yet, only created. To make this a fully functional class, we would need to add the mount location for the filesystem and ensure that the mount point exists, as shown in the following code:

```
file {'/var/www/html':
    ensure => 'directory',
    owner => '48',
    group => '48',
    mode    => '0755',
}
mount {'lvm_web_var_www':
    name  => '/var/www/html',
    ensure  => 'mounted',
    device  => "/dev/vg_web/lv_var_www",
    dump    => '1',
    fstype  => "ext4",
    options => "defaults",
    pass    => '2',
    target  => '/etc/fstab',
    require => [Lvm::Volume["lv_var_www"],File["/var/www/html"]],
}
```

Now when we run Puppet again, we can see that the directories are created and the filesystem is mounted:

```
node2# puppet agent -t --pluginsync --environment master

...

Info: Caching catalog for node2

Info: Applying configuration version '1391408851'

Notice: /Stage[main]/Lvm_web/File[/var/www]/ensure: created

Notice: /Stage[main]/Lvm_web/File[/var/www/html]/ensure: created

Notice: /Stage[main]/Lvm_web/Mount[lvm_web_var_www]/ensure: defined
'ensure' as 'mounted'

Info: /Stage[main]/Lvm_web/Mount[lvm_web_var_www]: Scheduling refresh of
Mount[lvm_web_var_www]

Info: Mount[lvm_web_var_www](provider=parsed): Remounting

Notice: /Stage[main]/Lvm_web/Mount[lvm_web_var_www]: Triggered 'refresh'
from 1 events

Info: /Stage[main]/Lvm_web/Mount[lvm_web_var_www]: Scheduling refresh of
Mount[lvm_web_var_www]

Notice: Finished catalog run in 1.21 seconds
```

Now when we run `lsblk`, we see the filesystem is mounted, as shown in the following screenshot:

```
node2# lsblk
NAME                          MAJ:MIN RM   SIZE RO TYPE MOUNTPOINT
vda                           252:0    0     8G  0 disk
├─vda1                        252:1    0   500M  0 part /boot
└─vda2                        252:2    0   7.5G  0 part
  ├─VolGroup-lv_root (dm-0)   253:0    0   6.7G  0 lvm  /
  └─VolGroup-lv_swap (dm-1)   253:1    0   816M  0 lvm  [SWAP]
sda                           8:0      0     8G  0 disk
└─vg_web-lv_var_www (dm-2)    253:2    0     4G  0 lvm  /var/www/html
node2#
```

This module can save you a lot of time. The steps required to set up a new volume group, add a logical volume, format the filesystem correctly, and then mount the filesystem can all be reduced to including a single class on a node.

stdlib

The **standard library (stdlib)** is a collection of useful facts, functions, types, and providers not included with the base language. Even if you do not use the items within `stdlib` directly, reading about how they are defined is useful to figure out how to write your own modules.

Several functions are provided by `stdlib`; these can be found at `https://forge.puppetlabs.com/puppetlabs/stdlib`. Also, several string-handling functions are provided by it, such as `capitalize`, `chomp`, and `strip`. There are functions for array manipulation and some arithmetic operations, such as absolute value (`abs`) and minimum (`min`). When you start building complex modules, the functions provided by the `stdlib` can occasionally reduce your code complexity.

Many parts of `stdlib` have been merged into facter and Puppet. One useful capability originally provided by `stdlib` is the ability to define custom facts based on text files or scripts on the node. This allows processes that run on nodes to supply facts to Puppet to alter the behavior of the agent. To enable this feature, we have to create a directory called `/etc/facter/facts.d` (Puppet enterprise uses `/etc/puppetlabs/facter/facts.d`), as shown in the following commands:

```
node2# facter -p myfact
node2# mkdir -p /etc/facter/facts.d
```

```
node2# echo "myfact=myvalue" >/etc/facter/facts.d/myfact.txt
node2# facter -p myfact
myvalue
```

The `facter_dot_d` mechanism can use text files (`.txt`), `.yaml`, or `.json` files based on the extension. If you create an executable file, then it will be executed and the results parsed for fact values as though you had a `.txt` file (fact = value). When using script files, you should create a **time-to-live** (**ttl**) file in the `/etc/facts/facts.d` directory to tell facter how long to wait between running the script.

> If you are using a facter version earlier than 1.7, then you will need the `facter.d` mechanism provided by `stdlib`. This was removed in `stdlib` version 3 and higher; the latest stable `stdlib` version that provides `facter.d` is 2.6.0. You will also need to enable `pluginsync` on your nodes (the default setting on Puppet 2.7 and higher).

To illustrate the usefulness, we will create a fact that returns the gems installed on the system. I'll run this on a host with a few gems to illustrate the point. Place the following script in `/etc/facter/facts.d/gems.sh` and make it executable (`chmod +x gems.sh`):

```bash
#!/bin/bash

gems=$(/usr/bin/gem list --no-versions | /bin/grep -v "^$" | /usr/bin/
paste -sd ",")
echo "gems=$gems"
echo $(date) >>/tmp/gems
```

Now run `facter` to see the output from the fact:

```
gemhost# facter -p gems
```

bigdecimal,bropages,builder,bundler,commander,hiera,hiera-
puppet,highline,io-console,json,json_pure,mime-types,net-http-
persistent,nokogiri,psych,puppet-lint,rbvmomi,rdoc,rest-client,smart_
colored,thor,trollop

```
gemhost# facter -p gems
```

bigdecimal,bropages,builder,bundler,commander,hiera,hiera-
puppet,highline,io-console,json,json_pure,mime-types,net-http-
persistent,nokogiri,psych,puppet-lint,rbvmomi,rdoc,rest-client,smart_
colored,thor,trollop

By default, the script will run every time we run facter. When we look in /tmp/gems, we see this happening:

```
gemhost# cat /tmp/gems
Sun Feb 2 23:33:02 PST 2014
Sun Feb 2 23:33:05 PST 2014
```

Now, we will create a ttl file and run facter -p twice again, as shown in the following commands;

```
gemhost# echo 600 >/etc/facter/facts.d/gems.sh.ttl
gemhost# facter -p gems
bigdecimal,bropages,builder,bundler,commander,hiera,hiera-
puppet,highline,io-console,json,json_pure,mime-types,net-http-
persistent,nokogiri,psych,puppet-lint,rbvmomi,rdoc,rest-client,smart_
colored,thor,trollop
gemhost# facter -p gems
bigdecimal,bropages,builder,bundler,commander,hiera,hiera-
puppet,highline,io-console,json,json_pure,mime-types,net-http-
persistent,nokogiri,psych,puppet-lint,rbvmomi,rdoc,rest-client,smart_
colored,thor,trollop
gemhost# cat /tmp/gems
Sun Feb 2 23:33:02 PST 2014
Sun Feb 2 23:33:05 PST 2014
Sun Feb 2 23:33:21 PST 2014
```

The ttl file prevents the script from running too often. We can now use these gems fact in our manifests to ensure that the gems we require are available. Another use of this fact mechanism could be to obtain the version of an installed application that doesn't use normal package-management methods. We can create a script that queries the application for its installed version and returns this as a fact. We will cover this in more detail when we build our own custom facts in a later chapter.

Summary

In this chapter, we explored how to pull in modules from the Puppet Forge and other locations. We looked at methods for keeping our public modules in order such as `librarian-puppet` and r10k. We revised our Git Hooks to use r10k and created an automatic system to update public modules. We then examined a selection of the Forge modules that are useful in the enterprise. In the next chapter, we will start writing our own custom modules.

5
Custom Facts and Modules

We have already created and used modules up to this point, when we installed and configured `tuned` using the `is_virtual` fact. We created a module called `virtual` in the process. Modules are nothing more than organizational tools; manifests, and plugin files that are grouped together.

We mentioned `pluginsync` in the previous chapter. By default, in Puppet 3.0 and higher, plugins in modules are synchronized from the master to the nodes. Plugins are special directories in modules that contain Ruby code.

Plugins are contained within the `/lib` subdirectory of a module, and there can be four possible subdirectories defined: `files`, `manifests`, `templates`, and `lib`. The `manifests` directory holds our manifests as we know, `files` has our files, and `templates` has the templates, and `lib` is where we extend augeas, hiera, facter, and/or Puppet depending on the files we place there. In this chapter, we will cover how to use the `modulename/lib/facter` directory to create custom facts, and in subsequent chapters, we will see how to use the `/lib/puppet` directory to create custom types.

The structure of a module is shown in the following diagram:

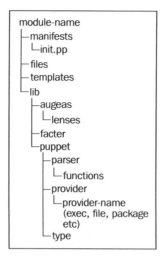

A module is a directory within the `modulepath` setting of Puppet that is searched when a module is included by name in a node manifest. If the module name is `base` and our `modulepath` is `$confdir/environments/$environment/modules:$confdir/environments/$environment/dist:$confdir/environments/production/modules`, then the search is done as follows (assuming `confdir` is `/etc/puppet`):

```
/etc/puppet/environments/$environment/modules/base/manifests/init.pp
/etc/puppet/environments/$environment/modules/dist/base/manifests/
init.pp
/etc/puppet/environments/production/modules/base/manifests/init.pp
```

Module manifest files

Each module is expected to have an `init.pp` file defined which has the top level class definition; in the case of our base example, `init.pp` is expected to contain `class base { }`.

Now, if we include `base::subitem` in our node manifest, then the file that Puppet would search for will be `base/manifests/subitem.pp`, and that file should contain `class base::subitem { }`.

It is also possible to have subdirectories of the manifests directory defined to split up the manifests even more. As a rule, a manifest within a module should only contain a single class. If we wish to define `base::subitem::subsetting`, then the file would be `base/manifests/subitem/subsetting.pp`, and it would contain `class base::subitem::subsetting { }`.

Naming your files correctly means they will be loaded automatically as needed, and you won't have to use the `import` function. By creating multiple subclasses, it is easy to separate a module into its various components; this is important later when you need to include only parts of the module in another module. As an example, say we have a database system called `judy`, and `judy` requires the `judy-server` package to run. The `judy` service requires the users `judy` and `judyadm` to run. Users `judy` and `judyadm` require the `judygrp` group, and they all require a filesystem to contain the database. We will split up these various tasks into separate manifests. We'll only sketch the contents of this fictional module as follows:

- In `judy/manifests/groups.pp`

```
class judy::groups {
  group {'judygrp': }

}
```

- In `judy/manifests/users.pp`:

```
class judy::users {
  include judy::groups
  user {'judy':
    require => Group['judygrp']
  }
  user {'judyadm':
    require => Group['judygrp']
  }
}
```

- In `judy/manifests/packages.pp`:

```
class judy::packages {
  package {'judy-server':
    require => User['judy','judyadm']
  }
}
```

- In `judy/manifests/filesystem.pp`:

```
class judy::filesystem {
  lvm {'/opt/judy':
    require => File['/opt/judy']
  }
  file {'/opt/judy': }
}
```

- Finally, our service is started from `judy/manifests/service.pp`:

```
class judy::service {
  service {'judy':
    require => [
      Package['judy-server'],
      File['/opt/judy'],
      Lvm['/opt/judy'],
      User['judy','judyadm']
    ],
  }
}
```

Now, we can include each one of these components separately, and our node can contain `judy::packages` or `judy::service` without using the entire `judy` module. We will define our top level module (`init.pp`) to include all these components, as shown in the following code:

```
class judy {
  include judy::users
  include judy::group
  include judy::packages
  include judy::filesystem
  include judy::service
}
```

Thus, a node that uses `include judy` will receive all of those classes, but if we have a node that only needs the `judy` and `judyadm` users, we need to include only `judy::users` in the code.

Module files and templates

Transferring files with Puppet is something best done within modules. When you define a file resource, you can use `content => "something"`, or you can push a file from the Puppet master using `source`. As an example, using our `judy` database, we can have `judy::config` with the following file definition:

```
class judy::config {
  file {'/etc/judy/judy.conf':
    source => 'puppet:///modules/judy/judy.conf'
  }
}
```

Now, Puppet will search for this file in the `judy/files` directory. It is also possible to add full paths and have your module mimic the filesystem. Thus, the previous source line will be changed to `source => 'puppet:///modules/judy/etc/judy/judy.conf'`, and the file will be found at `judy/files/etc/judy/judy.conf`.

The `puppet:///` url source line given previously has three backslashes; optionally, the name of a Puppet server may appear between the second and third backslash. If this field is left blank, the Puppet server that performs catalog compilation is used to retrieve the file. You can alternatively specify the server using `source => 'puppet://puppetfile.example.com/modules/judy/judy.conf'`.

> Having files that come from specific Puppet servers can make maintenance difficult. If you change the name of your Puppet server, you have to change all references to that name as well.

Templates are searched in a similar fashion. In this example, to specify the template in `judy/templates`, you will use `content => template('judy/template.erb')` to have the Puppet look for the template in your modules templates directory. As an example, another config file for `judy` can be as follows:

```
file {'/etc/judy/judyadm.conf':
  content => template('judy/judyadm.conf.erb')
}
```

Puppet will look for the `'judy/judyadm.conf.erb'` file at `modulepath/judy/templates/judyadm.conf.erb`. We haven't covered Ruby templates up to this point; templates are files that are parsed according to the `erb` syntax rules. If you need to distribute a file where you need to change some settings based on variables, then a template can help. The `erb` Syntax is covered in detail at `http://docs.puppetlabs.com/guides/templating.html`.

Modules can also include custom facts as we've already seen in this chapter. Using the `lib` subdirectory, it is possible to modify both facter and Puppet. In the next section, we will discuss module implementations in a large organization before writing custom modules.

Naming a module

Modules must begin with a lowercase letter and only contain lowercase letters, numbers, and the underscore (_) symbol. No other characters should be used. While writing modules that will be shared across the organization, use names that are obvious and won't interfere with other groups' modules or modules from the forge. A good rule of thumb is to insert your corporation's name at the beginning of the module name and, possibly, your group name.

While uploading to the forge, your forge username will be prepended to the module.

While designing modules, each module should have a specific purpose and not pull in manifests from other modules, and each module should be autonomous. Classes should be used within the module to organize functionality. For instance, you have a module called `example_foo` that installs a package and configures a service. Now, separating these two functions and their supporting resources into the `example_foo::pkg` and `example_foo:svc` classes makes it easier to find the code you need to work on, when you need to modify these different components. In addition, when you have all the service accounts and groups in another file, it makes it easy to find them as well.

Creating modules with a Puppet module

To start with a simple example, we will use Puppet's module command to generate empty module files with comments. The module name will be `example_phpmyadmin`, and `generate` expects the generated argument to be `[our username]` *hyphen* `[module name]`; thus, using our sample developer, samdev, the argument will be `samdev-example_phpmyadmin`, as shown in the following commands:

```
samdev@worker1$ cd puppet/dist
samdev@worker1$ puppet module generate samdev-example_phpmyadmin
Notice: Generating module at /home/samdev/puppet/dist/samdev-example_
phpmyadmin
samdev-example_phpmyadmin
samdev-example_phpmyadmin/manifests
samdev-example_phpmyadmin/manifests/init.pp
samdev-example_phpmyadmin/spec
samdev-example_phpmyadmin/spec/spec_helper.rb
samdev-example_phpmyadmin/Modulefile
samdev-example_phpmyadmin/README
samdev-example_phpmyadmin/tests
samdev-example_phpmyadmin/tests/init.pp
```

 If you plan on uploading your module to the forge or Github, use your forge/Github account name for the user portion of the module name (in the example, replace samdev with your Github account).

Comments in modules

The previous command generates `Modulefile` and `README` that can be modified for your use as needed. The `Modulefile` file is where you specify who wrote the module and which license it is released under. If your module depends on any other module, you can specify that in the dependency section of this file. In addition to the `README` text, an `init.pp` template is created in the `manifests` directory. At the top of this file, there are example comments that allow Puppet doc to parse the manifests and generate a documentation tree in RDoc.

 To see this in action, run the following command as any user, and use full paths so that the Puppet doc can find the modules:

```
$ puppet doc --all --mode rdoc --modulepath /etc/puppet/
environments/production/dist/ --manifestdir /etc/puppet/
manifests/
```

Then, point your web browser at the `index.html` file created inside the `doc` directory.

For Puppet to find your module, link the directory created as shown in the following command:

```
samdev@worker1$ ln -s samdev-example_phpmyadmin example_phpmyadmin
```

Our `phpmyadmin` package will need to install Apache (`httpd`) and configure the `httpd` service, so we'll create two new files in the manifests directory, `pkg.pp` and `svc.pp`.

 It's important to be consistent from the beginning; if you choose to use `package.pp` and `service.pp`, use that everywhere to save yourself time later.

In `init.pp`, we'll include our `example_phpmyadmin::pkg` and `example_phpmyadmin::svc` classes, as shown in the following code:

```
class example_phpmyadmin {
    include example_phpmyadmin::pkg
    include example_phpmyadmin::svc
}
```

`pkg.pp` will define `example_phpmyadmin::pkg`, as shown in the following code:

```
class example_phpmyadmin::pkg {
    package {'httpd':
      ensure => 'installed',
      alias  => 'apache'
    }
}
```

`svc.pp` will define `example_phpmyadmin::svc`, as shown in the following code:

```
class example_phpmyadmin::svc {
    service {'httpd':
      ensure => 'running',
      enable => true
    }
}
```

Now, we'll define another module called `example_phpldapadmin` using Puppet module in the following command:

```
samdev@worker1$ puppet module generate samdev-example_phpldapadmin
Notice: Generating module at /home/samdev/puppet/dist/samdev-example_
phpldapadmin
...

samdev@worker1$ ln -s samdev-example_phpldapadmin example_phpldapadmin
```

We'll define the `init.pp`, `pkg.pp`, and `svc.pp` files in this new module just as we did in our last module so that our three class files contain the following:

```
class example_phpldapadmin {
  include example_phpldapadmin::pkg
  include example_phpldapadmin::svc
}
class example_phpldapadmin::pkg {
  package {'httpd':
    ensure => 'installed',
    alias  => 'apache'
  }
}
class example_phpldapadmin::svc {
  service {'httpd':
    ensure => 'running',
    enable => true
  }
}
```

Now, we have a problem. `phpldapadmin` uses the `httpd` package, and so does `phpmyadmin`, and it's quite likely that these two modules may be included in the same node. We'll include both of them on our `node1` by editing `node1.yaml` and then we will run Puppet by using the following command:

```
node1# puppet agent -t --environment master
```

```
Error: Could not retrieve catalog from remote server: Error 400 on
SERVER: Duplicate declaration: Package[httpd] is already declared in file
/etc/puppet/environments/master/dist/example_phpmyadmin/manifests/pkg.
pp:5; cannot redeclare at /etc/puppet/environments/master/dist/example_
phpldapadmin/manifests/pkg.pp:5 on node node1
```

```
Warning: Not using cache on failed catalog
```

```
Error: Could not retrieve catalog; skipping run
```

Multiple definitions

A resource in Puppet can only be defined once per node. What this means is that if our module defines the `httpd` package, no other module can define `httpd`. There are several ways to deal with this problem, and we will work through two different solutions.

The first solution is the more difficult option—use **virtual resources** to define the package and then realize the package in each place you need it. Virtual resources are like a placeholder for a resource; you define the resource but you don't use it. This means that the Puppet master knows about the Puppet definition when you **virtualize** it, but it doesn't include the resource in the catalog at that point. Resources are included when you realize them later—the idea being that you can virtualize the resources multiple times and not have them interfere with each other. Working through our example, we will use the @ (at) symbol to virtualize our package and service resources. To use this model, it's helpful to create a container for the resources you are going to virtualize. In this case, we'll make modules for example_packages and example_services using Puppet module's generate command again. The init.pp file for example_packages will contain the following:

```
class example_packages {
  @package {'httpd':
    ensure => 'installed',
    alias  => 'apache',
  }
}
```

The init.pp file for example_services will contain the following:

```
class example_services {
  @service {'httpd':
    ensure  => 'running',
    enable  => true,
    require => Package['httpd'],
  }
}
```

These two classes define the package and service for httpd as virtual. We then need to include these classes in our example_phpmyadmin and example_phpldapadmin classes. The modified example_phpmyadmin::pkg class will now look as follows:

```
class example_phpmyadmin::pkg {
  include example_packages
  realize(Package['httpd'])
}
```

And the example_phpmyadmin::svc class will now be the following:

```
class example_phpmyadmin::svc {
  include example_services
  realize(Service['httpd'])
}
```

We will modify the `example_phpldapadmin` class in the same way and then attempt another Puppet run on `node1` (which still has `example_phpldapadmin` and `example_phpmyadmin` classes) as shown in the following command:

```
node1# puppet agent -t --environment master

...

Info: Caching catalog for node1
Info: Applying configuration version '1392191121'

...

Notice: /Stage[main]/Example_services/Service[httpd]/ensure: ensure
changed 'stopped' to 'running'
Info: /Stage[main]/Example_services/Service[httpd]: Unscheduling refresh
on Service[httpd]
Notice: Finished catalog run in 2.35 seconds
```

For this solution to work, you need to migrate any resource that may be used by multiple modules to your top-level resource module and include the resource module wherever you need to realize the resource.

In addition to the `realize` function used previously, a collector exists for virtual resources. A **collector** is a kind of glob that can be applied to virtual resources to realize resources based on a tag. A tag in Puppet is just a meta attribute of a resource that can be used for searching later. Tags are only used by collectors (for both virtual and exported resources, and exported resources will be explored in a later chapter) and do not affect the resource.

To use a collector in the previous example, we will have to define a tag in the virtual resources, for the `httpd` package this will be as follows:

```
class example_packages {
  @package {'httpd':
    ensure => 'installed',
    alias  => 'apache',
    tag    => 'apache',
  }
}
```

And then to realize the package using the collector, we will use the following code:

```
class example_phpldapadmin::pkg {
  include example_packages
  Package <| tag == 'apache' |>
}
```

The second solution would be to move the resource definitions into their own class and include that class wherever you need to realize the resource. This is considered to be the more correct way of solving the problem. Using the virtual resources described previously splits the definition of the package away from its use area.

For the previous example, instead of a class for all package resources, we will create one specifically for Apache and include that wherever we need to use Apache. We'll create the `example_apache` module monolithically with a single class for the package and the service as shown in the following code:

```
class example_apache {
  package {'httpd':
    ensure => 'installed',
    alias  => 'apache'
  }
  service {'httpd':
    ensure  => 'running',
    enable  => true,
    require => Package['httpd'],
  }
}
```

Now, in `example_phpldapadmin::pkg` and `example_phpldapadmin::svc`, we only need to include `example_apache`. This is because we can include a class any number of times in a catalog compilation without error. So, both our `example_phpldapadmin::pkg` and `example_phpldapadmin::svc` classes are going to receive definitions for the package and service of `httpd`; however, this doesn't matter as they only get included once in the catalog, as shown in the following code:

```
class example_phpldapadmin::pkg {
  include example_apache
}
```

Both these methods solve the issue of having a resource used in multiple packages. The rule is that a resource can only be defined once per catalog, but you should think of that rule as once per organization so that your modules won't interfere with those of another group within your organization.

Custom facts

While managing a complex environment, facts can be used to bring order out of chaos. If your manifests have large case statements or nested if statements, a custom fact may help reduce the complexity or allow you to change your logic.

When you work in a large organization, keeping the number of facts to a minimum is important as several groups may be working on the same system and thus interaction between users may adversely affect one another's work or they may find it difficult to understand how everything fits together.

As we have already seen in the previous chapter, if our facts are simple text values that are node specific, we can just use stdlib's `facts.d` directory to create static facts that are node specific.

This `facts.d` mechanism is included by default on facter Versions 1.7 and higher, and they are referred to as external facts.

Creating custom facts

We will be creating some custom facts, so we will create our Ruby files in the `module_name/lib/facter` directory. While designing your facts, choose names that are specific to your organization. Unless you plan on releasing your modules on the forge, avoid calling your fact something similar to a predefined fact or using a name that another developer might use. The names should be meaningful and specific—a fact named foo is probably not a good idea. Facts should be placed in the specific module that requires them. Keeping the fact name related to the module name will make it easier to determine where the fact is being set later.

For our `example.com` organization, we'll create a module named `example_facts` and place our first fact in there. As a first example, we'll create a fact that returns 1 (true) if the node is running the latest installed kernel or 0 (false) if not. As we don't expect this fact to become widely adopted, we'll call it `example_latestkernel`. The idea here is that we can apply modules to nodes that are not running the latest installed kernel, such as locking them down or logging them more closely.

To begin writing the fact, we'll start writing a Ruby script, you can also work in `irb` while you're developing your fact. Interactive Ruby (`irb`) is like a shell to write the Ruby code, where you can test your code instantly. Our fact will use a function from Puppet, so we will require `puppet` and `facter`. Fact scripts are run from within facter so that the `require` lines are removed once we are done with our development work. The script is written as follows:

```ruby
#!/usr/bin/env ruby
require 'puppet'
require 'facter'
# drop alpha numeric endings
def sanitize_version (version)
   temp = version.gsub(/.(el5|el6|fc19|fc20)/,'')
   return temp.gsub(/.(x86_64|i686|i586|i386)/,'')
   end
```

We define a function to remove textual endings on kernel versions and architectures. Textual endings like el5 and el6 will make our version comparison return incorrect results. For example, `2.6.32-431.3.1.el6` is less than `2.6.32-431.el6` because the e in `el6` is higher in ASCII than 3. It greatly simplifies our script if we simply remove known endings. We then obtain a list of installed kernel packages; the easiest way is with rpm, as shown in the following command:

```
kernels = %x( rpm -q kernel --qf '%{version}-%{release}\n' )
kernels = sanitize_version(kernels)
latest = ''
```

We will then set the `latest` variable to empty, and we'll loop through the installed kernels by comparing them to `latest`—if their values are greater than `latest`, then we convert `latest` such that it is equal to the value of the kernels. At the end of the loop, we have the `latest` (largest version number) kernel in the variable. For kernel in kernels, we will use the following commands:

```
kernel=kernel.chomp()
  if latest == ''
    latest = kernel
  end
  #print "%s > %s = %s\n" % [kernel,latest,Puppet::Util::Package.
versioncmp(kernel,latest)]
  if Puppet::Util::Package.versioncmp(kernel,latest) > 0
  latest = kernel
  end
end
```

We use `versioncmp` from `puppet::util::package` to compare the versions. I've included a debugging statement in the following code that we will remove later. At the end of this loop, the variable `latest` contains the largest version number and the latest installed kernel.

```
kernelrelease = Facter.value('kernelrelease')
kernelrelease = sanitize_version(kernelrelease)
```

Now, we will ask facter for the value of `kernelrelease`. We don't need to run `uname` or a similar tool as we'll rely on facter to get the value using the `Facter.value('kernelrelease')` command. Here, `Facter.value()` returns the value of a known fact. We will run the result of `Facter.value()` through our `sanitize_version` function to remove textual endings. We will then compare the value of `kernelrelease` with `latest` and update the `kernellatest` variable accordingly:

```
if Puppet::Util::Package.versioncmp(kernelrelease,latest) == 0
  kernellatest = 1
else
  kernellatest = 0
end
```

At this point, `kernellatest` will contain 1 if the system is running the kernel installed with `latest` and 0 if not. We will then print some debugging information to confirm whether our script is doing the right thing, as shown in the following command:

```
print "running kernel = %s\n" % kernelrelease
print "latest installed kernel = %s\n" % latest
print "kernellatest = %s\n" % kernellatest
```

We'll now run the script on `node1` and compare the results with the output of `rpm -q kernel` to see whether our fact is calculating the correct value:

```
node1# rpm -q kernel
kernel-2.6.32-431.el6.x86_64
kernel-2.6.32-431.1.2.el6.x86_64
kernel-2.6.32-431.3.1.el6.x86_64
node1# ./latestkernel.rb
running kernel = 2.6.32-431.3.1
latest installed kernel = 2.6.32-431.3.1
kernellatest = 1
```

Now that we've verified that our fact is doing the right thing, we need to call `Facter.add()` to add a fact to facter. The reason behind this will become clear in a moment, but we will place all our code within the `Facter.add` section, as shown in the following code:

```
Facter.add("example_latestkernel") do
  kernels = %x( rpm -q kernel --qf '%{version}-%{release}\n' )
  ...
End

Facter.add("example_latestkernelinstalled") do
  setcode do latest end
end
```

This will add two new facts to facter. We now need to go back and remove our require lines and print statements. The complete fact should look like the following script:

```
# drop alpha numeric endings
def sanitize_version (version)
 temp = version.gsub(/.(el5|el6|fc19|fc20)/,'')
 return temp.gsub(/.(x86_64|i686|i586|i386)/,'')
end
Facter.add("example_latestkernel") do
  kernels = %x( rpm -q kernel --qf '%{version}-%{release}\n' )
  kernels = sanitize_version(kernels)

  latest = ''
  for kernel in kernels do
    kernel=kernel.chomp()
    if latest == ''
      latest = kernel
    end
    if Puppet::Util::Package.versioncmp(kernel,latest) > 0
    latest = kernel
    end
  end
  kernelrelease = Facter.value('kernelrelease')
```

```
  kernelrelease = sanitize_version(kernelrelease)
  if Puppet::Util::Package.versioncmp(kernelrelease,latest) == 0
    kernellatest = 1
  else
    kernellatest = 0
  end
  setcode do kernellatest end
end
Facter.add("example_latestkernelinstalled") do
  setcode do latest end
end
```

Now, we need to create our module on our Git repository on `worker1` and have that checked out by `node1` to see the fact in action. Switch back to the `samdev` account to add the fact to Git as follows:

```
worker1# sudo -iu samdev
samdev@worker1$ cd puppet
samdev@worker1$ git checkout master
samdev@worker1$ cd dist
samdev@worker1$ mkdir -p example_facts/lib/facter
samdev@worker1$ cd example_facts/lib/facter
samdev@worker1$ cp ~/latestkernel.rb .
samdev@worker1$ git add latestkernel.rb
samdev@worker1$ git commit -m "adding first fact to example_facts"
[master d42bc22] adding first fact to example_facts
 1 files changed, 33 insertions(+), 0 deletions(-)
 create mode 100755 dist/example_facts/lib/facter/latestkernel.rb
samdev@worker1$ git push origin master
...
To /var/lib/git/puppet.git
   3bf0c18..d42bc22  master -> master
```

Now, we will go back to `node1`, run the Puppet agent and see that `latestkernel.rb` is placed in /var/lib/puppet/lib/facter/latestkernel.rb so that facter can now use the new fact.

This fact will be in the `/dist` folder of the environment. In the previous chapter, we added `/etc/puppet/environments/$environment/dist` to `modulepath` in `puppet.conf`; if you haven't done this already, do so now.

```
node1# puppet agent -t --environment master
InfoInfo: Retrieving plugin
Notice: /File[/var/lib/puppet/lib/facter/latestkernel.rb]/ensure: defined
content as '{md5}361cc146c5ab4fde8a948d9b503bd3c2'
...
Notice: Finished catalog run in 1.18 seconds
node1# facter -p |grep example
example_latestkernel => 1
example_latestkernelinstalled => 2.6.32-431.3.1
```

Now, this fact works fine for systems that use rpm for package management; it will not work on an apt system. To ensure our fact doesn't fail on these systems, we can use a `confine` statement to confine the fact calculation to systems where it will succeed. We can assume our script will work on all systems that report `RedHat` for the `osfamily` fact, so we will confine on that fact.

For instance, if we run Puppet on a Debian-based node to apply our custom fact, it fails when we run facter, as shown in the following code:

```
# cat /etc/debian_version
wheezy/sid
# facter -p example_latestkernelinstalled
sh: 1: rpm: not found
Could not retrieve example_latestkernelinstalled: undefined local
variable or method `latest' for #<Facter::Util::Resolution:0xb6bd386c>
```

Now, if we add a `confine` statement to confine the fact to nodes where `osfamily` is `RedHat`, this doesn't happen, as shown in the following code:

```
Facter.add("example_latestkernel") do
  confine :osfamily => RedHat
...
End
Facter.add("example_latestkernelinstalled") do
  confine :osfamily => RedHat
  setcode do latest end
end
```

When we run facter on the Debian node again, we will see that the fact is simply not defined by using the following command:

```
# facter -p example_latestkernelinstalled
##
```

> In the previous command, the prompt is returned without an error, and confine statements prevent the fact from being defined, so there is no error to return.

This simple example creates two facts that can be used in modules. You can, for instance, add a warning to motd to say that the node needs to reboot based on this fact.

> If you want to become really popular at work, have the node turn off SSH until it's running the latest kernel in the name of security.

While implementing a custom fact such as this, every effort should be made to ensure that the fact doesn't break facter compilation on any OS's within your organization. Using confine statements is one way to ensure your facts stay where you designed them.

So, why not just use the external fact (/etc/facter/facts.d) mechanism all the time? We could have easily written the previous fact script in bash and put the executable script in /etc/facter/facts.d. Indeed, there is no problem in doing it that way. We can also have the script run every so often by including a [script_name].ttl file as well. The problem with using the external fact mechanism is timing and precedence. Fact files placed in lib/facter are synced to nodes when pluginsync is set to true, so the custom fact is available for use during the initial catalog compilation. If you use the external fact mechanism, you have to send your script or text file to the node during the agent run so that the fact isn't available until after the file has been placed there (after the first run, any logic built around that fact will be broken until the next Puppet run). The second problem is preference. External facts are given a very high weight by default. Weight in the facter world is used to determine when a fact is calculated, and facts with low weight are calculated first and cannot be overridden by facts with higher weight.

> Weights are often used when a fact may be determined by one of the several methods. The preferred method is given the lowest weight. If the preferred method is unavailable (due to a confine), then the next higher weight fact is tried.

One great use case for external facts is having a system task (something that runs out of cron perhaps) that generates the text file in `/etc/facter/facts.d`. Initial runs of the Puppet agent won't see the fact until after cron runs the script, so you can use this to trigger further configuration by having your manifests key off the new fact. As a concrete example, you can have your node installed as a web server for a load-balancing cluster as part of modules that run a script from cron to ensure that your web server is up and functioning and ready to take part of the load. The cron script would then define a `load_balancer_ready=true` fact. It would then be possible to have the next Puppet agent run and add the node to the load balancer configuration.

Creating a custom fact for use in hiera

The most useful custom facts are those that return a calculated value that you can use to organize your nodes. Such facts allow you to group your nodes into smaller groups or create groups with `like` functionality or locality. These facts allow you to separate the data component of your modules from the logic or code components. This is a common theme that will be addressed again in *Chapter 9, Roles and Profiles*. Such a fact can be used in your `hiera.yaml` file to add a level to the hierarchy. One aspect of the system that can be used to determine information about the node is the IP address. Assuming you do not reuse IP addresses within your organization, the IP address can be used to determine where or in which part a node resides on a network, that is, the zone. In this example, we will define three zones in which machines reside: production, development, and sandbox. The IP addresses in each zone are on different subnets. We'll start by building up a script to calculate the zone and then turn it into a fact like our last example. Our script will need to calculate IP ranges using netmasks, so we'll import the `ipaddr` library and use `IPAddr` objects to calculate ranges.

```
require('ipaddr')
require('facter')
require('puppet')
```

Next, we'll define a function that takes an IP address as the argument and returns the zone to which that IP address belongs:

```
def zone(ip)
  zones = {
    'production' => [IPAddr.new('192.168.122.0/24'),IPAddr.
new('192.168.124.0/23')],
    'development' => [IPAddr.new('192.168.123.0/24'),IPAddr.
new('192.168.126.0/23')],
    'sandbox' => [IPAddr.new('192.168.128.0/22')]
  }
```

```
    for zone in zones.keys do
      for subnet in zones[zone] do
        if subnet.include?(ip)
          return zone
        end
      end
    end
    return 'undef'
  end
```

This function will loop through the zones looking for a match on the IP address. If no match is found, the value of undef is returned. We then obtain the IP address for the machine that is using the IP address fact from facter.

ip = IPAddr.new(Facter.value('ipaddress'))

Then, we will call the zone function with this IP address to obtain the zone.

print zone(ip),"\n"

Now, we can make this script executable and test it:

node1# facter ipaddress

192.168.122.132

node1# ./example_zone.rb

production

Now, all we have to do is replace print zone(ip),"\n" with the following code to define the fact:

```
    Facter.add('example_zone') do
      setcode do zone(ip) end
    end
```

Now, when we insert this code into our example_facts module and run Puppet on our nodes, the custom fact is available:

 # facter -p example_zone

production

Now that we can define a zone based on a custom fact, we can go back to our `hiera.yaml` file and add `%{::example_zone}` to the hierarchy. The `hiera.yaml` hierarchy will now contain the following:

```
---
:hierarchy:
  - "zones/%{::example_zone}"
  - "hosts/%{::hostname}"
  - "roles/%{::role}"
  - "%{::kernel}/%{::osfamily}/%{::lsbmajdistrelease}"
  - "is_virtual/%{::is_virtual}"
  - common
```

After restarting `httpd` to have the `hiera.yaml` file reread, we create a `zones` directory in `hieradata` and add `production.yaml` with the following content:

```
---
welcome: "example_zone - production"
```

Now when we run Puppet on our `node1`, we see `motd` updated with the new welcome message as follows:

```
node1# cat /etc/motd
PRODUCTION
example_zone - production
Managed Node: node1
Managed by Puppet version 3.4.2
```

Creating a few key facts that can be used to build up your hierarchy can greatly reduce the complexity of your modules. There are several workflows available, in addition to the custom fact we just described previously. You can use the `/etc/facter/facts.d` directory with static files or scripts, or you can have tasks run from other tools that dump files into that directory to create custom facts.

While writing Ruby scripts, you can use any other fact by calling `Facter.value('factname')`. If you write your script in Ruby, you can access any Ruby library using `require`. Your custom fact can query the system using `lspci` or `lsusb` to determine which hardware is specifically installed on that node. As an example, you can use `lspci` to determine the make and model of graphics card on the machine and return that as a fact, such as `videocard`. In the next section, we'll write our own custom modules that will take such a fact and install the appropriate driver for the video card based on the custom fact.

Summary

In this chapter, we used ruby to extend facter and define custom facts. Custom facts can be used in `hiera` hierarchies to reduce complexity and organize our nodes. We then began writing our own custom modules and ran into a few problems with multiple defined resources. Two solutions were presented, virtual resources and refactoring the code. In the next chapter, we will be making our custom modules more useful with custom types.

6

Custom Types

Puppet is about configuration management. As you write more and more code in puppet, patterns will begin to emerge—sections of code that repeat with only minor differences. If you were writing your code in a regular scripting language, you'd reach for a function or subroutine definition at this point. Puppet, like other languages, supports the blocking of code in multiple ways; where you'd reach for functions, you can use defined types; and where you might overload an operator, you can use a parameterized class. In this chapter, we will show you how to use parameterized classes and introduce the define function to define new user-defined types. Following that we will introduce custom types written in Ruby.

Parameterized classes

Parameterized classes are classes where you have defined several parameters that can be overridden when you instantiate the class for your node. The use case for parameterized classes is when you have something that won't be repeated within a single node. You cannot define the same parameterized class more than once per node. As a simple example, we'll create a class that installs a database program and starts that database's service. We'll call this class example::db; the definition will live in modules/example/manifests/db.pp as follows:

```
class example::db ($db) {
  case $db {
    'mysql': {
      $dbpackage = 'mysql-server'
      $dbservice = 'mysqld'
    }
    'postgresql': {
      $dbpackage = 'postgresql-server'
      $dbservice = 'postgresql'
    }
```

```
  }
  package { "$dbpackage": }
  service { "$dbservice":
    ensure  => true,
    enable => true,
    require => Package["$dbpackage"]
  }
}
```

This class takes a single parameter ($db) that specifies the type of the database, in this case either postgresql or mysql. To use this class, we have to instantiate it as follows:

```
class { 'example::db':
  db => 'mysql'
}
```

Now when we apply this to a node, we see that mysql-server is installed, and mysqld is started and enabled at boot. This works great for something like a database since we don't think we will have more than one type of database server on a single node. If we try to instantiate the example::db class with postgresql on our node, we'll get an error, as shown in the following screenshot:

Defined types

A situation where you have a block of code that is repeated within a single node can be managed with defined types. You create a defined type with a call to define. define is a block of Puppet code that receives a set of parameters when instantiated. Our previous database example could be rewritten as a defined type to allow more than one type of database server to be installed on a single node.

Another example of where a defined type is useful is building filesystems with the LVM module. When we used the LVM module to build a filesystem, there were three steps required: we needed a filesystem (a logical volume or LVM resource), a location to mount the filesystem (a file resource), and a mount command (a mount resource). Every time we liked to mount a filesystem, we'll need these three things. To make our code cleaner, we'll create a defined type for filesystem. Since we don't believe this will be used outside our example organization, we'll call it `example::fs`.

Defined types start with the keyword `define`, and then the name of the defined type and the parameters wrapped in parenthesis as shown in the following code:

```
define example::fs
(
    $mnt       = "$title",   # where to mount the filesystem
    $vg        = 'VolGroup', # which volume group
    $pv,                     # which physical volume
    $lv,                     # which logical volume
    $fs_type = 'ext4',       # the filesystem type
    $size,                   # how big
    $owner     = '0',        # who owns the mount point
    $group     = '0',        # which group owns the mount point
    $mode      = '0755'      # permissions on mount point
)
```

These are all the parameters for our defined type. Every defined type has to have a `$title` variable defined. An optional `$name` variable can be defined.

Both `$title` and `$name` are available within the attribute list, so you specify other attributes using these variables. This is why we are able to specify our `$mnt` attributes using `$title`. In this case, we'll use the mount point for the filesystem as `$title`, it should be unique on the node. Any of the previous parameters that are not given a default value, with = syntax, must be provided or Puppet will fail catalog compilation with the error message `must pass param to Example::Fs[title]` at `/path/to/fs.pp:lineno on node nodename`.

Providing sane defaults for parameters means most of the time you won't have to pass parameters to your defined types, making your code cleaner and easier to read.

Now that we've defined all the parameters required for our filesystem and mount combination type, we need to define the type; we can use any of the variables we've asked for as parameters. The definition follows the same syntax as a class definition as follows:

```
{
 # create the filesystem
 lvm::volume {"$lv":
   ensure => 'present',
   vg     => "$vg",
   pv     => "$pv",
   fstype => "$fs_type",
   size   => "$size",
 }

 # create the mount point (mnt)
 file {"$mnt":
   ensure => 'directory',
   owner  => "$owner",
   group  => "$group",
   mode   => "$mode",
 }
 # mount the filesystem $lv on the mount point $mnt
 mount {"$lv":
   name    => "$mnt",
   ensure  => 'mounted',
   device  => "/dev/$vg/$lv",
   dump    => '1',
   fstype  => "$fs_type",
   options => "defaults",
   pass    => '2',
   target  => '/etc/fstab',
   require => [Lvm::Volume["$lv"],File["$mnt"]],
 }
}
```

Note that we use the **CamelCase** notation for requiring `Lvm::Volume` for the mount. CamelCase is the practice of capitalizing each word of a compound word or phrase. This will become useful in the next example where we have nested filesystems that depend on one another. Now, we can redefine our `lvm_web` class using the new define to make our intention much clearer as follows:

```
class lvm_web {
  example::fs {'/var/www/html':
    vg     => 'vg_web',
    lv     => 'lv_var_www',
    pv     => '/dev/sda',
```

```
      owner    => '48',
      group    => '48',
      size     => '4G',
      mode     => '0755',
      require => File['/var/www'],
    }
    file {'/var/www':
      ensure => 'directory',
      mode     => '0755',
    }
  }
```

Now it's clear that we are making sure /var/www exists for our /var/www/html directory to exist and then creating and mounting our filesystem at that point. Now, when we need to make another filesystem on top of /var/www/html, we will need to require the first example::fs resource. To illustrate, we will define a subdirectory /var/www/html/drupal and require /var/www/html Example::Fs; the code becomes easier to follow, which is shown as follows:

```
    example::fs {'/var/www/html/drupal':
      vg       => 'vg_web',
      lv       => 'lv_drupal',
      pv       => '/dev/sda',
      owner    => '48',
      group    => '48',
      size     => '2G',
      mode     => '0755',
      require => Example::Fs['/var/www/html']
    }
```

The capitalization of Example::Fs is important; it needs to be Example::Fs in order for Puppet to recognize this as a reference to the defined type example::fs.

Encapsulation makes this sort of chaining much simpler. Also, any enhancements we make to our defined type are then added to all the instances of it. This keeps our code modular and makes it more flexible. For instance, what if we wanted to use our example::fs type for a directory that may be defined somewhere else in the catalog. We could add a parameter to our definition and set the default value so that previous uses of the type won't cause compilation errors, as shown in the following code:

```
    define example::fs
    (
    ...
    $managed = true,        # do we create the file resource or not.
    ...
    )
```

Now we can use the `if` conditional to either create the file and require it or not, as shown in the following code:

```
if ($managed) {
    file {"$mnt":
       ensure => 'directory',
       owner  => "$owner",
       group  => "$group",
       mode   => "$mode",
    }
    mount {"$lv":
       name    => "$mnt",
       ensure  => 'mounted',
       device  => "/dev/$vg/$lv",
       dump    => '1',
       fstype  => "$fs_type",
       options => "defaults",
       pass    => '2',
       target  => '/etc/fstab',
       require => [Lvm::Volume["$lv"],File["$mnt"]],
    }
} else {
    mount {"$lv":
       name    => "$mnt",
       ensure  => 'mounted',
       device  => "/dev/$vg/$lv",
       dump    => '1',
       fstype  => "$fs_type",
       options => "defaults",
       pass    => '2',
       target  => '/etc/fstab',
       require => Lvm::Volume["$lv"],
    }
}
```

None of our existing uses of the `example::fs` type will need modification, but now those cases where we only want the filesystem created and mounted are able to use this type.

For any portion of code that has repeatable parts, defined types can help abstract your classes to make your meaning more obvious. As another example, we'll develop the idea of an admin user—a user that should be in certain groups, have certain files in their home directory defined, and SSH keys added to their account. The idea here is that your admin users could be defined outside your enterprise authentication system and only be defined on the nodes to which they have admin rights.

We'll start small using the file and user types to create the users and their home directories. The user has a managehome parameter that creates the home directory, but with default permissions and ownership, we'll be modifying those in our type.

 If you rely on managehome, do understand that managehome just passes an argument to the user provider asking the OS specific tool to create the directory using whatever default permissions are provided by that tool. In the case of useradd on Linux, the -m option is added.

We'll define ~/.bashrc and ~/.bash_profile for our user, so we'll need parameters to hold those. An SSH key is useful for admin users, so we'll include a mechanism to include that as well. This isn't an exhaustive solution, just an outline of how you can use defines to simplify your life. In real-world admin scenarios, I've seen the admin define a sudoers file for the admin user as well and set up command logging with the audit daemon. Taking all the information we need to define an admin user, we have the following list of parameters:

```
define example::admin
(
  $user = $title,
  $ensure = 'present',
  $uid,
  $home = "/var/home/$title",
  $mode = '0750',
  $shell = "/bin/bash",
  $bashrc = undef,
  $bash_profile = undef,
  $groups = ['wheel','bin'],
  $comment = "$title Admin User",
  $expiry = 'absent',
  $forcelocal = true,
  $key,
  $keytype = 'ssh-rsa',
)
```

Now since define will be called multiple times and we need the admin group to exist before we start defining our admin users, we put the group into a separate class and include it here as follows:

```
include example::admin::group
```

The definition of `example::admin::group` is as follows:

```
class example::admin::group {
  group {'admin':
    gid => 1001,
  }
}
```

With `example::admin::group` included, we move on to define our user, being careful to require the group as follows:

```
user { "$user":
    ensure     => $ensure,
    allowdupe  => 'true',
    comment    => "$comment",
    expiry     => "$expiry",
    forcelocal => $forcelocal,
    groups     => $groups,
    home       => "$home",
    shell      => "$shell",
    uid        => $uid,
    gid        => 1001,
    require    => Group['admin']
}
```

Now our problem turns to ensuring that the directory containing the home directory exists, the logic here could get very confusing. Since we are defining our admin group by name rather than by `gid`, we need to ensure that the group exists before we create the home directory (so that the permissions can be applied correctly). We are also allowing the home directory location not to exist, so we need to make sure that the directory containing our home directory exists by using the following code:

 We are accounting for a scenario where admin users have their home directories under `/var/home`. This example complicates the code somewhat but also shows the usefulness of a defined type.

```
# ensure the home directory location exists
$grouprequire = Group['admin']
$dirhome = dirname($home)
```

Since we will require the group in all cases, we make a variable hold a copy of that resource definition, as shown in the following code:

```
case $dirhome {
  '/var/home': {
  include example::admin::varhome
  $homerequire = [$grouprequire,File['/var/home']]
}
```

If the home directory is under /var/home, we know that the home directory requires the class example::admin::varhome and also File['/var/home']. Next, if the home directory is under /home, then the home directory only needs the group require, as shown in the following code:

```
    '/home': {
      # do nothing, included by lsb
      $homerequire = $grouprequire
    }
```

As the default for our case statement, we assume the home directory needs to require that the directory ($dirhome) exist, but the user of this define will have to create that resource themselves (File[$dirhome]) as follows:

```
    default: {
      # rely on definition elsewhere
      $homerequire = [$grouprequire,File[$dirhome]]
    }
  }
```

Now we create the home directory using our $homerequire variable to define require for the resource as follows:

```
file {"$home":
  ensure  => 'directory',
  owner   => "$uid",
  group   => 'admin',
  mode    => "$mode",
  require => $homerequire
}
```

Next, we create the .ssh directory as shown in the following code:

```
# ensure the .ssh directory exists
 file {"$home/.ssh":
   ensure  => 'directory',
   owner   => "$uid",
   group   => 'admin',
   mode    => "0700",
   require => File["$home"]
 }
```

Then, we create an SSH key for the admin user; we require the .ssh directory, which requires the home directory, making a nice chain of existence. The home directory has to be made first, then the .ssh directory, and then the key added to authorized_keys, as shown in the following code:

```
ssh_authorized_key { "$user-admin":
   user    => "$user",
   ensure  => present,
   type    => "$keytype",
   key     => "$key",
   require => [User[$user],File["$home/.ssh"]]
 }
```

Now we can do something fancy. We know that not every admin likes to work in the same way, so we can have them add custom code to their .bashrc and .bash_profile files using a concat for the two files. In each case, we'll include the system default file from /etc/skel and then permit the instance of the admin user to add to the files using concat, as shown in the following code:

```
# build up the bashrc from a concat
 concat { "$home/.bashrc":
   owner => $uid,
   group => $gid,
 }
 concat::fragment { "bashrc_header_$user":
   target => "$home/.bashrc",
   source => '/etc/skel/.bashrc',
   order  => '01',
 }
 if $bashrc != undef {
   concat::fragment { "bashrc_user_$user":
     target  => "$home/.bashrc",
     content => $bashrc,
     order   => '10',
   }
 }
```

And the same goes for `.bash_profile`, as shown in the following code:

```
#build up the bash_profile from a concat as well
 concat { "$home/.bash_profile":
   owner => $uid,
   group => $gid,
 }
 concat::fragment { "bash_profile_header_$user":
   target => "$home/.bash_profile",
   source => '/etc/skel/.bash_profile',
   order  => '01',
 }
 if $bash_profile != undef {
   concat::fragment { "bash_profile_user_$user":
     target  => "$home/.bash_profile",
     content => $bash_profile,
     order   => '10',
   }
 }
```

We then close our definition with a right brace:

```
}
```

Now to define an admin user, we call our defined type as shown in the following code and let the type do all the work.

```
example::admin {'theresa':
   uid  => 1002,
   home => '/home/theresa',
   key  => 'BBBB...z',
 }
```

We can add another user easily using the following code:

```
example::admin {'thomas':
   uid    => 1001,
   key    => 'AAAA...z',
   bashrc => "alias vi=vim\nexport EDITOR=vim\n"
 }
```

Now when we add these resources to a node and run Puppet, we see the users created.

In this example, we defined a type that created a user and a group, created the user's home directory, added an SSH key to the user, and created their dotfiles. There are many examples where a defined type can streamline your code. Common examples of defined types include apache vhosts and Git repositories.

Defined types work well when you can express the thing you are trying to create with types that are already defined. If the new type can be expressed better with Ruby, then you might have to create your own type by extending Puppet with a custom type.

Types and providers

Puppet separates the implementation of a type into the type definition and any one of many providers for that type. For instance, the package type in Puppet has multiple providers depending on the platform in use (apt, yum, rpm, and others). Early on in Puppet development there were only a few core types defined. Since then, the core types have expanded to the point where anything that I feel should be a type is already defined by core Puppet. The modules presented in *Chapter 5, Custom Facts and Modules*, each created their own types using this mechanism. The LVM module created a type for defining logical volumes; the concat module created types for defining file fragments. The firewall module created a type for defining firewall rules. Each of these types represents something on the system with the following properties:

- Unique
- Searchable
- Atomic
- Destroyable
- Creatable

When creating a new type, you have to make sure your new type has these properties. The resource defined by the type has to be unique, which is why the file type uses the path to a file as the naming variable (namevar). A system may have files with the same name (not unique), but it cannot have more than one file with an identical path. As an example, the ldap configuration file for openldap is /etc/openldap/ldap.conf, the ldap configuration file for the name services library is /etc/ldap.conf. If you used filename, then they would both be the same resource. Resources must be unique. By atomic, I mean it is indivisible; it cannot be made of smaller components. For instance, the firewall module creates a type for single iptables rules. Creating a type for the tables (INPUT, OUTPUT, FORWARD) within iptables wouldn't be atomic—each table is made up of multiple smaller parts, the rules. Your type has to be searchable so that Puppet can determine the state of the thing you are modifying. A mechanism has to exist to know what the current state is of the thing in question. The last two properties are equally important. Puppet must be able to remove the thing, destroy it, and likewise, Puppet must be able to create the thing anew.

Given these criteria, there are several modules that define new types, with some examples including types that manage:

- Git repositories
- Apache virtual hosts
- LDAP entries
- Network routes
- Gem modules
- Perl CPAN modules
- Databases
- Drupal multisites

Creating a new type

As an example, we will create a gem type for managing Ruby gems installed for a user. Ruby gems are packages for Ruby that are installed on the system and can be queried like packages.

 Installing gems with Puppet can already be done using the gem provider with the package type.

To create a custom type requires some knowledge of Ruby. In this example, we assume the reader is fairly literate in Ruby. We start by defining our type in the lib/puppet/type directory of our module. We'll do this in our example module, modules/example/lib/puppet/type/gem.rb.

The file will contain the newtype method and a single property for our type, version as shown in the following code:

```
Puppet::Type.newtype(:gem) do
  ensurable
  newparam(:name, :namevar => true) do
    desc 'The name of the gem'
  end
  newproperty(:version) do
    desc 'version of the gem'
    validate do |value|
      fail("Invalid gem version #{value}") unless value =~
/^[0-9]+[0-9A-Za-z\.-]+$/
    end
  end
end
```

The `ensurable` keyword creates the ensure property for our new type, allowing the type to be either present or absent. The only thing we require of the version is that it start with a number and only contain numbers, letters, periods, or dashes.

 A more thorough regular expression here could save you time later, such as checking that the version ends with a number or letter.

Now we need to start making our provider. The name of the provider is the name of the command used to manipulate the type. For packages, the providers are named things like `yum`, `apt`, and `dpkg`. In our case we'll be using the `gem` command to manage gems, which makes our path seem a little redundant. Our provider will live at `modules/example/lib/puppet/provider/gem/gem.rb`.

We'll start our provider with a description of the provider and the commands it will use as shown in the following code:

```
Puppet::Type.type(:gem).provide :gem do
  desc "Manages gems using gem"

  commands :gem => "gem"
```

Then we'll define a method to list all the gems installed on the system as shown in the following code, which defines the `self.instances` method:

```
def self.instances
    gems = []
    begin
        execpipe("#{command(:gem)} list -l") { |process|
            process.each_line { |line|
                (name,version) = line.split(' ')
                hash = {}
                hash[:provider] = self.name
                hash[:name] = name
                hash[:ensure] = :present
                hash[:version] = version.tr('()','')
                gems << new(hash)
            }
        }
    rescue Puppet::ExecutionFailure
        raise Puppet::Error, "Failed to list gems"
    end

    gems
  end
end
```

This method runs `gem list -l` and then parses the output looking for lines such as `gemname (version)`. We then strip the parenthesis from the version and appends the lines to an instance hash, named `gems`. The gems hash is returned and then Puppet knows all about the gems installed on the system.

Puppet needs two more methods at this point and a method to determine if the gem exists (is installed), and if it does exist, which version is installed. We already populated the ensure parameter, so as to use that to define our exists method as follows:

```
def exists?
   @property_hash[:ensure] == :present
end
```

To determine the version of an installed gem, we can use the `property_hash` variable as follows:

```
def version
   @property_hash[:version] || :absent
 end
```

To test this, add the module to a node and pluginsync the module over to the node as follows:.

```
node1# puppet plugin download
```

Notice: /File[/var/lib/puppet/lib/puppet/provider/gem/gem.rb]/ensure: defined content as '{md5}48749efcd33ce06b401d5c008d10166c'

Notice: /File[/var/lib/puppet/lib/puppet/type/gem.rb]/ensure: defined content as '{md5}78a1f1b995beb2852a60da72c6879904'

This will install our `type/gem.rb` and `provider/gem/gem.rb` files into `/var/lib/puppet` on the node. After that, we are free to run `puppet resource` on our new type to list the available gems as shown in the following code:

```
# puppet resource gem
gem { 'bigdecimal':
  ensure  => 'present',
  version => '1.2.0',
}
gem { 'bropages':
  ensure  => 'present',
  version => '0.1.0',
}
...
```

Now, if we want to manage gems, we'll need to create and destroy them, and we'll need to provide methods for those operations. If we try at this point, Puppet will fail, as we can see from the following output:

So we'll need a method to destroy (remove) gems, `gem uninstall` should do the trick, as shown in the following code:

```
def destroy
        g = @resource[:version] ? [@resource[:name], '--version', @
resource[:version]] : @resource[:name]
        gem('uninstall', g, '-q', '-x')
        @property_hash.clear
    end
```

Using the ternary operator, we either run `gem uninstall name -q -x` if no version is defined, or `gem uninstall name --version version -q -x` if a version is defined. We finish by calling `@property_hash.clear` to remove the gem from the `property_hash` since the gem is now removed.

Now we need to let Puppet know about the state of the `bropages` gem using our instances method we defined earlier, we'll need to write a new method to prefetch all the available gems. This is done with `self.prefetch`, as shown in the following code:

```
def self.prefetch(resources)
  gems = instances
  resources.keys.each do |name|
    if provider = gems.find{ |gem| gem.name == name }
      resources[name].provider = provider
    end
  end
end
```

We can see this in action using the `--debug` option to Puppet resource as shown in the following screenshot:

Almost there, now we want to add `bropages` back, we'll need a `create` method, as shown in the following code:

```
def create
  g = @resource[:version] ? [@resource[:name], '--version', @
resource[:version]] : @resource[:name]
  gem('install', g)
  @property_hash[:ensure] = :present
end
```

Now when we run `puppet resource` to create the gem, we see the installation, as shown in the following screenshot:

```
# puppet resource --debug gem bropages ensure=present
Debug: Loaded state in 0.00 seconds
Debug: Prefetching gem resources for gem
Debug: Executing '/bin/gem list -l'
Debug: Executing '/bin/gem install bropages'
Notice: /Gem[bropages]/ensure: created
Debug: Finishing transaction 16503240
Debug: Storing state
Debug: Stored state in 0.01 seconds
gem { 'bropages':
  ensure => 'present',
}
# gem list bropages

*** LOCAL GEMS ***

bropages (0.1.0)
#
```

Nearly done now, we need to handle versions. If we want to install a specific version of the gem, we'll need to define methods to deal with versions.

```
def version=(value)
  begin
    gem('install',@resource[:name],'--version',@resource[:version])
  rescue Puppet::ExecutionFailure
    raise Puppet::Error, "Failed to install gem #{resource[:name]}
(#{resource[:version]})"
  end
  @property_hash[:version] = value
end
```

Now, we can tell Puppet to install a specific version of the gem and have the correct results. This is where our choice of gem as an example breaks down as gem provides for multiple versions of a gem to be installed. Our gem provider, however, works well enough for use at this point. We can specify the gem type in our manifests and have gems installed or removed from the node.

Summary

Using parameterized classes and defined types, it is possible to increase the readability and resiliency of your code. Encapsulating sections of your code within a defined type makes your code more modular and easier to support. When defined types are not enough, you can extend Puppet with custom types and providers written in Ruby. The details of writing providers are best learned by reading the already written providers and referring to the documentation on the Puppet Labs website. The public modules covered in an earlier chapter make use of defined types and custom types and providers and can serve as a starting point to writing your own types. The module `augeasproviders` is another module to read when looking to write your own types and providers. In the next chapter, we will set up reporting and look at Puppet Dashboard and The Foreman.

7
Reporting and Orchestration

Reports return all the log messages from the Puppet nodes to the master. In addition to log messages, reports send other useful metrics such as timing (time spent performing different operations) and statistical information (counts of resources and number of failed resources). With reports, you can know when your Puppet runs fail and most importantly, why. In this chapter, we will cover the following reporting mechanisms.

- Syslog
- Store (YAML)
- IRC
- Foreman
- Puppet Dashboard

In addition to reporting, we will configure the **marionette collective (mcollective)** system to allow for orchestration tasks. In the course of configuring reporting, we will show different methods of signing and transferring SSL keys for systems that are subordinate to our master, `puppet.example.com`.

Turning on reporting

To turn on reporting, set `report = true` in the `[agent]` section of `puppet.conf` on all your nodes.

Once you have done that, you need to configure the master to deal with reports. There are several report types included with Puppet; they are listed at `http://docs.puppetlabs.com/references/latest/report.html`.

There are two simple reporting options included with Puppet: `log` and `store`. The `log` option uses syslog to output messages from the nodes via syslog on the master. This is a reasonable option if you cannot guarantee syslog connectivity at your nodes due to a firewall or other restrictions. The other option is `store`, which simply stores the report as a file in the `reportdir` of the master.

To use a report, add it by name to the `reports` section on the master. This is a comma-separated list of reports. You can have many different report handlers. Report handlers are stored at `site_ruby/[version]/puppet/reports/` and `/var/lib/puppet/lib/puppet/reports`. The latter directory is where modules can send report definitions to be installed on clients (using the `pluginsync` mechanism; remember that things get purged from the `pluginsync` directories, so unless you are placing files there with Puppet, they will be removed).

Syslog

To use `syslog`, set `reports = log` in the `main` section of `/etc/puppet/puppet.conf` and `report=true` on all the nodes, as shown in the following snippet:

```
[main]
    reports = log
[agent]
    report = true
```

After restarting `httpd` on our masters, we'll see catalog compilation messages from nodes appearing in our `syslog` logs. By default, Puppet will use the `daemon` facility to change the facility set `syslogfacility` in the `[main]` section of `puppet.conf`. To determine your current facility, use the following command:

```
# puppet master --configprint syslogfacility
daemon
```

On our system using `rsyslog`, we can have all Puppet report messages go into a Puppet logfile using `syslogfacility = local5`, as shown in the following snippet:

```
[main]
   reports = log
   syslogfacility = local5
```

Then, in `/etc/rsyslog.conf` or `/etc/syslog.conf` (similar syntax), redirect all `local5` level messages to `puppet.log`, as shown in the following snippet:

```
local5.*              /var/log/puppet.log
```

Even if you use one of the GUIs in the next few sections, having your catalog compilation logs going into `syslog` can be useful. If you have a log aggregation and searching mechanism such as Splunk or **Elasticsearch/Logstash/Kibana** (ELK), you can quickly correlate catalog compilation problems.

Store

To enable the store mechanism, use `reports = store`. We'll add this to our log destination in this example, as shown in the following snippet:

```
[main]
  reports = log, store
```

The default location for reports is `reportdir`. To see your current `reportdir` directory, use the `--configprint` option of master, as shown in the following snippet:

```
# puppet master --configprint reportdir
/var/lib/puppet/reports
```

The `store` option is on by default; however, once you specify the `reports` setting as anything in the `main` section of `puppet.conf`, you disable `store`. By placing `log` and `store` in `reports`, we will have both reports. Remember though, once you enable `store` for `reports`, report files will start accumulating on the master. It's a good idea to enable purging of those reports. In our multiple worker scenario, it's a good idea to set `report_server` in the `agent` section of the nodes if you are using `log` or `store`, as shown in the following commands. The default setting for `report_server` is the same as the server parameter.

```
node1# puppet agent --configprint report_server
puppet.example.com
node1# puppet agent --configprint server
puppet.example.com
```

IRC

If you have an internal **Internet Relay Chat** (IRC) server, using the IRC report plugin can be useful. This report sends failed catalog compilations to an IRC chatroom. You can have this plugin installed on all your catalog workers; each catalog worker will login to the IRC server and send failed reports. That works very well, but in this example we'll configure a new worker called `reports.example.com`. It will be configured as though it were a standalone worker; the reports machine will need the same packages as a regular worker (`puppet`, `httpd`, and `mod_passenger`). We'll enable the IRC logging mechanism on this server. That way we only have to install the dependencies for the IRC reporter on one worker.

The reports server will need certificates signed by `puppet.example.com`. There are two ways you can have the keys created; the simplest way is to make your reports server a client node of `puppet.example.com` and have Puppet generate the keys. We will show how to use `puppet certificate generate` to manually create and download keys for our reports server.

First, generate certificates for this new server on `puppet.example.com` using `puppet certificate generate`.

The command `puppet certificate generate` may be issued from either `puppet.example.com` or `reports.example.com`. When running from `puppet.example.com`, the command looks as follows:

```
# puppet certificate generate --ca-location local
reports.example.com
```

When running from reports.example.com, the command looks as follows:

```
# puppet certificate generate --ca-location remote
--server puppet.example.com reports.example.com
```

You will then need to sign the certificate on `puppet.example.com` using the following command:

```
# puppet cert sign reports.example.com
Notice: Signed certificate request for reports.example.com
Notice: Removing file Puppet::SSL::CertificateRequest reports.example.com
at '/var/lib/puppet/ssl/ca/requests/reports.example.com.pem'
```

If you used `puppet certificate generate`, then you will need to download the public and private keys from `puppet.example.com` to `reports.example.com`. The private key will be in `/var/lib/puppet/ssl/private_keys/reports.example.com.pem`, and the public key will be in `/var/lib/puppet/ssl/ca/signed/reports.example.com.pem`.

We can use `puppet certificate` to do this as well. On the reports machine, run the following command:

```
# puppet certificate find reports.example.com --ca-location remote
--server puppet.example.com
-----BEGIN CERTIFICATE-----
...
2jU/DvBAhWVxZEd674ATk2llyfncm3CDapW7/hiyb/eG
-----END CERTIFICATE-----.
```

The report machine will need the the certificate authority files as well (`/var/lib/puppet/ssl/ca/ca_crt.pem` and `/var/lib/puppet/ssl/ca/ca_crl.pem`); the CRL should be kept in sync using an automated mechanism.

To download the CA from `puppet.example.com`, use the following command:

```
# puppet certificate find ca --ca-location remote --server puppet.example.com
```

The CRL will have to be downloaded manually. Create a passenger configuration file for this new server, as shown in the following configuration file:

```
PassengerHighPerformance on
PassengerMaxPoolSize 12
PassengerPoolIdleTime 1500
# PassengerMaxRequests 1000
PassengerStatThrottleRate 120
RackAutoDetect Off
RailsAutoDetect Off


Listen 8140


LoadModule ssl_module modules/mod_ssl.so
<VirtualHost *:8140>
   ServerName reports.example.com
   # SSL settings
   SSLEngine on
   SSLProtocol -ALL +SSLv3 +TLSv1
   SSLCipherSuite ALL:!ADH:RC4+RSA:+HIGH:+MEDIUM:-LOW:-SSLv2:-EXP
   SSLCertificateFile      /var/lib/puppet/ssl/certs/reports.example.com.pem
   SSLCertificateKeyFile   /var/lib/puppet/ssl/private_keys/reports.example.com.pem
   SSLCertificateChainFile /var/lib/puppet/ssl/ca/ca_crt.pem
   SSLCACertificateFile    /var/lib/puppet/ssl/ca/ca_crt.pem
   SSLCARevocationFile     /var/lib/puppet/ssl/ca/ca_crl.pem
   SSLVerifyClient optional
   SSLVerifyDepth  1
   SSLOptions +StdEnvVars +ExportCertData

   # Pass SSL information to puppet
   RequestHeader set X-SSL-Subject %{SSL_CLIENT_S_DN}e
   RequestHeader set X-Client-DN %{SSL_CLIENT_S_DN}e
   RequestHeader set X-Client-Verify %{SSL_CLIENT_VERIFY}e

   DocumentRoot /etc/puppet/rack/public/
```

```
      RackBaseURI /
      # where to find config.ru
      <Directory /etc/puppet/rack/>
        Options None
        AllowOverride None
        Order allow,deny
        allow from all
      </Directory>
    </VirtualHost>
```

Now, you can run Puppet on your nodes that are configured to send reports to `report_server=reports.example.com`, and the reports will show up in `$reportdir`. With that in place, we'll turn to installing the IRC plugin. First use `puppet module` to install the module.

```
# puppet module install jamtur01/irc
Notice: Preparing to install into /etc/puppet/modules ...
Notice: Downloading from https://forge.puppetlabs.com ...
Notice: Installing -- do not interrupt ...
/etc/puppet/modules
└── jamtur01-irc (v0.0.6)
# cp /etc/puppet/modules/irc/lib/puppet/reports/irc.rb /usr/lib/ruby/
site_ruby/1.8/puppet/reports
```

 Search for `puppet/reports` to find the `reports` directory.

Now copy the `irc.yaml` configuration file into `/etc/puppet`, and edit as appropriate. Our IRC server is `irc.example.com`. We'll use the username `puppetbot` and password `PacktPubBot`, as shown in the following snippet:

```
    ---
    :irc_server: 'irc://puppetbot:PacktPubBot@irc.example.com:6667#puppet'
    :irc_ssl: false
    :irc_register_first: false
    :irc_join: true
    :report_url: 'http://foreman.example.com/hosts/%h/reports/last'
```

We are almost ready; the IRC `report` plugin uses The RubyGem `carrier-pigeon` to do the IRC work, so we'll need to install that now, as shown in the following command:

```
reports# gem install carrier-pigeon
Successfully installed addressable-2.3.5
Successfully installed carrier-pigeon-0.7.0
2 gems installed
```

Now we can restart `httpd` on our `reports` worker and create a catalog compilation problem on `node1` (I sent it multiple definitions of a resource), as shown in the following screenshot:

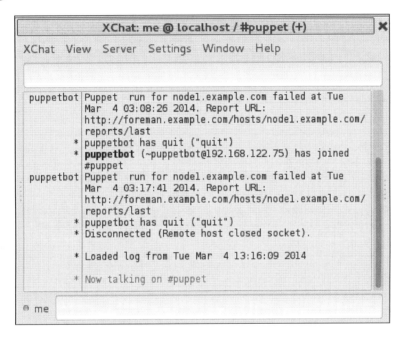

So, whenever there is a catalog compilation issue, the `puppetbot` user will login to our #puppet channel and let us know. Now for our next task—the given URL requires that Foreman is configured; we'll set up that now.

Foreman

Foreman is more than just a Puppet reporting tool, it bills itself as a complete life cycle management platform. Foreman can act as the **External Node Classifier** (ENC) for your entire installation and configure DHCP, DNS, and PXE booting. It's a one-stop shop. We'll configure Foreman to be our report backend in this example.

Installing Foreman

To install Foreman, we'll need the **Extra Packages for Enterprise Linux (EPEL)** (`https://fedoraproject.org/wiki/EPEL`) and **Software Collections (SCL)** (`https://fedorahosted.org/SoftwareCollections/`), which are the YUM repositories for ruby193 and its dependencies. We have previously used the EPEL repository; the SCL repository is used for updated versions of packages that already exist on the system, in this case, Ruby 1.9.3 (Ruby 1.8.7 is the default on Enterprise Linux 6.5). The SCL repositories have updated versions of other packages as well.

```
# yum -y install http://yum.theforeman.org/releases/1.4/el6/x86_64/
foreman-release.rpm
```

```
# yum -y install foreman-installer
```

The `foreman-installer` command uses `puppet apply` to configure Foreman on the server. Since we will only be using Foreman for reporting in this example, we can just use the installer, as shown in the following command:

```
foreman# foreman-installer --no-enable-foreman-proxy --no-enable-puppet
--puppet-ca-server puppet.example.com
Installing              Done                        [100%] [............
.................................................]
  Success!
  * Foreman is running at https://foreman.example.com
      Default credentials are 'admin:changeme'
  The full log is at /var/log/foreman-installer/foreman-installer.log
```

The installer will pull down all the RubyGems required for Foreman and install and configure PostgreSQL by default. The database will be populated and started with all using `puppet apply`. The Foreman web application will be configured using `mod_passenger` and Apache.

Attaching Foreman to Puppet

With Foreman installed and configured, create certificates for `foreman.example.com` on `puppet.example.com` ,and copy the keys over to Foreman; they will go in `/var/lib/puppet/ssl` using the same procedure as we did for `reports.example.com` at the beginning of the chapter.

We need our `report` server to send reports to Foreman, so we need the `foreman-report` file. You can download this from `https://raw.github.com/theforeman/puppet-foreman/master/templates/foreman-report_v2.rb.erb` or use the one that `foreman-installer` installed for you. This file will be located in `/usr/lib/ruby/site_ruby/1.8/puppet/reports/foreman.rb`.

Copy this file to `reports.example.com` into `/usr/lib/ruby/site_ruby/1.8/puppet/reports/foreman.rb`. Edit the file so that the Foreman URL and SSL settings are as follows:

```
# URL of your Foreman installation
$foreman_url='https://foreman.example.com'
# if CA is specified, remote Foreman host will be verified
$foreman_ssl_ca = "/var/lib/puppet/ssl/certs/ca.pem"
# ssl_cert and key are required if require_ssl_puppetmasters is
enabled in Foreman
$foreman_ssl_cert = "/var/lib/puppet/ssl/certs/reports.example.com.
pem"
$foreman_ssl_key = "/var/lib/puppet/ssl/private_keys/reports.example.
com.pem"
```

So far we have our Puppet nodes sending reports to our reporting server, which is in turn sending reports to Foreman. Foreman will reject the reports at this point until we allow `reports.example.com`. Login to `https://foreman.example.com` using `admin:changeme`, as shown in the following screenshot:

Then navigate to the **Settings** section as shown in the following screenshot, click on the **Auth** tab, and update the `trusted_puppetmaster_hosts` setting:

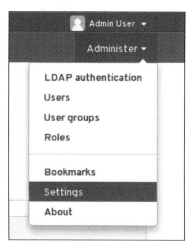

Note that this must be an array, so keep the `[ ]` brackets around `reports.example.com` as shown in the following screenshot:

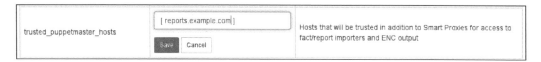

With all this in place, when a node compiles a catalog, it will send the report to `reports.example.com`, which will send the report on to `foreman.example.com`. After a few reports arrive, our Foreman homepage will list hosts and reports.

Using Foreman

Let's first look at the **Hosts** window:

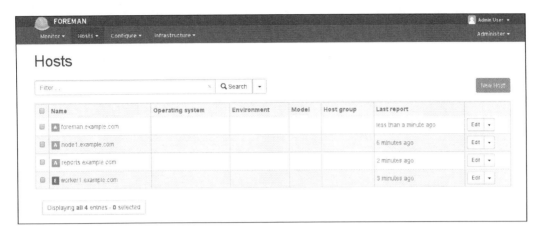

The icons next to the hostnames indicate the status of the last Puppet run. You can also navigate to the **Monitor | Reports** section to see the latest reports, as shown in the following screenshot:

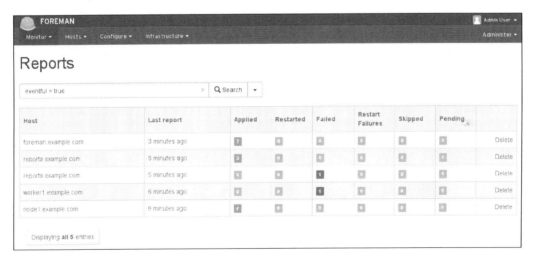

Clicking on `worker1.example.com` shows the failed catalog run and the contents of the error message, as shown in the following screenshot:

Another great feature of Foreman is that when a file is changed by Puppet, Foreman will show the `diff` file for the change in a pop-up window. When we configured our IRC bot to inform us of failed Puppet runs in the last section, the bot presented URLs for reports; those URLs were Foreman specific and will now work as intended. The Foreman maintainers recommend purging your Puppet reports to avoid filling the database and slowing down Foreman. They have provided a rakefile that can be run with `foreman-rake` to delete old reports, as shown in the following command:

```
# foreman-rake reports:expire days=7
```

To complete this example, we will have our worker facts sent to Foreman. This is something that can be run from `cron`. Copy the `node.rb` ENC script from `foreman.example.com` to `worker1.example.com`, as shown in the following command:

```
# scp /etc/puppet/node.rb worker1.example.com:/etc/puppet
```

Edit `node.rb` and change the SSL information as follows:

```
    :ssl_cert      => "/var/lib/puppet/ssl/certs/worker1.example.com.pem",
    :ssl_key       => "/var/lib/puppet/ssl/private_keys/worker1.example.
com.pem"
```

Again, go back into Foreman and add `worker1.example.com` to `trusted_puppetmaster_hosts`. Then, from `worker1` run the `node.rb` script with `--push-facts` to push all the facts to Foreman, as shown in the following command:

```
# /etc/puppet/node.rb --push-facts
```

Now when you view hosts in Foreman, they will have their facts displayed. Foreman also includes rakefiles to produce e-mail reports on a regular basis. Information on configuring this is available at `http://projects.theforeman.org/projects/foreman/wiki/Mail_Notifications`.

With this configuration, Foreman is only showing us the reports. Foreman can be used as a full ENC implementation and take over the entire life cycle of provisioning hosts. I recommend looking at the documentation and exploring the GUI to see if you might benefit from using more of Foreman's features.

Puppet Dashboard

The Dashboard is an open source GUI. It was previously used by Puppet enterprise. Dashboard uses MySQL as its backend unlike Foreman.

 New versions of Puppet enterprise use the Puppet console, which uses PostgreSQL as its backend.

We'll create another vm for Dashboard. Starting with an empty image, we will add the `puppetlabs` repository and the `mysql-server` packages using the following commands:

```
# yum install  https://yum.puppetlabs.com/el/6/products/x86_64/
puppetlabs-release-6-7.noarch.rpm mysql-server
```
```
# yum install puppet-dashboard
```

With MySQL installed, we'll start MySQL with `service mysqld start`, and then run the secure installation script to set a root password before connecting to the database, as shown in the following command:

```
# mysql_secure_installation
```

```
# mysql -p
Enter password:
Welcome to the MySQL monitor.  Commands end with ; or \g.
Your MySQL connection id is 10
Server version: 5.1.73 Source distribution

Copyright (c) 2000, 2013, Oracle and/or its affiliates. All rights reserved.

Oracle is a registered trademark of Oracle Corporation and/or its
affiliates. Other names may be trademarks of their respective
owners.

Type 'help;' or '\h' for help. Type '\c' to clear the current input statement.

mysql> CREATE DATABASE dashboard CHARACTER SET utf8;
Query OK, 1 row affected (0.00 sec)

mysql> GRANT ALL ON dashboard.* TO 'dashboard'@'localhost' IDENTIFIED BY 'PacktP
ubDashboard';
Query OK, 0 rows affected (0.00 sec)

mysql> FLUSH PRIVILEGES;
Query OK, 0 rows affected (0.00 sec)

mysql> quit
Bye
#
```

The Dashboard works with reports from the nodes, some of which can be very large. To accommodate this, change the maximum size of a commit message, as noted in the Dashboard installation manual (`http://docs.puppetlabs.com/dashboard/manual/1.2/bootstrapping.html`), as shown in the following snippet. Puppet can sometimes send very large results.

```
[mysqld]
...
max_allowed_packet=32M
```

Restart `mysqld` after this to make the change take effect.

Create or edit the `database.yml` file in `/usr/share/puppet-dashboard/config` to reflect our new database and database user we just created:

```
production:
  database: dashboard
  username: dashboard
  password: PacktPubDashboard
  encoding: utf8
  adapter: mysql
```

With the database defined, it's now time to create the tables (schema) in our database; this is done with a rake task:

```
# rake RAILS_ENV=production db:migrate
==  BasicSchema: migrating ==================================================
...
==  RemoveUrlFromNodes: migrating ===========================================
-- remove_column(:nodes, :url)
  -> 0.0383s
==  RemoveUrlFromNodes: migrated (0.0386s) ==================================
```

Using passenger with Dashboard

For production, we'll run Dashboard through mod_passenger with Apache, so install mod_passenger from EPEL, and then install Puppet, as shown in the following command:

```
# yum -y install mod_passenger mod_ssl puppet
```

The Dashboard RPM includes an Apache vhost configuration file that can be used as a reference. With mod_passenger installed, create a dashboard.conf file in /etc/httpd/conf.d with the following:

```
# Passenger configuration
PassengerHighPerformance on
PassengerMaxPoolSize 12
PassengerPoolIdleTime 1500
# PassengerMaxRequests 1000
PassengerStatThrottleRate 120
RailsAutoDetect On

<VirtualHost *:80>
  ServerName dashboard.example.com
  DocumentRoot /usr/share/puppet-dashboard/public/
  <Directory /usr/share/puppet-dashboard/public/>
    Options None
    Order allow,deny
    allow from all
  </Directory>
  ErrorLog /var/log/httpd/dashboard.example.com_error.log
  LogLevel warn
```

```
    CustomLog /var/log/httpd/dashboard.example.com_access.log combined
    ServerSignature On
</VirtualHost>

Listen 443
<VirtualHost *:443>
  SSLEngine on
  SSLProtocol -ALL +SSLv3 +TLSv1
  SSLCipherSuite ALL:!ADH:RC4+RSA:+HIGH:+MEDIUM:-LOW:-SSLv2:-EXP
  SSLCertificateFile        /usr/share/puppet-dashboard/certs/
dashboard.example.com.pem
  SSLCertificateKeyFile     /usr/share/puppet-dashboard/dashboard.
example.com-private.pem
  SSLCACertificateFile      /usr/share/puppet-dashboard/certs/ca.pem
  SSLCARevocationFile       /usr/share/puppet-dashboard/certs/ca_crl.
pem

  SSLVerifyClient optional
  SSLVerifyDepth  1
  SSLOptions +StdEnvVars
  ServerName dashboard.example.com
  DocumentRoot /usr/share/puppet-dashboard/public
  <Directory    /usr/share/puppet-dashboard/public>
    Options None
    AllowOverride None
    Order allow,deny
    allow from all
  </Directory>
  <Location / >
    Order deny,allow
    Allow from ALL
  </Location>
</VirtualHost>
```

mod_passenger creates a passenger.conf file with the required LoadModule and PassengerRoot values.

This configuration references certificates for `dashboard.example.com`. We'll need to generate those certificates now. We installed Puppet, so we'll use `puppet certificate generate` on the Dashboard machine, as shown in the following commands:

```
# cd /usr/share/puppet-dashboard/certs
# puppet certificate generate dashboard.example.com --ca-location remote
--server puppet.example.com
```

Now go sign the certificate on `puppet.example.com` with `puppet cert sign dashboard.example.com`. Then, back on Dashboard, download the signed certificate using the following command:

```
# puppet certificate find dashboard.example.com --ca-location remote
--server puppet.example.com
-----BEGIN CERTIFICATE-----
...
2jU/DvBAhWVxZEd674ATk21lyfncm3CDapW7/hiyb/eG
-----END CERTIFICATE-----
```

Download the CA from `puppet.example.com`, as shown in the following command:

```
# puppet certificate find ca --ca-location remote --server puppet.
example.com
```

Copy `ca_crl.pem` from `/var/lib/puppet/ssl/ca` on `puppet.example.com` to `ca_crl.pem` in `/usr/share/puppet-dashboard/certs`. Copy the other three files into the directory as well, as shown in the following commands:

```
# cd /usr/share/puppet-dashboard/certs
# cp /var/lib/puppet/ssl/private_keys/dashboard.example.com.pem
dashboard.example.com-private.pem
# cp /var/lib/puppet/ssl/certs/dashboard.example.com.pem .
# cp /var/lib/puppet/ssl/certs/ca.pem .
```

Now with all the files in place, we can start `httpd` and view our Dashboard at `https://dashboard.example.com`.

You may have to comment out `VirtualHost` in the `ssl.conf` file created by `mod_ssl` before you can start `httpd`. You may also have to change the ownership on `production.log`, as shown in the following command:

```
# chown puppet-dashboard:puppet-dashboard /usr/share/
puppet-dashboard/log/production.log
```

The following screenshot shows our Dashboard:

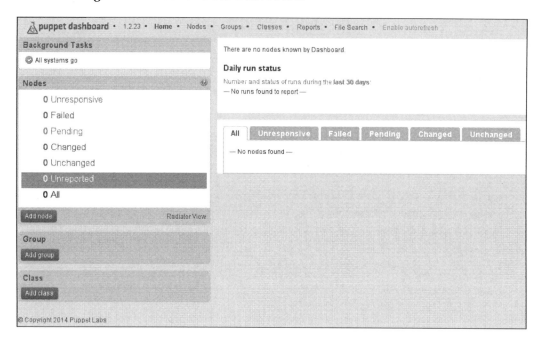

Linking Dashboard to Puppet

Dashboard is operational but not functional yet. Just as we had to do for Foreman, we need to configure reports.example.com to forward reports to Dashboard (or configure our catalog workers to send reports directly to Dashboard). On reports.example.com, we change /etc/puppet/puppet.conf to add the new Dashboard report, as shown in the following snippet:

```
[main]
...
    reports = irc,foreman,http
    reporturl = http://dashboard.example.com/reports/upload
```

Restart httpd on reports.example.com, and wait for a node to run; you will see the report in Dashboard. Well, not really; you'll see it waiting in Dashboard, as shown in the following screenshot:

Processing reports

Dashboard processes report asynchronously, so we need to start some Dashboard worker processes to handle these reports. With our RPM installation, these processes are controlled via the init script `puppet-dashboard-workers`. Puppet Labs recommends you to run as many of these workers as you have CPU cores on the system. To do this, create a file `/etc/sysconfig/puppet-dashboard-workers`, and place the following:

```
CPUS=xxx
```

Here xxx is the number of CPU cores on the system. Then start the `workers` as shown in the following line:

```
# service puppet-dashboard-workers
```

Now go back to the Dashboard GUI, and see that the pending tasks have been dealt with, as shown in the following screenshot:

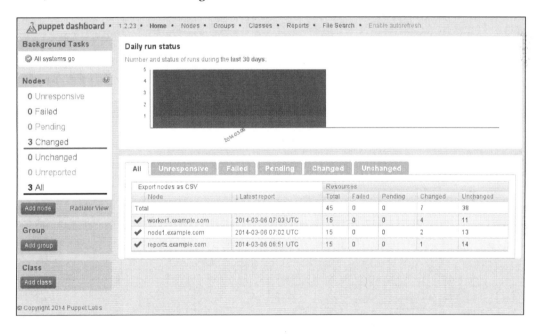

The background tasks box now shows **All systems go**. If the load on your Dashboard worker ever becomes too great, or the `delayed_job` processes (`puppet-dashboard-workers`) are unable to keep up, this will change to a list of jobs pending execution.

Dashboard is now configured to show us the reports from the nodes; we would use `chkconfig` to ensure the workers and `puppet-dashboard-httpd` process start automatically on reboot, if this were a production system.

All of these reporting mechanisms so far have dealt with collecting information from Puppet runs. If you wish to query nodes live, then the **marionette collective** is the tool of choice.

mcollective

mcollective is an orchestration tool created by Puppet Labs that is not specific to Puppet. Plugins exist to work with other configuration management systems. mcollective uses a **Message Queue (MQ)** tool with active connections from all active nodes to enable parallel job execution on large numbers of nodes.

To understand how mcollective works, we'll consider the following high-level diagram and work through the various components. The configuration of mcollective is somewhat involved and prone to errors. Still, once mcollective is working properly, the power it provides can become addictive. It will be worth the effort, I promise.

In the following diagram, we see that the client executing the `mcollective` command communicates with the MQ server. The MQ server then sends the query to each of the nodes connected to the queue.

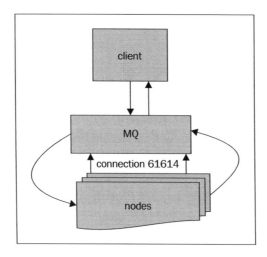

The default MQ installation for marionette uses `activemq`. The `activemq` package provided by the Puppet Labs repository is known to work.

 mcollective uses a generic message queue and can be configured to use your existing message queue infrastructure.

If using `activemq`, a single server can handle 800 nodes. After that, you'll need to spread out to multiple MQ servers. We'll cover the standard mcollective installation using Puppet's certificate authority to provide SSL security to mcollective. The theory here is that we trust Puppet to configure the machines already; we can trust it a little more to run arbitrary commands. We'll also require that users of mcollective have proper SSL authentication.

> You can install mcollective using the `mcollective` module from Forge (`https://forge.puppetlabs.com/puppetlabs/mcollective`). In this section, we will install mcollective manually to explain the various components.

Installing activemq

activemq is the recommended messaging server for mcollective. If you already have a messaging server in your infrastructure, you can use your existing server and just create a message queue for mcollective.

- We will install activemq from the Puppet Labs repository to `puppet.example.com` using the following command:

  ```
  # yum install activemq
  ...
  Installed:
    activemq.noarch 0:5.8.0-3.el6
  ```

- Next, download the sample activemq config file using the following commands:

  ```
  # cd /etc/activemq
  # mv activemq.xml activemq.xml.orig
  # wget -q https://raw.github.com/puppetlabs/marionette-collective/
  master/ext/activemq/examples/single-broker/activemq.xml
  ```

- This will create `activemq.xml`. This file needs to be owned by the user `activemq`, and since we will be adding passwords to the file shortly, we'll set its access permissions to user only:

  ```
  # chown activemq activemq.xml
  # chmod 0600 activemq.xml
  ```

- Now create an mcollective password and admin password for your message queue using the following code. The defaults in this file are `marionette` and `secret` respectively.

```
<simpleAuthenticationPlugin>
  <users>
    <authenticationUser username="mcollective"
password="PacktPubSecret" groups="mcollective,everyone"/>
    <authenticationUser username="admin"
password="PacktPubSuperSecret" groups="mcollective,admins,everyo
ne"/>
  </users>
</simpleAuthenticationPlugin>
```

- Next, change the `transportConnectors` section to use SSL, as shown in the following snippet:

```
<transportConnectors>
  <transportConnector name="openwire" uri="tcp://0.0.0.0:61616"/>
  <transportConnector name="stomp+ssl" uri="stomp+ssl://0.0.0.0:61
614?needClientAuth=true"/>
</transportConnectors>
```

- Immediately following the `transportConnectors`, we'll define an `sslContext`, which will contain the SSL keys from our Puppet master in a format compatible with activemq (`keystores`):

```
<sslContext>
  <sslContext
    keyStore="keystore.jks" keyStorePassword="PacktPubKeystore"
    trustStore="truststore.jks" trustStorePassword="PacktPubTru
st"
  />
</sslContext>
```

This section should be within the `<broker>` definition. For simplicity, just stick it right after the `<transportConnectors>` section.

- Now we need to create `keystore.jks` and `truststore.jks`. Start by copying the certificates from Puppet into a temporary directory, as shown in the following commands:

```
# cd /etc/activemq
# mkdir tmp
# cd tmp
# cp /var/lib/puppet/ssl/certs/ca.pem .
# cp /var/lib/puppet/ssl/certs/puppet.example.com.pem .
```

```
# cp /var/lib/puppet/ssl/private_keys/puppet.example.com.pem
puppet.example.com.private.pem
# keytool -import -alias "Example CA" -file ca.pem -keystore
truststore.jks
Enter keystore password: PacktPubTrust
Re-enter new password: PacktPubTrust
Owner: CN=Puppet CA: puppet.example.com
Issuer: CN=Puppet CA: puppet.example.com
...
Trust this certificate? [no]:  yes
Certificate was added to keystore
```

- The `truststore.jks` keystore is now complete. We next need to create the `keystore.jks` keystore. We start by combining the public and private portions of the Puppet server certificate. The combined file is then fed to OpenSSL's `pkcs12` command to create a pkcs12 file suitable for import using `keytool`.

```
# cat puppet.example.com.pem puppet.example.com.private.pem
>puppet.pem
# openssl pkcs12 -export -in puppet.pem -out activemq.p12 -name
puppet.example.com
Enter Export Password: PacktPubKeystore
Verifying - Enter Export Password: PacktPubKeystore
# keytool -importkeystore -destkeystore keystore.jks -srckeystore
activemq.p12 -srcstoretype PKCS12 -alias puppet.example.com
Enter destination keystore password: PacktPubKeystore
Re-enter new password: PacktPubKeystore
Enter source keystore password:  PacktPubKeystore
```

- Now that these files are created, move them into `/etc/activemq`, and make sure they have appropriate permissions.

```
# chown activemq truststore.jks keystore.jks
# chmod 0600 truststore.jks keystore.jks
# mv truststore.jks keystore.jks /etc/activemq/
```

- We can now start `activemq`; make sure that your firewall allows connections inbound on port 61614, which is the port specified in the `transportConnector` line in `activemq.xml`, as shown in the following command:

```
# service activemq start
Starting ActiveMQ Broker...
```

- Verify that the broker is listening on 61614 using `lsof`:

```
# lsof -i |grep 61614
java      17734 activemq  138u  IPv6  72619      0t0  TCP *:61614
(LISTEN)
```

Configuring nodes to use activemq

Now we need to create a module to install mcollective on every node and have the nodes `mcollective` configuration point back to our message broker. Each node will use a shared key which we will now generate and sign on `puppet.example.com` as shown in the following commands:

```
# puppet certificate generate mcollective-servers --ca-location local
Notice: mcollective-servers has a waiting certificate request
true
# puppet cert sign mcollective-servers
Notice: Signed certificate request for mcollective-servers
Notice: Removing file Puppet::SSL::CertificateRequest mcollective-servers
at '/var/lib/puppet/ssl/ca/requests/mcollective-servers.pem'
```

We'll now copy the certificate and private keys for this new certificate into our modules files directory and add these files to our module definition. The certificate will be in `/var/lib/puppet/ssl/ca/signed/mcollective-servers.pem` and the private key will be in `/var/lib/puppet/ssl/private_keys/mcollective-servers.pem`. The definitions for these files would be as shown in the following snippet:

```
    file {'mcollective_server_cert':
      path   => '/etc/mcollective/ssl/mcollective_public.pem',
      owner  => 0,
      group  => 0,
      mode   => 0640,
      source => 'puppet:///modules/example/mcollective/mcollective_
public.pem',
    }
    file {'mcollective_server_private':
      path   => '/etc/mcollective/ssl/mcollective_private.pem',
      owner  => 0,
      group  => 0,
      mode   => 0600,
      source => 'puppet:///modules/example/mcollective/mcollective_
private.pem',
    }
```

With the certificates in place, we'll move on to the configuration of the service as shown in the following snippet:

```
class example::mcollective {
  $mcollective_server = 'puppet.example.com'
  package {'mcollective':
    ensure => true,
  }
  service {'mcollective':
    ensure  => true,
    enable  => true,
    require => [Package['mcollective'],File['mcollective_server_
config']]
  }
  file {'mcollective_server_config':
    path     => '/etc/mcollective/server.cfg',
    owner    => 0,
    group    => 0,
    mode     => 0640,
    content => template('example/mcollective/server.cfg.erb'),
    require => Package['mcollective'],
    notify   => Service['mcollective'],
  }
```

This is a pretty clean package-file-service relationship. We need to define the mcollective `server.cfg` configuration file. We'll define this with a template as shown in the following code:

```
main_collective = mcollective
collectives = mcollective
libdir = /usr/libexec/mcollective
daemonize = 1

# logging
logger_type = file
logfile = /var/log/mcollective.log
loglevel = info
logfile = /var/log/mcollective.log
logfacility = user
keeplogs = 5
max_log_size = 2097152

# activemq
```

```
connector = activemq
plugin.activemq.pool.size = 1
plugin.activemq.pool.1.host = <%= mcollective_server %>
plugin.activemq.pool.1.port = 61614
plugin.activemq.pool.1.user = mcollective
plugin.activemq.pool.1.password = PacktPubSecret
plugin.activemq.pool.1.ssl = 1
plugin.activemq.pool.1.ssl.ca = /var/lib/puppet/ssl/certs/ca.pem
plugin.activemq.pool.1.ssl.cert = /var/lib/puppet/ssl/certs/<%= @fqdn
%>.pem
plugin.activemq.pool.1.ssl.key = /var/lib/puppet/ssl/private_keys/<%=
@fqdn %>.pem
plugin.activemq.pool.1.ssl.fallback = 0

# SSL security plugin settings:
securityprovider = ssl
plugin.ssl_client_cert_dir = /etc/mcollective/ssl/clients
plugin.ssl_server_private = /etc/mcollective/ssl/mcollective_private.
pem
plugin.ssl_server_public = /etc/mcollective/ssl/mcollective_public.pem

# Facts, identity, and classes:
identity = <%= @fqdn %>
factsource = yaml
plugin.yaml = /etc/mcollective/facts.yaml
classesfile = /var/lib/puppet/state/classes.txt

registerinterval = 600
```

The next thing we need is a `facts.yaml` file populated, as shown in the following snippet, so that we can query facts on the nodes and filter results:

```
file {'facts.yaml':
    path      => '/etc/mcollective/facts.yaml',
    owner     => 0,
    group     => 0,
    mode      => 0640,
    loglevel  => debug,
    content   => inline_template("---\n<% scope.to_hash.reject { |k,v|
k.to_s =~ /(uptime_seconds|timestamp|free)/ }.sort.each do |k, v| %>
<%= k %>: \"<%= v %>\"\n<% end %>\n"),
    require   => Package['mcollective'],
  }
}
```

In the previous example, the `inline_template` uses a call to sort due to random ordering in the hash. Without the sort, the resulting `facts.yaml` file is completely different on each Puppet run, resulting in the entire file being rewritten every time.

Almost there; now we have all our nodes pointing to our activemq server. We need to configure a client to connect to the server.

Connecting a client to activemq

Clients would normally be installed on the admin user's desktop. We will use `puppet certificate generate` here just as we have in previous examples. We will now outline the steps needed to have a new client connect to `mcollective`:

1. Create certificates for Thomas and name his certificates `thomas`:

    ```
    $ puppet certificate generate thomas --ssldir ~/.mcollective.d/
    credentials --ca-location remote --ca_server puppet.example.com
    ```

2. Sign the cert on `puppet.example.com` (our SSL master):

    ```
    # puppet cert sign thomas
    ```

    ```
    Notice: Signed certificate request for thomas
    ```

    ```
    Notice: Removing file Puppet::SSL::CertificateRequest thomas at '/
    var/lib/puppet/ssl/ca/requests/thomas.pem'
    ```

3. Retrieve the signed certificate on your client:

    ```
    $ puppet certificate find thomas --ssldir ~/.mcollective.d/
    credentials --ca-location remote --ca_server puppet.example.com
    ```

    ```
    -----BEGIN CERTIFICATE-----
    ```

    ```
    MIIFTjCCAzagAwIBAgIBEjANBgkqhkiG9w0BAQsFADAoMSYwJAYDVQQDDB1QdXBw
    ```

    ```
    ...
    ```

    ```
    36ZEB0C+UZij9VVy/ekN2AV0
    ```

    ```
    -----END CERTIFICATE-----
    ```

    This certificate gets downloaded to `~/.mcollective.d/credentials/certs/thomas.pem`.

4. Download the `mcollective-servers` key:

```
$ puppet certificate find mcollective-servers --ssldir
~/.mcollective.d/credentials --ca-location remote --ca_server
puppet.example.com
-----BEGIN CERTIFICATE-----
MIIFWzCCA00gAwIBAgIBEzANBgkqhkiG9w0BAQsFADAoMSYwJAYDVQQDDB1QdXBw
...
Vd5M0lfdYSDKOA+b1AXXoMaAn9n9j7AyBhQhie52Og==
-----END CERTIFICATE-----
```

This gets downloaded into `~/.mcollective.d/credentials/certs/mcollective-servers.pem`.

5. Download our main CA for certificate verification purposes using the following command:

```
$ puppet certificate find ca --ssldir ~/.mcollective.d/credentials
--ca-location remote --ca_server puppet.example.com
-----BEGIN CERTIFICATE-----
MIIFRjCCAy6gAwIBAgIBATANBgkqhkiG9w0BAQsFADAoMSYwJAYDVQQDDB1QdXBw
...
XO+dgA5aAhUUMg==
-----END CERTIFICATE-----
```

This gets downloaded into `~/.mcollective.d/credentials/certs/ca.pem`.

6. Now we need to create the configuration file of `mco` at `~/.mcollective`:

```
connector = activemq
direct_addressing = 1
# ActiveMQ connector settings:
plugin.activemq.pool.size = 1
plugin.activemq.pool.1.host = puppet.example.com
plugin.activemq.pool.1.port = 61614
plugin.activemq.pool.1.user = mcollective
plugin.activemq.pool.1.password = PacktPubSecret
plugin.activemq.pool.1.ssl = 1
plugin.activemq.pool.1.ssl.ca = /home/thomas/.mcollective.d/
credentials/certs/ca.pem
plugin.activemq.pool.1.ssl.cert = /home/thomas/.mcollective.d/
credentials/certs/thomas.pem
plugin.activemq.pool.1.ssl.key = /home/tuphill/.mcollective.d/
credentials/private_keys/thomas.pem
plugin.activemq.pool.1.ssl.fallback = 0
```

```
securityprovider = ssl
plugin.ssl_server_public = /home/thomas/.mcollective.d/
credentials/certs/mcollective-servers.pem
plugin.ssl_client_private = /home/thomas/.mcollective.d/
credentials/private_keys/thomas.pem
plugin.ssl_client_public = /home/thomas/.mcollective.d/
credentials/certs/thomas.pem
default_discovery_method = mc
direct_addressing_threshold = 10
ttl = 60
color = 1
rpclimitmethod = first
libdir = /usr/libexec/mcollective
logger_type = console
loglevel = warn
main_collective = mcollective
```

7. Now, we need to add our public key to all the nodes so that they will accept our signed messages. We do this by copying our public key into `example/files/mcollective/clients` and creating a file resource to manage that directory with `recurse => true`, as shown in the following snippet:

```
file {'mcollective_clients':
ensure  => 'directory',
path    => '/etc/mcollective/ssl/clients',
mode    => '0700',
owner   => 0,
group   => 0,
recurse => true,
source  => 'puppet:///modules/example/mcollective/clients',
}
```

Using mcollective

With everything in place, our client will now pass messages that will be accepted by the nodes, and we in turn will accept the messages signed by the `mcollective-servers` key.

```
thomas@host $ mco ping
worker1.example.com                     time=86.03 ms
node2.example.com                       time=96.21 ms
node1.example.com                       time=97.64 ms
---- ping statistics ----
3 replies max: 97.64 min: 86.03 avg: 93.29
```

Any admin that you wish to add to your team will need to generate a certificate for themselves and have the puppet CA sign the key. Then they can copy your .mcollective file and change the keys to their own. After adding their public key to the example/mcollective/clients directory, the nodes will start to accept their messages. You can also add a key for scripts to use; in those cases, using the hostname of the machine running the scripts will make it easier to distinguish the host that is running the mco queries.

Now that mco is finally configured, we can use it to generate reports as shown in the following command. The inventory service is a good place to start.

```
$ mco inventory node1.example.com
Inventory for node1.example.com:

    Server Statistics:
                    Version: 2.4.1
                 Start Time: 2014-03-03 00:33:29 -0800
                Config File: /etc/mcollective/server.cfg
                Collectives: mcollective
            Main Collective: mcollective
                 Process ID: 885
             Total Messages: 5
     Messages Passed Filters: 5
           Messages Filtered: 0
           Expired Messages: 0
                Replies Sent: 4
        Total Processor Time: 0.46 seconds
                System Time: 0.19 seconds
```

> The facts returned in the inventory command, and in fact in any mco command, are the redacted facts from the /etc/mcollective/facts. yaml file we created.

Other common uses of mco are to find nodes that have classes applied to them, as shown in the following command:

```
$ mco find --wc webserver
www.example.com
```

Another use of mco is to find nodes that have a certain value for a fact. You can use regular expression matching using /something/ notation, as shown in the following command:

```
$ mco find --wf hostname=/^node/
node2.example.com
node1.example.com
```

Using the built-in modules, it's possible to start and stop services. Check file contents and write your own modules to perform tasks.

Summary

Reports help you understand when things go wrong. Using some of the built-in report types, it's possible to alert your admins of Puppet failures. The two GUIs outlined here, Foreman and Dashboard, allow you to review Puppet run logs. Both GUIs have more advanced features, and each can be used as an ENC. Of the two, Foreman has the most polished feel and makes it easier to link directly to reports and search for reports. Dashboard was produced by Puppet Labs and is the predecessor of the Puppet console used in the enterprise product line. mcollective is an orchestration utility that allows you to actively query and modify all the nodes in an organized manner interactively via a message broker.

In the next chapter, we will be installing puppetdb and creating exported resources.

8

Exported Resources

When automating tasks among many servers, information from one node may affect the configuration of another node or nodes. For example, if you configure DNS servers using Puppet, then you can have Puppet tell the rest of your nodes where all the DNS servers are located. This sharing of information is called catalog storage and searching in Puppet.

Catalog storage and searching was previously known as **storeconfigs** and enabled using the storeconfig option in puppet.conf. Storeconfigs was able to use sqlite, MySQL, and PostgreSQL; it is now deprecated in favor of **puppetdb**.

The currently supported method of supporting exported resources is puppetdb, which uses Java and PostgreSQL and can support hundreds to thousands of nodes with a single puppetdb instance. Most scaling issues with puppetdb can be solved by beefing up the PostgreSQL server, either adding a faster disk or more CPU, depending on the bottleneck.

We will begin our discussion of exported resources by configuring puppetdb. We will then discuss exported resource concepts and some example usage.

Configuring puppetdb – using the forge module

The easy way to configure puppetdb is to use the puppetdb Puppet module on Puppet Forge at `https://forge.puppetlabs.com/puppetlabs/puppetdb`. The steps to install and use puppetdb that we will outline are as follows:

1. Install the puppetdb module on Puppet master/worker.

2. Install puppetlabs-repo and Puppet on puppetdb host.

3. Deploy the puppetdb module onto puppetdb host.

4. Update configuration of the Puppet master to use puppetdb.

We will start with a vanilla EL6 machine and install puppetdb using the puppetdb module. In *Chapter 4*, *Public Modules*, we used a `Puppetfile` in combination with `librarian-puppet` or `r10k` to download modules. We used the puppetdb module since it was a good example of dependencies; we will rely on puppetdb being available to our catalog worker for this example. If you do not already have puppetdb downloaded, do so now using one of those methods or simply use `puppet module install puppetlabs/puppetdb` as shown in the following screenshot:

```
# puppet module install puppetlabs/puppetdb
Notice: Preparing to install into /etc/puppet/modules ...
Notice: Downloading from https://forge.puppetlabs.com ...
Notice: Installing -- do not interrupt ...
/etc/puppet/modules
└─┬ puppetlabs-puppetdb (v3.0.1)
  ├── puppetlabs-firewall (v1.0.2)
  ├── puppetlabs-inifile (v1.0.3)
  └─┬ puppetlabs-postgresql (v3.3.3)
    ├── puppetlabs-apt (v1.4.2)
    └── puppetlabs-concat (v1.1.0-rc1)
#
```

After installing the puppetdb module, we need to install the `puppetlabs` repo on our puppetdb machine and install Puppet using the following command:

```
# yum -q -y install puppetlabs-release-6-7.noarch.rpm
# yum -q -y install puppet
```

Our next step is to deploy puppetdb on the puppetdb machine using Puppet. We'll create a wrapper class to install and configure puppetdb on our worker as shown in the following code (in the next chapter this will become a profile). Wrapper classes, or profiles, are classes that bundle lower-level classes (building blocks) into higher-level classes.

```
class pdb {
  # puppetdb class
  class { 'puppetdb::server': }
  class { 'puppetdb::database::postgresql': listen_addresses => '*' }
}
```

At this point, the puppetdb server also needs network ports opened in `iptables`; the two ports are 5432 (`postgresql`) and 8081 (`puppetdb`). Using our knowledge of the firewall module, we could do this with the following snippet included in our pdb class:

```
firewall {'5432 postgresql':
  action => 'accept',
  proto  => 'tcp',
  dport  => '5432',
}
firewall {'8081 puppetdb':
  action => 'accept',
  proto  => 'tcp',
  dport  => '8081',
}
```

We then apply this pdb class to our puppetdb machine. For this example, I used the `hiera_include` method and the following `puppetdb.yaml` file:

```
---
classes: pdb
```

Now we run the Puppet agent on puppetdb to have puppetdb installed (running the Puppet agent creates the SSL keys for our puppetdb server as well; remember to sign those on the master).

Back on our workers, we need to tell Puppet to use puppetdb; we can do this by defining a worker class that configures Puppet and applying it to our workers:

```
class worker {
  class {'puppetdb::master::config':
    puppetdb_server     => 'puppetdb.example.com',
    puppet_service_name => 'httpd',
  }
}
```

In the previous puppetdb class definition, `puppetdb::master::config` expects the Puppet master service to be `puppetmaster`, but since we are using passenger, we need to change this name to `httpd` so that Puppet will restart Apache and not try to start the `puppetmaster` service. Now we configure our `worker1.yaml` file to include the previous class as follows:

```
---
classes: worker
```

The worker will need to be able to resolve puppetdb.example.com, either through DNS or static entries in `/etc/hosts`. Now run Puppet on our worker to have the worker configured to use puppetdb. The worker will attempt to communicate with the puppetdb machine over port 8081. You'll need the firewall (iptables) rules to allow this access in place at this point.

Now we can test that puppetdb is operating by using Puppet node status as follows:

```
worker1# puppet node status puppetdb.example.com
puppetdb.example.com
Currently active
Last catalog: 2014-03-13T06:59:31.773Z
Last facts: 2014-03-13T06:59:26.681Z
```

Manually installing puppetdb

The `puppetlabs/puppetdb` module does a great job of installing puppetdb and getting you running quickly. Unfortunately it also obscures a lot of the configuration details. In the enterprise, you'll need to know how all the parts fit together. We will now install puppetdb manually in the following five steps:

1. Install Puppet and puppetdb
2. Install and configure PostgreSQL
3. Configure puppetdb to use PostgreSQL

4. Start puppetdb and open firewall ports

5. Configure the Puppet master to use puppetdb

Installing Puppet and puppetdb

To manually install puppetdb, start with a fresh machine and install the `puppetlabs` repository, as in previous examples. We'll call this new server puppetdb_manual. example.com to differentiate it from our automatically installed puppetdb instance (puppetdb.example.com).

Install Puppet, do a Puppet agent run as shown in the following command to generate certificates, and sign them on the master as we did when we used the `puppetlabs/puppetdb` module. Alternatively use `puppet certificate generate` as we have shown in previous chapters.

```
# yum -q -y install puppetlabs-release-6-7.noarch.rpm
# yum -q -y install puppet
# puppet agent -t
```

Sign the certificate on the master as follows:

```
puppet# puppet cert sign puppetdb_manual.example.com
Notice: Signed certificate request for puppetdb_manual.example.com
Notice: Removing file Puppet::SSL::CertificateRequest puppetdb_manual.
example.com at '/var/lib/puppet/ssl/ca/requests/puppetdb_manual.example.
com.pem'
```

Install puppetdb as follows:

```
# yum -q -y install puppetdb
```

Installing and configuring PostgreSQL

If you already have an enterprise PostgreSQL server configured, you can simply point puppetdb at that instance. To install PostgreSQL, install the `postgresql-server` package, and initialize the database as follows:

```
# yum -q -y install postgresql-server
# service postgresql initdb
Initializing database:                              [  OK  ]
# service postgresql start
Starting postgresql service:                        [  OK  ]
```

Next create a puppetdb `postgres` user, and create the `puppetdb` database (allowing the puppetdb user to access that database) as follows:

```
# sudo -iu postgres
$ createuser -DRSP puppetdb
Enter password for new role: PacktPub
Enter it again: PacktPub
$ createdb -E UTF8 -O puppetdb puppetdb
```

Allow puppetdb to connect to the PostgreSQL server using md5 on the localhost since we'll keep puppetdb and the PostgreSQL server on the same machine (puppetdb_manual.example.com).

> You would need to change the allowed address rules from 127.0.0.1/32 to that of the puppetdb server, if puppetdb was on a different server than the PostgreSQL server.

Edit `/var/lib/pgsql/data/pg_hba.conf` and add the following:

```
local    puppetdb       puppetdb                       md5
host     puppetdb       puppetdb       127.0.0.1/32    md5
host     puppetdb       puppetdb       ::1/128         md5
```

> The default configuration uses `ident` authentication; you must remove the following lines:
> ```
> local    all      all                             ident
> host     all      all        127.0.0.1/32    ident
> host     all      all          ::1/128       ident
> ```

Restart PostgreSQL and test connectivity as follows:

```
# service postgresql restart
Stopping postgresql service:                          [  OK  ]
Starting postgresql service:                          [  OK  ]
# psql -h localhost puppetdb puppetdb
Password for user puppetdb: PacktPub
psql (8.4.20)
Type "help" for help.

puppetdb=> \d
No relations found.
puppetdb=> \q
```

Now that we've verified that PostgreSQL is working, we need to configure puppetdb to use PostgreSQL.

Configuring puppetdb to use PostgreSQL

Locate the database.ini file in /etc/puppetdb/conf.d, and replace it with the following code snippet:

```
[database]
classname = org.postgresql.Driver
subprotocol = postgresql
subname = //localhost:5432/puppetdb
username = puppetdb
password = PacktPub
```

If it's not present in your file, configure automatic tasks of puppetdb, such as garbage collection (gc-interval) as shown in the following code. Puppetdb will remove stale nodes every 60 minutes. For more information on the other settings refer to the Puppet Labs documentation at http://docs.puppetlabs.com/puppetdb/latest/configure.html.

```
gc-interval = 60
log-slow-statements = 10
report-ttl = 14d
syntax_pgs = true
conn-keep-alive = 45
node-ttl = 0s
conn-lifetime = 0
node-purge-ttl = 0s
conn-max-age = 60
```

Start puppetdb using the following command:

```
# service puppetdb start
Starting puppetdb:                                      [  OK  ]
Allow external connections to port 8081
# iptables -I INPUT -p tcp -m state --state NEW -m tcp --dport 8081 -j
ACCEPT
```

Configuring Puppet to use puppetdb

Perform the following steps to configure Puppet to use puppetdb:

1. To use puppetdb, the worker will need the puppetdb node terminus package; we'll install that first by using the following command:

```
# yum -y install puppetdb-terminus
```

2. Create /etc/puppet/puppetdb.conf, and point puppetdb at puppetdb_manual.example.com:

```
[main]
port = 8081
soft_write_failure = false
server = puppetdb_manual.example.com
```

3. Tell Puppet to use puppetdb for storeconfigs by adding the following in the [master] section:

```
[master]
storeconfigs = true
storeconfigs_backend = puppetdb
```

4. Next, create a routes.yaml file that will make Puppet use puppetdb for inventory purposes:

```
---
master:
  facts:
    terminus: puppetdb
    cache: yaml
```

5. Restart httpd to restart the worker's passenger process and start using puppetdb. Verify that puppetdb is working by running the puppet agent again on puppetdb_manual.example.com. After the second Puppet agent runs, you can inspect the PostgreSQL database for a new catalog as follows:

```
puppetdb=> \x
Expanded display is on.
puppetdb=> SELECT * from catalogs;
-[ RECORD 1 ]----+-------------------------------------------
id               | 1
hash             | 0e8749558ee701f26de4eedcc15b00cbb1bc7fc9
api_version      | 1
```

```
catalog_version   | 1394781065
transaction_uuid  | 04a5c02f-5a52-4c37-8a91-99686502733c
timestamp         | 2014-03-14 03:11:05.502-04
certname          | puppetdb_manual.example.com
```

Exported resource concepts

Now that we have puppetdb configured, we can begin exporting resources into puppetdb. In *Chapter 5, Custom Facts and Modules*, we introduced virtual resources. Virtual resources are resources that are defined but not instantiated. The concept with virtual resources is that a node has several resources defined, but only one or a few resources are instantiated. Unstantiated resources are not used in catalog compilation. This is one method of overcoming some "duplicate definition" type problems. The concept with exported resources is much the same, the difference being that exported resources are published to puppetdb and made available to any node in the enterprise. In this way, resources defined on one node can be instantiated (realized) on another node.

What actually happens is quite simple. Exported resources are put into the catalog_resources table in the PostgreSQL backend of puppetdb. The table contains a column named exported. This column is set to true for exported resources. When trying to understand exported resources, just remember that exported resources are just entries in a database.

To illustrate exported resources, we will walk through a few simple examples. Before we start, you need to know two terms used with exported resources: declaring and collecting.

Declaring exported resources

Exported resources are declared with the @@ operator. You define the resource as you would normally but prepend the definition with @@. For example, the following host resource:

```
host {'exported':
  host_aliases => 'exported-resources',
  ip    => '1.1.1.1',
}
```

It can be declared as the exported resource:

```
@@host {'exported':
  host_aliases => 'exported-resources',
  ip    => '1.1.1.1',
}
```

Any resource can be declared as an exported resource. The process of realizing exported resources is known as collecting.

Collecting exported resources

Collecting is performed using a special form of the collecting syntax. When we collected virtual resources, we used `<| |>` to collect the resources. For exported resources, we use `<<| |>>`. To collect the previous host resource, we would use the following:

```
Host <<| |>>
```

To take advantage of exported resources, we need to think about what we are trying to accomplish. We'll start with a simplified example.

Simple example: a host entry

It makes sense to have static host entries in `/etc/hosts` for some nodes since DNS outages may disrupt the services provided by those nodes. Examples of such services are backups, authentication, and kerberos. We'll use LDAP (authentication) in this example. In this scenario, we'll apply the `ldap::server` class to any LDAP server and add a collector for `Host` entries to our `base` class (the `base` class will be a default applied to all nodes). First, declare the exported resource in `ldap::server`, as shown in the following code snippet:

```
class ldap::server {
  @@host {"ldap-$::hostname":
    host_aliases => ["$::fqdn",'ldap'],
    ip           => "$::ipaddress",
  }
}
```

This will create an exported entry on any host to which we apply the `ldap::server` class. We'll apply this class to `node2` and then run Puppet to have the resource exported. After running the Puppet agent on `node2`, we will examine the contents of puppetdb, as shown in the following screenshot:

```
                            root@puppetdb_manual:~                          [x]
puppetdb=> \x on
Expanded display is on.
puppetdb=> SELECT * FROM catalog_resources WHERE exported=TRUE AND title LIKE 'l
ap-node2';
-[ RECORD 1 ]----------------------------------------------------------------
catalog_id | 2
resource   | 0301142923d5ac0614d094f3087a0b0a8664c374
type       | Host
title      | ldap-node2
tags       | {default,node,server,ldap,host,ldap-node2,ldap::server,class}
exported   | t
file       | /etc/puppet/environments/production/dist/ldap/manifests/server.pp
line       | 5

puppetdb=>
```

The `catalog_resources` table holds the catalog resource mapping information. Using the resource ID from this table, we can retrieve the contents of the resource from the `resource_params` table, as shown in the following screenshot:

```
                            root@puppetdb_manual:~                          [x]
puppetdb=> SELECT * FROM resource_params WHERE resource='0301142923d5ac0614d094f
3087a0b0a8664c374';
-[ RECORD 1 ]-----------------------------------------
resource | 0301142923d5ac0614d094f3087a0b0a8664c374
name     | host_aliases
value    | ["node2.example.com","ldap"]
-[ RECORD 2 ]-----------------------------------------
resource | 0301142923d5ac0614d094f3087a0b0a8664c374
name     | ip
value    | "192.168.122.133"

puppetdb=> 
```

As we can see, the `node2` host entry has been made available in puppetdb. The `host_aliases` and `ip` information has been stored in puppetdb.

To use this exported resource, we will need to add a collector to our `base` class as follows:

```
class base {
  Host <<| |>>
}
```

Now when we run `puppet agent` on any host in our network (any host that has the `base` class applied), we will see the following host entry:

```
node1# grep ldap /etc/hosts
192.168.122.133  ldap-node2  node2.example.com ldap
```

The problem with this example is that every host with `ldap::server` applied will be sent to every node in the enterprise. To make things worse, any exported host resource will be picked up by our collector. We need a method to be specific when collecting our resources. Puppet provides tags for this purpose.

Resource tags

Resource tags are **metaparameters** available to all resources in Puppet. They are used in collecting only and do not affect the definition of resources.

> Metaparameters are part of how Puppet compiles the catalog and not part of the resource to which they are attached. Metaparameters include `before`, `notify`, `require`, and `subscribe`. More information on metaparameters is available at `http://docs.puppetlabs.com/references/latest/metaparameter.html`.

Any tags explicitly set on a resource will be appended to the array of tags. In our previous example, we saw the tags for our host entry in the PostgreSQL output as follows, but we didn't address what the tags meant:

```
{default,node,server,ldap,host,ldap-node2,ldap::server,class}
```

All these tags are defaults set by puppet. To illustrate how tags are used, we can create multiple exported host entries with different tags. We'll start with adding a tag search to our `Host` collector in the `base` class as follows:

```
Host <<| tag == 'ldap-server' |>>
```

Then we'll add an `ldap-client` exported host resource to the base class with the tag `'ldap-client'` as follows:

```
@@host {"ldap-client-$::hostname":
    host_aliases => ["$::fqdn","another-$::hostname"],
    ip           => "$::ipaddress",
    tag          => 'ldap-client',
  }
```

Now all nodes will only collect `Host` resources marked as ldap-server. Every node will create an `ldap-client` exported host resource, we'll add a collector for those to the `ldap::server` class:

```
Host <<| tag == 'ldap-client' |>>
```

One last change: we need to make our ldap-server resource-specific, so we'll add a tag to it in `ldap::server` as follows:

```
@@host {"ldap-$::hostname":
    host_aliases => ["$::fqdn",'ldap'],
    ip           => "$::ipaddress",
    tag          => 'ldap-server',
}
```

Now every node with the `ldap::server` class exports a host resource tagged with `ldap-server` and collects all host resources tagged with `ldap-client`. After running Puppet on our worker1 and nodes 1 and 2, we see the following on node2 as the host resources tagged with `ldap-client` get defined:

```
root@node2:~
Info: Caching catalog for node2.example.com
Info: Applying configuration version '1395036786'
Notice: /Stage[main]/Ldap::Server/Host[ldap-client-node1]/ensure: created
Notice: /Stage[main]/Base/Host[ldap-client-node2]/ensure: created
Notice: /Stage[main]/Ldap::Server/Host[ldap-client-worker1]/ensure: created
Notice: Finished catalog run in 0.24 seconds
node2# grep ldap /etc/hosts
192.168.122.133 ldap-node2 node2.example.com ldap
192.168.122.132 ldap-client-node1 node1.example.com another-node1
192.168.122.133 ldap-client-node2 node2.example.com another-node2
192.168.122.150 ldap-client-worker1 worker1.example.com another-worker1
node2#
```

Exported SSH keys

Most exported resource documentation starts with an SSH key example. `sshkey` is a Puppet type that creates or destroys entries in the `ssh_known_hosts` file used by SSH to verify the validity of remote servers. The `sshkey` example is a great use of exported resources, but since most examples put the declaration and collecting phases in the same class, it may be a confusing example for those starting out learning exported resources. It's important to remember that exporting and collecting are different operations.

sshkey collection for laptops

We'll outline an enterprise application of the sshkey example. We'll define a class for login servers—any server that allows users to login directly. Using that class to define exported resources for ssh_host_keys, we'll then create an ssh_client class that collects all the login server ssh_keys. In this way, we can apply the ssh_client class to any laptops that might connect and have them get updated SSH host keys. To make this an interesting example, we'll run Puppet as non-root on the laptop and have Puppet update the user's known_hosts file ~/.ssh/known_hosts instead of the system file.

> This is a slightly novel approach to run Puppet without root privileges.

We'll begin by defining our example::login_server class that exports the RSA and DSA SSH host keys. RSA and DSA are the two types of encryption keys that can be used by the SSH daemon; the name refers to the encryption algorithm used by each key type. We will need to check if a key of each type is defined as it is only a requirement that one type of key be defined for the SSH server to function, as shown in the following code:

```
class example::login_server {
  if ( $::sshrsakey != undef ) {
    @@sshkey {"$::fqdn-rsa":
      host_aliases => ["$::hostname","$::ipaddress"],
      key          => "$::sshrsakey",
      type         => 'rsa',
      tag          => 'example::login_server',
    }
  }
  if ( $::sshdsakey != undef ) {
    @@sshkey {"$::fqdn-dsa":
      host_aliases => ["$::hostname","$::ipaddress"],
      key          => "$::sshdsakey",
      type         => 'dsa',
      tag          => 'example::login_server',
    }
  }
}
```

This class will export two SSH key entries, one for the rsa key and another for the dsa key. It's important to populate the host_aliases array as we have done so that both the IP address and short hostname are verified with the key when using SSH.

Now we could define an example::laptop class that simply collects the keys and applies them to the system-wide ssh_known_hosts file. Instead, we will define a new fact, homedir in base/lib/facter/homedir.rb to determine if Puppet is being run by a non-root user as follows:

```
Facter.add(:homedir) do
  if Process.uid != 0 and ENV['HOME'] != nil
        setcode do
          begin
            ENV['HOME']
          rescue LoadError
            nil
          end
        end
    end
end
```

This simple fact checks the UID of the running Puppet process, if it is not 0 (root), it looks for the environment variable HOME and sets the fact homedir equal to the value of that environment variable.

Now we can key off this fact as a top scope variable in our definition of the example::laptop class as follows:

```
class example::laptop {
  # collect all the ssh keys
  if $::homedir != undef {
    Sshkey <<| tag == 'login_server' |>> {
      target => "$::homedir/.ssh/known_hosts"
    }
  } else {
    Sshkey <<| tag == 'login_server' |>>
  }
}
```

Depending on the value of the $::homedir fact, we either define system-wide SSH keys or userdir keys. The SSH key collector (Sshkey <<| tag == 'login_server' |>>) uses the tag login_server to restrict the SSH key resources to those defined by our example::login_server class.

To test this module, we apply the `example::login_server` class to both node1 and node2, thereby creating the exported resources. Now on our laptop, we run Puppet as ourselves and sign the key on the Puppet master.

 If Puppet has already run as root or another user, the certificate may have already been generated for your laptop hostname; use the `--certname` option to `puppet agent` to request a new key.

We add the `example::laptop` class to our laptop machine and examine the output of our Puppet run.

Our laptop is likely not a normal client of our Puppet master, so when calling the Puppet agent, we define the Puppet server and environment as follows:

```
$ puppet agent -t --environment production --server puppet.example.com
--waitforcert 60
...
Info: Applying configuration version '1395123100'
Notice: /Stage[main]/Example::Laptop/Sshkey[node1.example.com-dsa]/
ensure: created
Info: FileBucket adding {md5}36209b6aed02c7a30ac2351a777590b4
Notice: /Stage[main]/Example::Laptop/Sshkey[node1.example.com-rsa]/
ensure: created
Notice: Finished catalog run in 0.15 seconds
```

Since we ran the agent as non-root, the system-wide SSH keys in `ssh_known_hosts` cannot have been modified, looking at `~/.ssh/known_hosts`, we see the new entries at the bottom of the file as follows:

```
node2.example.com-dsa,node2,192.168.122.133 ssh-dss AAAA...91+
node2.example.com-rsa,node2,192.168.122.133 ssh-rsa AAAA...w==
node1.example.com-dsa,node1,192.168.122.132 ssh-dss AAAA...91+
node1.example.com-rsa,node1,192.168.122.132 ssh-rsa AAAA...w==
```

Putting it all together

Any resource can be exported, including defined types and your own custom types. Tags may be used to limit the set of exported resources collected by a collector. Tags may include local variables, facts, and custom facts. Using exported resources, defined types and custom facts, it is possible to have Puppet generate complete interactions without intervention (automatically).

As an abstract example, think of any clustered service where members of a cluster need to know about the other members of the cluster. You could define a custom fact, `clustername`, that defines the name of the cluster based on information either on the node or in a central **Configuration Management DataBase (CMDB)**.

 CMDBs are the data warehouses of an organization. Examples of CMDBs include OneCMDB, Itop, or BMC Atrium.

You would then create a cluster module, which would export firewall rules to allow access from each node. The nodes in the cluster would collect all the exported rules based on the relationship `tag=="clustername"`. Without any interaction, a complex firewall rule relationship would be built up between cluster members. If a new member is added to the cluster, the rules will be exported, and with the next Puppet run, the node will be permitted access to the other cluster members.

Another useful scenario is where there are multiple slave nodes that need to be accessed by a master node, such as with backup software or a software distribution system. The master node needs the slave nodes to allow it access to them. The slave nodes need to know which node is the master node. In this relationship, you would define a master and a slave module and apply them accordingly. The slave node would export its host configuration information, and the master would export both its firewall access rule and master configuration information. The master would collect all the slave configuration resources. The slaves would each collect the firewall and configuration information from the master. The great thing about this sort of configuration is that you can easily migrate the master service to a new node. As slaves check into Puppet, they will receive the new master configuration and begin pointing at the new master node.

To illustrate this concept, we will go through a DNS configuration example. We will configure a DNS server with the `example::dns::server` class. We will then configure clients using a `example::dns::client` class. DNS servers are configured with `zone` files. Zone files come in two forms: the forward zones map hostnames to IP addresses and the reverse zones map IP address to hostnames. To make a fully functioning DNS implementation, our clients will export a `concat::fragment` resource which will be collected on the master and used to build both the forward and reverse DNS zone files.

The following diagram outlines the process where two nodes export
`concat::fragment` resources that are assembled with a header into a
zone file on the DNS server node:

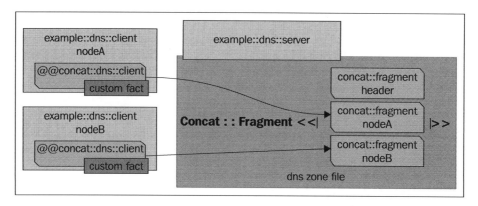

To start, we will define two custom facts that produce the reverse of the IP address
suitable for use in a DNS reverse zone and the network in **Classless Inter-Domain
Routing (CIDR)** notation used to define the reverse zone file as follows:

```
# reverse.rb
# Set a fact for the reverse lookup of the network on eth0

require 'ipaddr'
require 'puppet/util/ipcidr'

# define 2 facts for each interface passed in
def reverse(dev)
  # network of device
  ip = IPAddr.new(Facter.value("network_#{dev}"))
  # network in cidr notation (uuu.vvv.www.xxx/yy)
  nm = Puppet::Util::IPCidr.new(Facter.value("network_#{dev}")).
mask(Facter.value("netmask_#{dev}"))
  cidr = nm.cidr

  # set fact for network in reverse vvv.www.uuu.in-addr.arpa
  Facter.add("reverse_#{dev}") do
    setcode do ip.reverse.to_s[2..-1] end
  end

  # set fact for network in cidr notation
  Facter.add("network_cidr_#{dev}") do
    #
    setcode do cidr end
  end
end
```

We put these two fact definitions into a Ruby function so that we can loop through the interfaces on the machine and define the facts for each interface as follows:

```
# loop through the interfaces, defining the two facts for each
interfaces = Facter.value('interfaces').split(',')
interfaces.each do
  |eth| reverse(eth)
end
```

Save this definition in `example/lib/facter/reverse.rb`, and then run Puppet to synchronize the fact definition down to the nodes. After the fact definition has been transferred, we can see its output for `node1` (IP address `192.168.122.132`) as follows:

```
node1# facter -p ipaddress
192.168.122.132
node1# facter -p reverse_eth0
122.168.192.in-addr.arpa
node1# facter -p network_cidr_eth0
192.168.122.0/24
```

In our earlier custom fact example, we built a custom fact for the zone based on the IP address. We could use the fact here to generate zone-specific DNS zone files. To keep this example simple, we will skip this step. With our fact in place, we can export our client's DNS information in the form of `concat::fragments` that can be picked up by our master later. To define the clients, we'll create an `example::dns::client` class as follows:

```
class example::dns::client
  (
    $domain = 'example.com',
    $search = 'prod.example.com example.com'
  ) {
```

We start with defining the search and domain settings and providing defaults. If we need to override the settings, we can do so from hiera. These two settings would be defined as the following in a hiera YAML file:

```
example::dns::client::domain: 'subdomain.example.com'

example::dns::client::search: 'sub.example.com prod.example.com'
```

Be careful when modifying /etc/resolv.conf. This can change the way Puppet defines certname used to verify the nodes' identity to the Puppet server. If you change your domain, a new certificate will be requested, and you will have to sign the new certificate before you can proceed.

We then define a concat container for /etc/resolv.conf as follows:

```
concat {'/etc/resolv.conf':
  mode => 0644,
}

# search and domain settings
concat::fragment{'resolv.conf search/domain':
  target  => '/etc/resolv.conf',
  content => "search $search\ndomain $domain\n",
  order   => 07,
}
```

The concat::fragment will be used to populate the /etc/resolv.conf file on the client machines. We then move on to collect the nameserver entries, which we will later export in our example::dns::server class using the tag 'resolv.conf'. We use the tag to make sure we only receive resolv.conf-related fragments as follows:

```
Concat::Fragment <<| tag == 'resolv.conf' |>> {
  target => '/etc/resolv.conf'
}
```

We use a piece of syntax we haven't used yet for exported resources called **modify on collect**. With modify on collect, we are overriding settings in the exported resource when we collect. In this case, we are utilizing modify on collect to modify the exported concat::fragment to include a target. When we define the exported resource, we leave the target off so that we do not need to define a concat container on the server. We'll be using this same trick when we export our DNS entries to the server.

Next we export our zone file entries as concat::fragments and close the class definition as follows:

```
@@concat::fragment {"zone example $::hostname":
  content => "$::hostname A $::ipaddress\n",
  order   => 10,
  tag     => 'zone.example.com',
}
```

```
$lastoctet = regsubst($::ipaddress_eth0,'^([0-9]+)[.]([0-9]+)[.]([0-9]+)[.]([0-9]+)$','\4')
  @@concat::fragment {"zone reverse $::reverse_eth0 $::hostname":
    content => "$lastoctet PTR $::fqdn.\n",
    order   => 10,
    tag     => "reverse.$::reverse_eth0",
  }
}
```

In the previous code, we used the `regsubst` function to grab the last octet from the nodes' IP address. We could have made another custom fact for this, but the `regsubst` function is sufficient for this usage.

Now we move on to the DNS server; to install and configure bind's `named` daemon, we need to configure the `named.conf` file and the zone files. We'll define the `named.conf` file from a template first as follows:

```
class example::dns::server {

  # setup bind
  package {'bind': }
  service {'named': require => Package['bind'] }

  # configure bind
  file {'/etc/named.conf':
    content => template('example/dns/named.conf.erb'),
    owner   => 0,
    group   => 'named',
    require => Package['bind'],
    notify  => Service['named']
  }
```

Next we'll define an exec that reloads `named` whenever the zone files are altered as follows:

```
exec {'named reload':
  refreshonly => true,
  command     => 'service named reload',
  path        => '/usr/sbin:/sbin',
  require     => Package['bind'],
}
```

At this point we'll export an entry from the server defining it as `nameserver` as follows (we already defined the collection of this resource in the client class):

```
@@concat::fragment {"resolv.conf nameserver $::hostname":
  content => "nameserver $::ipaddress\n",
  order   => 10,
  tag     => 'resolv.conf',
}
```

Now for the zone files, we'll define concat containers for the forward and reverse zone files, and then header fragments for each as follows:

```
concat {'/var/named/zone.example.com':
  mode   => 0644,
  notify => Exec['named reload'],
}
concat {'/var/named/reverse.122.168.192.in-addr.arpa':
  mode   => 0644,
  notify => Exec['named reload'],
}
concat::fragment {'zone.example header':
  target  => '/var/named/zone.example.com',
  content => template('example/dns/zone.example.com.erb'),
  order   => 01,
}
concat::fragment {'reverse.122.168.192.in-addr.arpa header':
  target => '/var/named/reverse.122.168.192.in-addr.arpa',
  content => template('example/dns/reverse.122.168.192.in-addr.arpa.
erb'),
  order   => 01,
}
```

Our clients exported `concat::fragments` for each of the previous zone files. We collect them here and use the same modify on collect syntax as we did for the client as follows:

```
Concat::Fragment <<| tag == "zone.example.com" |>> {
  target => '/var/named/zone.example.com'
}
Concat::Fragment <<| tag == "reverse.122.168.192.in-addr.arpa" |>> {
  target => '/var/named/reverse.122.168.192.in-addr.arpa'
}
}
```

The server class is now defined. We only need to create the template and header files to complete our module. The `named.conf.erb` template makes use of our custom facts as well, as shown in the following code:

```
options {
    listen-on port 53 { 127.0.0.1; <%= @ipaddress_eth0 -%>;};
    listen-on-v6 port 53 { ::1; };
    directory     "/var/named";
    dump-file     "/var/named/data/cache_dump.db";
        statistics-file "/var/named/data/named_stats.txt";
        memstatistics-file "/var/named/data/named_mem_stats.txt";
    allow-query     { localhost; <%- interfaces.split(',').each do
|eth| if has_variable?("network_cidr_#{eth}") then -%><%= scope.
lookupvar("network_cidr_#{eth}") -%>;<%- end end -%> };
    recursion yes;

    dnssec-enable yes;
    dnssec-validation yes;
    dnssec-lookaside auto;

    /* Path to ISC DLV key */
    bindkeys-file "/etc/named.iscdlv.key";

    managed-keys-directory "/var/named/dynamic";
};
```

This is a fairly typical DNS configuration file. The `allow-query` setting makes use of the `network_cidr_eth0` fact to allow hosts in the same subnet as the server to query the server.

`named.conf` then includes definitions for the various zones handled by the server, as shown in the following code:

```
zone "." IN {
    type hint;
    file "named.ca";
};

zone "example.com" IN {
    type master;
    file "zone.example.com";
    allow-update { none; };
};
```

```
zone "<%= @reverse_eth0 -%>" {
  type master;
  file "reverse.<%= @reverse_eth0 -%>";
};
```

The zone file headers are defined from templates that use the local time to update the zone serial number.

> DNS zone files must contain a **Start Of Authority (SOA)** record that contains a timestamp used by downstream DNS servers to determine if they have the most recent version of the zone file. Our template will use the Ruby function `Time.now.gmtime` to append a timestamp to our zone file.

The zone for `example.com` is as follows:

```
$ORIGIN example.com.
$TTL 1D
@       IN SOA    root hostmaster (
                        <%= Time.now.gmtime.strftime("%Y%m%d%H") %> ;
serial
                        8H         ; refresh
                        4H         ; retry
                        4W         ; expire
                        1D )       ; minimum
            NS        ns1
            MX        10 ns1
;
; just in case someone asks for localhost.example.com
localhost       A        127.0.0.1
ns1             A        192.168.122.1
; exported resources below this point
```

The definition of the reverse zone file template contains a similar SOA record and is defined as follows:

```
$ORIGIN 122.168.192.in-addr.arpa.
$TTL 1D
@       IN SOA   dns.example. hostmaster.example. (
                <%= Time.now.gmtime.strftime("%Y%m%d%H") %> ; serial
                28800           ; refresh (8 hours)
                14400           ; retry (4 hours)
                2419200         ; expire (4 weeks)
                86400           ; minimum (1 day)
                )
                NS        ns.example.
; exported resources below this point
```

With all this in place, we need to only apply the `example::dns::server` class to a machine to turn it into a DNS server for `example.com`. As more and more nodes are given the `example::dns::client` class, the DNS server receives their exported resources and builds up zone files. Eventually, when all the nodes have the `example::dns::client` class applied, the DNS server knows about all the nodes under Puppet control within the enterprise. Although this is a simplified example, the usefulness of this technique is obvious; it is applicable to many situations.

Summary

In this chapter, we installed and configured puppetdb. Once installed, we used puppetdb as our storeconfigs container for exported resources. We then showed how to use exported resources to manage relationships between nodes. Finally we used many of the concepts from earlier chapters to build up a complex node relationship for the configuration of DNS services. In the next chapter, we will explore a design paradigm that reduces clutter in node configuration and makes understanding the ways in which your modules interact easier to digest.

9
Roles and Profiles

In *Chapter 2, Organizing Your Nodes and Data*, we showed you how to organize your nodes using an ENC or hiera, and ideally both. At that point, we hadn't covered the forge modules or writing your own modules as we did in *Chapter 4, Public Modules* and *Chapter 5, Custom Facts and Modules*. In this chapter, we will cover a popular design concept in large installations of Puppet. The idea was originally made popular by Craig Dunn in his blog, which can be found at `http://www.craigdunn.org/2012/05/239/`.

Design pattern

The concept put forth by Craig Dunn in his blog is one that most Puppet masters arrive at independently. Modules should be nested in such a way that common components can be shared among nodes. The naming convention generally accepted is that roles contain one or more profiles. Profiles in turn contain one of more modules. Using the roles and profiles design pattern together with an ENC and hiera, you can have node-level logic that is very clean and elegant. The ENC and or hiera can be used to enforce standards on your nodes without interfering with the roles and profiles. We showed in *Chapter 2, Organizing Your Nodes and Data*, that with the virtual module, it is possible to have classes automatically applied by hiera to any system where the `is_virtual` fact is true. Using the same logic applied to facts such as `osfamily`, we can ensure that all the nodes for which `osfamily` is RedHat receive an appropriate module.

Putting all these elements together, we arrive at the following diagram of how modules are applied to a node.

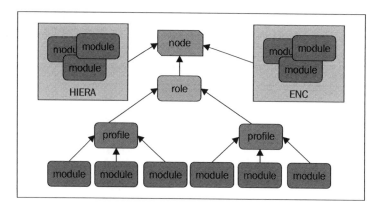

Roles are the high level abstraction of what a node will do.

Creating an example CDN role

We will start by constructing a module for a web server (the cliché example). What though, is a web server? Is a web server an Apache server or a Tomcat server or both, or maybe even nginx? What filesystems are required? What firewall rules should always be applied? The design problem is figuring out what the commonalities are going to be and where to divide. In most enterprises, creating a blanket "web server" module won't solve any problems and will potentially generate huge case statements. If your modules follow the roles-and-profiles design pattern, you shouldn't need huge case statements keyed off $::hostname; nodes shouldn't be mentioned in your role module. To illustrate this point, we'll look at an example for our companies' **Content Delivery Network (CDN)** implementation. Nodes in the CDN will be running nginx.

The use of nginx for a CDN is only given as an example. This in no way constitutes an endorsement of nginx for this purpose.

We'll create an nginx module, but we'll keep it simple so that it just does the following:

* Installs nginx
* Configures the service to start
* Starts the service

To configure nginx, we need to create the global configuration file, `/etc/nginx/nginx.conf`. We will also need to create site configuration files for any site that we wish to include in `/etc/nginx/conf.d/<sitename>.conf`. Changes to either of these files need to trigger a refresh of the `nginx` service. This is a great use case for a parameterized class. We'll make the `nginx.conf` file a template and allow some settings to be overridden, as shown in the following code:

```
class nginx (
  $worker_connections = 1024,
  $worker_processes = 1,
  $keepalive_timeout = 60,
  $nginx_version = 'installed',
) {
  file {'nginx.conf':
    path    => '/etc/nginx/nginx.conf',
    content => template('nginx/nginx.conf.erb'),
    mode    => 0644,
    owner   => '0',
    group   => '0',
    notify  => Service['nginx'],
    require => Package['nginx'],
  }
  package {'nginx':
    ensure => $nginx_version,
  }
  service {'nginx':
    require => Package['nginx'],
    ensure  => true,
    enable  => true,
  }
}
```

The `nginx.conf.erb` template will be very simple, as shown in the following code:

```
# HEADER: created by puppet
# HEADER: do not edit, contact puppetdevs@example.com for changes
user  nginx;
worker_processes  <%= @worker_processes -%>;

error_log  /var/log/nginx/error.log;
pid         /var/run/nginx.pid;

events {
  worker_connections  <%= @worker_connections -%>;
}
```

```
http {
    include         /etc/nginx/mime.types;
    default_type    application/octet-stream;
    log_format  main  '$remote_addr - $remote_user [$time_local]
"$request" '
                        '$status $body_bytes_sent "$http_referer" '
                        '"$http_user_agent" "$http_x_forwarded_for"';
    access_log  /var/log/nginx/access.log  main;
    sendfile            on;
    keepalive_timeout  <%= @keepalive_timeout -%>;
    include /etc/nginx/conf.d/*.conf;
}
```

Now, we need to create the `define` for an nginx server (not specific to the CDN implementation), as shown in the following code:

```
define nginx::server (
    $server_name,
    $error_log,
    $access_log,
    $root,
    $listen = 80,
) {
    include nginx
    file {"nginx::server::$server_name":
        path      => "/etc/nginx/conf.d/${server_name}.conf",
        content => template('nginx/server.conf.erb'),
        mode      => 0644,
        owner     => '0',
        group     => '0',
        notify  => Service['nginx'],
        require => Package['nginx']
    }
}
```

To ensure that the autoloader finds this file, we put the definition in a file called `server.pp` within the manifest's directory of the nginx module (`nginx/manifests/server.pp`). With the defined type for `nginx::server` in hand, we create a CDN profile to automatically configure a node with nginx and create some static content as follows:

```
class profile::cdn{
    (

        $listen = "80",
```

```
  ) {

  nginx::server {"profile::nginx::cdn::$::fqdn":
    server_name => "${::hostname}.cdn.example.com",
    error_log   => "/var/log/nginx/cdn-${::hostname}-error.log",
    access_log  => "/var/log/nginx/cdn-${::hostname}-access.log",
    root        => "/srv/www",
    listen      => "$listen",

  }
  file {'/srv/www':
    ensure  => 'directory',
    owner   => 'nginx',
    group   => 'nginx',
    require => Package['nginx'],
  }
  file {'/srv/www/index.html':
    mode    => '0644',
    owner   => 'nginx',
    group   => 'nginx',
    content => "<html><head><title>${::hostname} cdn node</title></
head>\n<body><h1>${::hostname} cdn node</h1><h2>Sample Content</h2>\
n</body></html>",
    require => [Package['nginx'],File['/srv/www']],
  }
}
```

Now all that is left is to define the role to include this profile definition as follows:

```
class role::cdn {
  include profile::cdn
}
```

Now the node definition for a CDN node would only contain the `role::cdn` class as follows:

```
node firstcdn {
  include role::cdn
}
```

Creating a sub-CDN role

Now that we have a `role::cdn` class to configure a CDN node, we will now configure some nodes to run `varnish` in front of nginx.

 Varnish is a web accelerator (caching HTTP reverse proxy). More information on varnish is available at `http://www.varnish-cache.org`. In our implementation, varnish will be provided by the EPEL repository.

In this configuration, we will need to change nginx to only listen on `127.0.0.1` port 80 so that varnish can attach to port 80 on the default IP address. Varnish will accept incoming connections and retrieve content from nginx. Varnish will cache any data it retrieves and only retrieve from nginx when it needs to update its cache. We will start by defining a module for varnish that installs the package, updates the configuration, and starts the service, as shown in the following code:

```
class varnish
  (
    $varnish_listen_address = "$::ipaddress_eth0",
    $varnish_listen_port    = '80',
    $backend_host           = '127.0.0.1',
    $backend_port           = '80',
  ) {
  package {'varnish':
    ensure => 'installed'
  }
  service {'varnish':
    ensure  => 'running',
    enable  => true,
    require => Package['varnish'],
  }
  file {'/etc/sysconfig/varnish':
    mode    => 0644,
    owner   => 0,
    group   => 0,
    content => template('varnish/sysconfig-varnish.erb'),
    notify  => Service['varnish']
  }

  file {'/etc/varnish/default.vcl':
    mode    => 0644,
    owner   => 0,
```

```
    group    => 0,
    content => template('varnish/default.vcl.erb'),
    notify   => Service['varnish'],
  }
}
```

Now we need to create a profile for varnish as shown in the following code. In this example, it will only contain the varnish class, but adding this level allows us to add any extra modules to the profile later.

```
# profile::varnish
# default is to listen on 80 and use 127.0.0.1:80 as backend
class profile::varnish{
  include ::varnish
}
```

> We need to specify ::varnish to include the module called varnish. Puppet will look for varnish at the current scope (profile) and find profile::varnish.

Next, we create the role cdn::varnish, which will use role::cdn as a base class as follows:

```
class role::cdn::varnish inherits role::cdn {
  include profile::varnish
}
```

One last thing we need to do is to tell nginx to only listen on the loopback device (127.0.0.1). We can do that with hiera; we'll assign a top scope variable called role to our node. You can do this through your ENC or in site.pp as follows:

```
$role = hiera('role','none')
node default {
  hiera_include('classes',base)
}
```

Now create a YAML file for our cdn::varnish role at hieradata/roles/ role::cdn::varnish.yaml with the following content:

```
---
profile::cdn::listen: '127.0.0.1:80'
```

We made a parameter named listen in `profile::cdn` so that we could override that value. Now when we apply the `role::cdn::varnish role` to a node, the node will be configured with nginx to listen only to the loopback device. Varnish will listen on the public IP address (`::ipaddress_eth0`) on port 80. Varnish will cache content that it retrieves from nginx.

We didn't need to modify `role::cdn`, and we made `role::cdn::varnish` inherit `role::cdn`. This model allows you to create multiple sub roles to fit all the use cases. Using hiera to override certain values for different roles removes any ugly conditional logic from these definitions.

Dealing with exceptions

In a pristine environment, all your nodes with a certain role would be identical in every way, and there would be no exceptions. Unfortunately dealing with exceptions is a large part of the day-to-day business of running Puppet. Using roles and profiles together with hiera, it is possible to remove node level data from your code (roles, profiles, and modules).

Hiera can be used to achieve this separation of code from data. In *Chapter 2, Organizing Your Nodes and Data*, we configured `hiera.yaml` with `roles/%{::role}` in the hierarchy. The defaults for any role would be put in `hieradata/roles/` `[rolename].yaml`. The hierarchy determines the order in which files are searched for the hiera data. Our configuration is as follows:

```
---
:hierarchy:
    - "zones/%{::example_zone}"
    - "hosts/%{::hostname}"
    - "roles/%{::role}"
    - "%{::kernel}/%{::osfamily}/%{::lsbmajdistrelease}"
    - "is_virtual/%{::is_virtual}"
    - common
```

Any single host that requires an exception to the default value from the roles level YAML file, can be put in either the hosts level or zones level YAML files.

The idea here is to keep the top-level role definition as clean as possible, it should only include profiles. Any ancillary modules (such as the `virtual` module) that need to be applied to specific nodes will be handled by either hiera (via `hiera_include`) or the ENC.

Summary

In this chapter, we explored a design concept that aims to reduce complexity at the topmost level making your node definitions cleaner. Breaking up module application into multiple layers forces your Puppeteers to compartmentalize their definitions. If all the contributors to your code base keep this in mind, collisions will be kept to a minimum. Exceptions can be handled with host-level hiera definitions. In the next chapter, we will look at how to diagnose inevitable problems with catalog compilation and execution.

10
Troubleshooting

Inevitably, you will run into problems with your Puppet runs. Having good reporting is the key to knowing when failures occur. When most of your Puppet runs are error free, the IRC report mechanism we showed in *Chapter 7, Reporting and Orchestration*, is useful to detect errors quickly.

 If you have more than the occasional error, then the IRC report will just become noise that you'll learn to ignore. If you are having multiple failures in your code, you should start looking at the acceptance testing procedures provided by Puppet beaker. More information on Puppet beaker is available at `https://github.com/puppetlabs/beaker`.

Most of the Puppet failures I've come across end up in two buckets. These buckets are as follows:

- Connectivity to Puppet and certificates
- Catalog failure

We'll examine these separately and provide some methods to diagnose issues. We will also be covering debugging, in detail.

Connectivity issues

As we have seen in *Chapter 1, Dealing with Load/Scale*, by noticing that at its core, Puppet communication is done using a web service. When troubleshooting problems with the Puppet infrastructure, we should always start with that mindset. Assuming you are having trouble accessing the Puppet master, Puppet should be listening on port 8140 by default.

This port is configurable; you should verify the port is 8140 by running the following command:

```
# puppet config print masterport
```

```
8140
```

You should be able to successfully connect to `masterport`. Check that you get a successful connection using **netcat** (nc).

Netcat can be used to check the connectivity of TCP and UDP sockets. If you do not have netcat (nc) available, you can use telnet for the same purpose. To exit `telnet`, you would issue `Control-]` followed by quit.

```
root@node1:~
# nc -v puppet.example.com 8140
Connection to puppet.example.com 8140 port [tcp/*] succeeded!
#
```

To exit netcat after the successful connection, type `Control+D`. If you don't see **succeeded!** in the output, then you are having trouble reaching the Puppet server on port 8140. For this type of error, you'll need to check your network settings and diagnose the connection issue. The common tools for that are `ping`, which uses ICMP ECHO messages, and `mtr`, which mimics `traceroute` functionality. Don't forget your host-based firewall (`iptables`) rules, you'll need to allow the inbound connection on port 8140.

Assuming the previous connection was successful, the next thing you can do is either use `wget` or `curl` to try retrieving the CA certificate from the Puppet master.

wget and `curl` are simple tools used to download information using the HTTP protocol. Any tool that can communicate using HTTP with SSL encryption can be used for our purposes.

Retrieving the CA certificate and requesting a certificate to be signed are two operations that can occur without having certificates. Your nodes need to be able to verify the Puppet master and request certificates before they have had their certificates issued. We will use `wget` to download the CA certificate, as shown in the following screenshot:

```
root@node1:~                                          ✕
# wget --no-check-certificate \
> https://puppet.example.com:8140/production/certificate/ca
--2014-04-03 00:42:40--  https://puppet.example.com:8140/production/certificate/
ca
Resolving puppet.example.com... 192.168.122.100
Connecting to puppet.example.com|192.168.122.100|:8140... connected.
WARNING: cannot verify puppet.example.com's certificate, issued by "/CN=Puppet C
A: puppet.example.com":
  Self-signed certificate encountered.
HTTP request sent, awaiting response... 200
Length: 1891 (1.8K) [text/plain]
Saving to: "ca"

100%[========================================>] 1,891        --.-K/s   in 0s

2014-04-03 00:42:40 (27.3 MB/s) - "ca" saved [1891/1891]

# head -2 ca
-----BEGIN CERTIFICATE-----
MIIFRjCCAy6gAwIBAgIBATANBgkqhkiG9w0BAQsFADAoMSYwJAYDVQQDDB1QdXBw
# █
```

Another option is using `gnutls-cli` or the `openssl s_client` client programs. Each of these tools will help you diagnose certificate issues; you want to verify that the Puppet master is sending the certificate you think it should.

To use `gnutls-cli`, you install the `gnutls-utils package`. To connect to your Puppet master on port 8140, use the following command:

```
# gnutls-cli -p 8140 puppet.example.com

Resolving 'puppet.example.com'...

Connecting to '192.168.122.100:8140'...

- Successfully sent 0 certificate(s) to server.

...

- Simple Client Mode:
```

You will then have an SSL-encrypted connection to the server, and you may issue standard HTTP commands, such as GET. Attempt to download the CA certificate by typing the following command:

```
GET /production/certificate/ca HTTP/1.0
Accept: text/plain
```

The CA certificate will be returned as text, so we need to specify that we will accept a response that is not HTML. We use Accept: text/plain to do this. The CA certificate should be exported following the HTTP response header as shown in the following screenshot:

```
- Handshake was completed

- Simple Client Mode:

GET /production/certificate/ca HTTP/1.0
Accept: text/plain

HTTP/1.1 200
Date: Tue, 20 May 2014 04:39:13 GMT
Server: Apache/2.2.15 (Red Hat)
X-Powered-By: Phusion Passenger (mod_rails/mod_rack) 3.0.21
X-Puppet-Version: 3.6.0
Content-Length: 1891
Status: 200
Content-Type: text/plain; charset=UTF-8
Connection: close

-----BEGIN CERTIFICATE-----
MIIFRjCCAy6gAwIBAgIBATANBgkqhkiG9w0BAQsFADAoMSYwJAYDVQQDDB1QdXBw
ZXQgQ0E6IHB1cHBldC5leGFtcGxlLmNvbTAeFw0xMzExMjcwNzQzNTBaFw0xODEx
MjcwNzQzNTBaMCgxJjAkBgNVBAMMHVB1cHBldCBDQTogcHVwcGV0LmV4YW1wbGUu
Y29tMIICIjANBgkqhkiG9w0BAQEFAAOCAg8AMIICCgKCAgEA8s/lmkeKHXKz16SU
B7Sfb5UTnrSCNdnttDd/5FqQi4ZH5K/eshdCzFPeQ7NYOJs3V15dRmueZ6HZ90/U
Fi5/YmBXoRMXdcotDCbg2dB9WGEh8VS7Iqu8CwS3CAGkFiUpY5vxOAlXLkIW4oNi
```

Using OpenSSL's s_client program is similar to using gnutls-cli. You will need to specify the host and port using the -host and -port parameters as follows (s_client has a less verbose mode, -quiet, which we'll use to make our screenshot smaller):

```
node1# openssl s_client -host puppet.example.com -port 8140 -quiet
depth=1 CN = Puppet CA: puppet.example.com
verify error:num=19:self signed certificate in certificate chain
verify return:0
GET /production/certificate/ca HTTP/1.0
Accept: text/plain

HTTP/1.1 200
Date: Tue, 20 May 2014 04:49:23 GMT
Server: Apache/2.2.15 (Red Hat)
X-Powered-By: Phusion Passenger (mod_rails/mod_rack) 3.0.21
X-Puppet-Version: 3.6.0
Content-Length: 1891
Status: 200
Content-Type: text/plain; charset=UTF-8
Connection: close

-----BEGIN CERTIFICATE-----
MIIFRjCCAy6gAwIBAgIBATANBgkqhkiG9w0BAQsFADAoMSYwJAYDVQQDDB1QdXBw
```

Catalog failures

When the client requests a catalog, it is compiled on the master and sent down to the client. If the catalog fails to compile, the error is printed and can most likely be corrected easily. For example, the following base class has an obvious error:

```
class base {
  file {'one':
    path   => '/tmp/one',
    ensure => 'directory',
  }
  file {'one':
    path   => '/tmp/one',
    ensure => 'file',
  }
}
```

The file resource is defined twice with the same name. When we run Puppet, the error appears as shown in the following screenshot:

```
root@node1:~                                                    ✕
# puppet agent -t
Info: Retrieving plugin
Info: Loading facts in /var/lib/puppet/lib/facter/puppet_vardir.rb
Info: Loading facts in /var/lib/puppet/lib/facter/facter_dot_d.rb
Info: Loading facts in /var/lib/puppet/lib/facter/reverse.rb
Info: Loading facts in /var/lib/puppet/lib/facter/concat_basedir.rb
Info: Loading facts in /var/lib/puppet/lib/facter/pe_version.rb
Info: Loading facts in /var/lib/puppet/lib/facter/ip6tables_version.rb
Info: Loading facts in /var/lib/puppet/lib/facter/iptables_persistent_version.rb
Info: Loading facts in /var/lib/puppet/lib/facter/homedir.rb
Info: Loading facts in /var/lib/puppet/lib/facter/root_home.rb
Info: Loading facts in /var/lib/puppet/lib/facter/iptables_version.rb
Error: Could not retrieve catalog from remote server: Error 400 on SERVER: Dupli
cate declaration: File[one] is already declared in file /etc/puppet/environments
/production/dist/base/manifests/init.pp:12; cannot redeclare at /etc/puppet/envi
ronments/production/dist/base/manifests/init.pp:16 on node node1.example.com
Warning: Not using cache on failed catalog
Error: Could not retrieve catalog; skipping run
#
```

The duplicate declaration error is shown following `Error 400 on SERVER`.

HTTP 400 errors indicate that the request sent to the web server (Puppet server in this case) was malformed. In this case, the Puppet server are letting the client know that there was a problem with the request to compile a catalog. The previous versions of Puppet did not return error codes as useful as those shown in the preceding screenshot. Fixing this type of duplicate declaration is very straightforward, the line numbers to each declaration are printed in the error message. Simply locate the two files and remove one of the entries.

A more perplexing issue is when the catalog compiles cleanly but fails to apply on the node. To illustrate, we'll rewrite our base class to fail on application, and not compilation, as follows:

```
class base {
  file {'one':
    path    => '/tmp/one',
    ensure => 'directory',
  }
  file {"two":
    path    => "/tmp/one$one",
    ensure => 'file',
  }
}
```

Now, when we attempt to run the agent, we retrieve a good catalog, but it fails to apply. The agent displays an error message, as shown in the following screenshot:

```
root@node1:~                                                    ✕
Error: Could not retrieve catalog; skipping run
# puppet agent -t
Info: Retrieving plugin
Info: Loading facts in /var/lib/puppet/lib/facter/puppet_vardir.rb
Info: Loading facts in /var/lib/puppet/lib/facter/facter_dot_d.rb
Info: Loading facts in /var/lib/puppet/lib/facter/reverse.rb
Info: Loading facts in /var/lib/puppet/lib/facter/concat_basedir.rb
Info: Loading facts in /var/lib/puppet/lib/facter/pe_version.rb
Info: Loading facts in /var/lib/puppet/lib/facter/ip6tables_version.rb
Info: Loading facts in /var/lib/puppet/lib/facter/iptables_persistent_version.rb
Info: Loading facts in /var/lib/puppet/lib/facter/homedir.rb
Info: Loading facts in /var/lib/puppet/lib/facter/root_home.rb
Info: Loading facts in /var/lib/puppet/lib/facter/iptables_version.rb
Info: Caching catalog for node1.example.com
Error: Failed to apply catalog: Cannot alias File[two] to ["/tmp/one"] at /etc/p
uppet/environments/production/dist/base/manifests/init.pp:9; resource ["File", "
/tmp/one"] already declared at /etc/puppet/environments/production/dist/base/man
ifests/init.pp:5
#
```

In this example, it is still easy to see the problem. But if the problem is obscured or non-obvious, we can go look at the catalog. The catalog is stored in the agent's `client_data` directory (current versions use JSON files, earlier versions used YAML files). In this case, the file is stored in `/var/lib/puppet/client_data/catalog/node1.example.com.json`. Using `jq`, we can examine the JSON file and find the problem definitions.

`jq` is a JSON processor and is available in the EPEL repository on Enterprise Linux installations.

 You can always just read the JSON file directly, but using `jq` on extremely large files is useful. You can use `jq` as you would `grep` on a file, making searching within a JSON file much easier. More information on `jq` can be found at `http://stedolan.github.io/jq/`.

```
$ jq .data.resources[].title <node1.example.com.json
"main"
"Settings"
"Main"
"default"
"Base"
"one"
"two"
```

Now to look at our problem definition, we'll select the resource whose title is `"two"` as shown in the following command:

```
$ jq '.data.resources[] | select(.title=="two")' <node1.example.com.json
{
  "type": "File",
  "line": 9,
  "exported": false,
  "tags": [
    "default",
    "two",
    "class",
    "file",
    "base",
    "node"
  ],
  "parameters": {
    "path": "/tmp/one",
    "ensure": "file"
  },
  "file": "/etc/puppet/environments/production/dist/base/manifests/init.
pp",
  "title": "two"
}
```

From this JSON, we can see that the path for `File['two']` is /tmp/one, so in the definition "/tmp/one$one", the variable $one must be empty.

You can also manually download the catalog in yaml format if you find that easier to debug. Doing this with wget, you need to specify the certificate and CA files for your node so that Puppet grants access to the catalog. The following is a simple script to perform this action:

```
#!/bin/bash
SSL=$(puppet config print ssldir)
FQDN=$(facter fqdn)
PUPPET=puppet.example.com
ENV=production
exec wget --certificate ${SSL}/certs/${FQDN}.pem \
         --private-key ${SSL}/private_keys/${FQDN}.pem \
         --ca-certificate ${SSL}/certs/ca.pem \
         --header="Accept: yaml" \
         https://${PUPPET}:8140/$ENV/catalog/${FQDN}
```

The client catalog will also be available on the Puppet master in the `/var/lib/puppet/yaml/node` directory; however, in a multiple master environment, tracking down which master compiled the catalog may be slower than downloading a fresh copy. Alternatively, you may force a master to compile a catalog for a node as follows (Puppet will print out the catalog, in JSON format, to the terminal):

```
worker1# puppet master --compile node1.example.com
Notice: Compiled catalog for node1.example.com in environment production
in 1.16 seconds
{
  "data": {
    "edges": [
      {
        "source": "Stage[main]",
        "target": "Class[main]"
      },
...
```

Full trace of a catalog compile

Using `puppet master --compile`, you can also specify to run a full trace on the compilation with the `--trace` option. This option will show which providers were run and a much higher level of detail than the debug output. To do so, specify the log destination as well. Running a full trace will generate a lot of data and you'll want to store that in a logfile.

```
worker1# puppet master --compile node1.example.com --debug --trace --logdest /v
ar/log/puppet/node1.example.com.log
Debug: Using cached facts for node1.example.com
Info: Caching node for node1.example.com
Debug: hiera(): Hiera YAML backend starting
Debug: hiera(): Looking up role in YAML backend
Debug: hiera(): Looking for data source hosts/node1
Debug: hiera(): Found role in hosts/node1
Debug: importing '/etc/puppet/environments/production/dist/role/manifests/cdn/v
arnish.pp' in environment production
Debug: Automatically imported role::cdn::varnish from role/cdn/varnish into pro
duction
Debug: importing '/etc/puppet/environments/production/dist/role/manifests/cdn.p
p' in environment production
Debug: importing '/etc/puppet/environments/production/dist/profile/manifests/cd
n.pp' in environment production
Debug: Automatically imported profile::cdn from profile/cdn into production
Debug: hiera(): Looking up profile::cdn::listen in YAML backend
Debug: hiera(): Looking for data source hosts/node1
Debug: hiera(): Looking for data source roles/role::cdn::varnish
Debug: hiera(): Found profile::cdn::listen in roles/role::cdn::varnish
Debug: importing '/etc/puppet/environments/production/dist/nginx/manifests/init
.pp' in environment production
Debug: importing '/etc/puppet/environments/production/dist/nginx/manifests/serv
er.pp' in environment production
Debug: Automatically imported nginx::server from nginx/server into production
Debug: Executing '/bin/rpm --version'
Debug: Executing '/bin/rpm -ql rpm'
Debug: Executing '/bin/rpm --version'
Debug: importing '/etc/puppet/environments/production/dist/profile/manifests/va
rnish.pp' in environment production
Debug: Automatically imported profile::varnish from profile/varnish into produc
```

The output in the previous screenshot shows that we can see a lot more information than the normal --debug flag will show, including the low-level calls to /bin/rpm to determine the version of rpm installed on the system.

 The log file /var/log/puppet/node1.example.com.log will contain all of this output without the ANSI color codes, making it suitable for searching.

The logfile will also compile the catalog in the production environment by default. To compile for another environment, specify the environment with --environment as shown in the following command:

```
worker1# puppet master --compile node1.example.com --debug --trace
--logdest /var/log/puppet/node1.example.com.log --environment sandbox
```

The classes.txt file

The /var/lib/puppet/classes.txt file contains a list of the classes applied to the machine. If you are having trouble with a node, you can look here for the last set of classes that were successfully applied to a node. But, when you are having trouble, you are most interested in the classes in the current catalog, and which classes are different or missing.. We can use jq again to query the JSON of the current catalog as shown in the following command:

```
$ jq '.data.classes[]' <node1.example.com.json
"settings"
"default"
"base"
```

 Settings and default are classes internal to Puppet, and not user defined. In this output, only the base was defined by our manifests.

We can compare the list of classes returned by jq to those listed in classes.txt. The classes shown in classes.txt are from the last successful run of Puppet. The file is created at the end of the Puppet agent run. The classes returned by jq are from the catalog, which just fail to apply if we are debugging. These two lists would be consistent on a node with a successful Puppet agent run.

Debugging

Turning on the debugging option on your Puppet master isn't such a big deal with a few hundred nodes. However, in an environment with thousands of nodes, it isn't a viable option. Nevertheless, you sometimes need to enable debugging to figure out where catalog compilation is failing. Our proxy configuration comes to the rescue here. The idea is to have a worker dedicated to debugging. The debugging server will have debugging turned on, using the `--debug` and `--logdest` options in the `config.ru` file. The advantage of this method over that of running `puppet master --compile` as we showed earlier, is that while you are debugging your node, you place it in a debugging environment (`problem` for instance). While the node is in the debugging environment, it will be removed from your reporting infrastructure and not continue to alert you of failures.

To do this, we go back to our `proxy.conf` file on our Puppet master and define a new balancer named `puppetproblem` that goes to our debugging worker. We'll use worker2 (`192.168.100.102`) in the following example:

```
<Proxy balancer://puppetproblem>
BalancerMember http://192.168.100.102:18140
</Proxy>
```

We then add a new `ProxyPassMatch` line to our `VirtualHost` right after the certificate matching line:

```
ProxyPassMatch ^/(problem/.*)$ balancer://puppetproblem/$1
```

> Whenever adding a new `ProxyPassMatch` line to the `proxy.conf` file, make sure the first entry is always the certificate matching line. If you place anything before the certificate line, certificate requests will not be routed to your CA machines.

Restart `httpd` on the master to make the change effective. With this in place, we edit the `config.ru` on worker2 and add the following command lines:

```
ARGV << "--debug"
ARGV << "--logdest" << "/var/log/puppet/problem.log"
```

These two settings are passed as command-line arguments to Puppet master when passenger starts the master service. Any other configuration changes should be made to `/etc/puppet/puppet.conf` to avoid confusion.

Restart `httpd` on worker2 to make the change effective. Now, when you have a problem with a node, you can send it to worker2 by specifying the environment "problem" when running the agent. If you are using dynamic environments, the steps to diagnose a problem would be as follows:

1. Create the problem branch in Git.
2. Work on the issue.
3. Set the environment of a test node to the new environment.
4. Solve the problem.
5. Merge that branch back into the working branch or production.

Using this method, you also tie the catalog compilation to a specific worker, which makes tracking down bugs much easier. Without this, your catalog may compile on any one of your workers, and some large installations have several workers.

Personal and bugfix branches

When working through a catalog compilation issue, it is sometimes useful to start attacking the problem and changing things on the fly. To avoid problems with other nodes, you should work in a new branch (which will create a new environment, just as we configured our Puppet masters to have dynamic environments in *Chapter 3, Git and Environments*). If you are frequently creating branches, you can create one named after yourself or your username, for instance. In an example in *Chapter 3, Git and Environments*, we created a `thomas` branch and worked in the `thomas` branch by specifying `--environment thomas` when running `puppet agent`. Working through problems in a personal branch is a great troubleshooting technique that allows the rest of the nodes to continue working against the main branch or master. If multiple members of your team are working on an issue, it is useful to create a working branch for your team, possibly named either after the issue or more likely after the trouble ticket created by the issue.

Echo statements

When working on a problem branch, you are free to add any number of debugging print or echo statements to your code. In Puppet, these take the form of `notice` or `notify` lines. I prefer notify lines since notify lines will be printed when I run `puppet agent -t` on a node. I usually place all the variables in the affected module in a single notify statement to verify that the variables are getting set to the values I believe they should. This method is very useful when working with data from hiera, where you would like to know the value returned by hiera is correct, as shown in the following example:

```
$importantSetting = hiera('importantSetting','defaultValue')
notify {"importantSetting is $importantSetting": }
```

It is not uncommon to have many notify lines throughout a module during the development phase.

Scope

When working on a large code base, occasionally you will have naming conflicts with variables or modules. For variables, using an echo statement can quickly determine if your code is using the variable you believe it should. For modules it can sometimes be difficult to determine if the module you intended is being included. For example, you have two modules called `packages` and `example::ntp::packages`. The `packages` module contains a single `notify` statement in `packages/manifests/init.pp` as shown in the following code:

```
class packages {

  notify {"this is packages":}

}
```

The `example::ntp::packages` module has a similar notify statement in `example/manifests/ntp/packages.pp` as shown in the following code:

```
class example::ntp::packages {

  notify {"this is example::ntp::packages": }

}
```

Now in `example/manifest/ntp.pp,` we use `include packages,` as shown in the following code:

```
class example::ntp {

    include packages

}
```

You may be surprised by the following result from `puppet agent`:

```
# puppet agent -t

...

Notice: this is example::ntp::packages


Notice: /Stage[main]/Example::Ntp::Packages/Notify[this is
example::ntp::packages]/message: defined 'message' as 'this is
example::ntp::packages'
```

We might have expected `include packages` to use the top-scope `packages` class, but it actually searched the local scope and used `example::ntp::packages` instead. When working in a large environment, it is advisable to use very specific names for classes or always specify the scope. We could achieve the result we expected using the following code for the definition of `example::ntp`:

```
class example::ntp {
    include ::packages
}
```

If we run Puppet agent against this version, we see the notify we were expecting, as follows:

```
# puppet agent -t

...

Notice: this is packages


Notice: /Stage[main]/Packages/Notify[this is packages]/message: defined
'message' as 'this is packages'
```

Profiling and summarizing

If your Puppet runs are taking a long time to complete, it is useful to see where there are bottlenecks. From the command line, you can pass the `--summarize` option to `puppet agent` to tell the agent to keep track of how long operations took to complete and display a summary at the end of compilation as shown in the following screenshot:

```
Time:
            Resources: 0.00
           Filebucket: 0.00
                 Host: 0.00
                Group: 0.00
             Schedule: 0.00
               Notify: 0.00
              Yumrepo: 0.00
            File line: 0.00
             Firewall: 0.01
              Package: 0.01
   Ssh authorized key: 0.01
                 User: 0.02
              Service: 0.77
                 File: 0.92
                 Exec: 1.46
             Last run: 1397103601
                Total: 15.58
     Config retrieval: 4.71
               Augeas: 7.67
```

After you have configured one of your workers to be your debugging worker, as we showed in the *Debugging* section of this chapter, you can enable profiling support by adding the following code to `/etc/puppet/puppet.conf`:

```
profile = true
```

After making that change, when a node runs against that master, the profiling information will be written to the location pointed to by `logdest`, `/var/log/puppet/problem.log` in our example configuration. A sample of this output is shown as follows:

```
1.1 Setup server facts for compiling: took 0.0139 seconds
1.2 Found facts: took 0.2459 seconds
...
1.4.3 Compile: Evaluated main: took 0.0007 seconds
...
1.4.7 Compile: Finished catalog: took 0.0025 seconds
1.4 Compiled catalog for node1.example.com in environment problem:
took 0.0237 seconds
```

Using this information, you can determine where the slow operations are with your catalog compilation and delivery to the nodes.

Summary

In this chapter, we examined a few troubleshooting techniques that are useful in the enterprise. Troubleshooting basic network and system connectivity is the first thing to be checked. Using Puppet's rest API, we were able to talk directly to the master with the help of HTTP tools such as `wget` and `gnutls-cli`. We learned how to read the catalog and use `jq` to search the catalog on the client. Finally, we showed a method of enabling the expensive debugging feature for specific nodes by creating a debugging worker and directing nodes to that specific worker.

In this book, we took advantage of Puppet's rest API to scale out our Puppet infrastructure in order to accommodate a large number of nodes. Working in the enterprise, the division of code from data is important to allow modules to be reused and to reduce complexity. A large number of nodes will introduce its own set of complexities. Working to reduce the complexity in your environment will allow you to grow and adapt quickly.

Index

V

varnish
  about 238
  URL 238
virtual resources
  using 140

W

wget tool 244
workload
  catalog compilation 16-21
  certificate, signing 15
  code consistency 22
  reporting 15
  splitting up 15
  storeconfigs 15
wrapper class
  creating 209

Y

YAML
  about 40
  URL 40
YUM repository
  creating 33, 34

Z

zone file headers 230
zone files
  forward zones 223
  reverse zones 223
zone function 151

Thank you for buying
Mastering Puppet

About Packt Publishing

Packt, pronounced 'packed', published its first book "*Mastering phpMyAdmin for Effective MySQL Management*" in April 2004 and subsequently continued to specialize in publishing highly focused books on specific technologies and solutions.

Our books and publications share the experiences of your fellow IT professionals in adapting and customizing today's systems, applications, and frameworks. Our solution based books give you the knowledge and power to customize the software and technologies you're using to get the job done. Packt books are more specific and less general than the IT books you have seen in the past. Our unique business model allows us to bring you more focused information, giving you more of what you need to know, and less of what you don't.

Packt is a modern, yet unique publishing company, which focuses on producing quality, cutting-edge books for communities of developers, administrators, and newbies alike. For more information, please visit our website: www.packtpub.com.

About Packt Open Source

In 2010, Packt launched two new brands, Packt Open Source and Packt Enterprise, in order to continue its focus on specialization. This book is part of the Packt Open Source brand, home to books published on software built around Open Source licenses, and offering information to anybody from advanced developers to budding web designers. The Open Source brand also runs Packt's Open Source Royalty Scheme, by which Packt gives a royalty to each Open Source project about whose software a book is sold.

Writing for Packt

We welcome all inquiries from people who are interested in authoring. Book proposals should be sent to author@packtpub.com. If your book idea is still at an early stage and you would like to discuss it first before writing a formal book proposal, contact us; one of our commissioning editors will get in touch with you.

We're not just looking for published authors; if you have strong technical skills but no writing experience, our experienced editors can help you develop a writing career, or simply get some additional reward for your expertise.

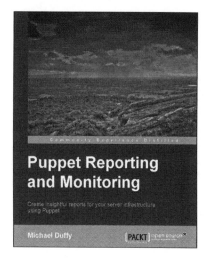

Puppet Reporting and Monitoring

ISBN: 978-1-78398-142-7   Paperback: 186 pages

Create insightful reports for your server infrastructure using Puppet

1. Learn how to prepare and set up Puppet to report on a wealth of data.

2. Develop your own custom plugins and work with report processor systems.

3. Explore compelling ways to utilize and present Puppet data with easy-to-follow examples.

Puppet 3 Beginner's Guide

ISBN: 978-1-78216-124-0   Paperback: 204 pages

Start from scratch with the Puppet configuration management system, and learn how to fully utilize Puppet through simple, practical examples

1. Shows you step-by-step how to install Puppet and start managing your systems with simple examples.

2. Every aspect of Puppet is explained in detail so that you really understand what you're doing.

3. Gets you up and running immediately, from installation to using Puppet for practical tasks in a matter of minutes.

Please check **www.PacktPub.com** for information on our titles

open source✲
community experience distilled

Puppet 3 Cookbook

ISBN: 978-1-78216-976-5   Paperback: 274 pages

Build reliable, scalable, secure, and high-performance systems to fully utilize the power of cloud computing

1. Use Puppet 3 to take control of your servers and desktops, with detailed step-by-step instructions.

2. Covers all the popular tools and frameworks used with Puppet: Dashboard, Foreman, and more.

3. Teaches you how to extend Puppet with custom functions, types, and providers.

4. Packed with tips and inspiring ideas for using Puppet to automate server builds, deployments, and workflows.

Instant Puppet 3 Starter

ISBN: 978-1-78216-174-5   Paperback: 50 pages

Gain complete consistency from your systems with minimal effort using Instant Puppet 3 Starter

1. Learn something new in an Instant! A short, fast, focused guide delivering immediate results.

2. Learn how deterministic results can vastly reduce your workload.

3. Deploy Puppet Server as a Ruby-on-Rails application to handle thousands of clients.

Please check **www.PacktPub.com** for information on our titles